CLASSIC DISPUTES IN SOCIOLOGY

Classic Disputes in Sociology

Edited by

R. J. ANDERSON
Manchester Polytechnic

J. A. HUGHES
University of Lancaster

W. W. SHARROCK
University of Manchester

London
ALLEN & UNWIN
Boston   Sydney   Wellington

Allen & Unwin, the academic imprint of

Unwin Hyman Ltd

PO Box 18, Park Lane, Hemel Hempstead, Herts HP2 4TE, UK
40 Museum Street, London WC1A 1LU, UK
37/39 Queen Elizabeth Street, London SE1 2QB, UK

Allen & Unwin Inc.,
8 Winchester Place, Winchester, Mass. 01890, USA

Allen & Unwin (Australia) Ltd,
8 Napier Street, North Sydney, NSW 2060, Australia

Allen & Unwin (New Zealand) Ltd in association with the Port
Nicholson Press Ltd,
60 Cambridge Terrace, Wellington, New Zealand

First published in 1987

British Library Cataloguing in Publication Data

Classic disputes in sociology.
1. Sociology – History
I. Anderson, R. J. (Robert John) II. Hughes,
J.A. III. Sharrock, W. W.
301'.01 HM24

ISBN 0-04-301243-4
ISBN 0-04-301244-2 Pbk

Library of Congress Cataloging-in-Publication Data

Classic disputes in sociology.
Includes index.
I. Sociology. 2. Sociology – History. I. Anderson,
R. J. II. Hughes, J. A., 1941–   . III. Sharrock,
W. W. (Wes W.)
HM51.C54 1987 301 86–20661
ISBN 0–04–301243–4 (alk. paper)
ISBN 0–04–301244–2 (pbk.: alk. paper)

Typeset in 10 on 12 pt Bembo by Computape (Pickering) Ltd, Yorkshire
and printed in Great Britain by
Billing and Sons Ltd, London and Worcester

Contents

Introduction

One of the most familiar features of sociology teaching is the immense presence, no doubt to the chagrin of many students, of the classical thinkers, particularly but not only, Marx, Weber and Durkheim. It is hard to think of another discipline, except perhaps philosophy though for different reasons, in which founding figures loom so large. For us this is not only a measure of the achievement of such thinkers but a testament to the very real difficulties involved in producing good and innovative sociological ideas. As a result, many of the current disputes in sociology have a classical character in that they draw their inspiration, their importance, their ideas even, from the fact that they are problems which also preoccupied earlier social thinkers. This is not to say, of course, that the problems, the ideas, the disputes are simply always a modern rehash of old problems and ideas. The discipline has moved on though this has not always been progress and, where it has, it has not always been a smooth, cumulative development of wisdom. Sociology is still a disputatious discipline: as much typified by its arguments as by the knowledge it has produced. And it is this argumentative quality that we wanted to reflect in the contributions to this introductory volume.

In referring to the collection as a series of contributions on some of the classical disputes in sociology, we are not only trying to provide an idea of the tradition behind contemporary debates and show why they are classic in the sense of being old and enduring, but in the sense that they are key contemporary issues. We do not pretend that the disputes covered here are the only ones currently of major concern in sociology or that the classic problems could not have been presented rather differently. Indeed, one of the difficulties with dealing with sociological ideas is that they have seemingly multiple relevances and ramifications across a wide range of sociological interests. The Protestant ethic debate, for example, has clear relevance for the methodological discussions on the nature of sociological explanation, among others. So, what we have done is not to aim for another over-strenuously coherent, but ultimately misleading, view of the discipline, rather to try to present the issues as they are normally packaged in sociology courses. One consequence of this is that three figures loom large in nearly every chapter: Marx, Weber and Durkheim. However, rather than trying to settle on *one* definitive interpretation of each of these thinkers, we have left it to each contributor to give the account he felt necessary to the debate being written about. So, although the penalty of this is a measure of repetitiveness, at the same time it illustrates not only the importance of these thinkers but also the way in which their importance is exhibited is also part of sociological debate.

One final point. Though for reasons of exegesis many of the chapters may well give the impression of an ongoing debate in which the pros and cons are clear, the sides well defined, and conducted in the civilized manner of debating society, it should be remembered that this is, in most cases, simply a heuristic device. Many of the disputes are not disputes in this sense. The Protestant ethic debate and the future of capitalism, to pick but two examples, suggest that what looks like an exchange of views is more a case of scholars shouting past each other. Again, this is not uncharacteristic of sociology. It is often, very often, hard to see quite what the arguments are about, what the issues are, where they might lead, let alone do so in a quietly uncommitted and dispassionate manner. What is clearer is that the arguments, the disputes, will continue.

R. J. Anderson, J. A. Hughes, W. W. Sharrock.

Chapter 1

The Great Transition

DAVE FRANCIS

Introduction

The idea of the 'great transition' by which modern, urban, industrial society emerged from a pre-modern, rural society is arguably the central motif of the history of sociology. In one form or another it has influenced every area of sociology and provided some of its most abiding theoretical and empirical questions, such as social class inequality, social change, urbanism, social mobility, bureaucracy and secularization. In recent years, however, the great transition thesis has been subjected to critical re-examination. Though the critics are few in number compared with the legions of sociologists and social historians who have uncritically imbibed the great transition concept, their arguments strike at the roots of sociology's intellectual tradition. They suggest not just that there is a different way of telling the same story, but that there may be a quite different kind of story to be told.

The thesis of the great transition rests upon two key methodological assumptions. One is the idea of *holism*, the other the idea of *contrast*. The thesis posits two types of society, both characterized by a distinct set of interconnected features. The connections between these features are such that social change is fundamentally holistic, that is, it ramifies the various elements which make up society, resulting in a transformation of the whole. The new type of society which thus comes about stands in contrast to what went before. Each of its components stands in more or less direct opposition to the corresponding feature found in the other

type. The great transition thesis therefore presents the sociologist
with two analytic tasks. The first is to describe the components
which make up the societal forms in their 'before' and 'after'
states. The second is to chart the process of change itself. Which
components 'lead' the change and which 'resist' it? How does
change in one dimension of social organization transmit its
effects to other dimensions? How do 'new' social structures arise
from within the 'old'?

To these questions sociology has produced no universally
agreed answers. Instead it offers a variety of different theories.
There is much less of a problem about what these theories have
to explain. Many sociologists are in agreement, in broad outline
at least, on the nature of the contrast between the 'pre-modern'
and 'modern' societal types. A list of their features, which many
sociologists of different theoretical persuasions could agree,
looks like the following: 'pre-modern' society is overwhelmingly rural and agricultural; has a non-market economy based
upon the family; has little division of labour and a rigidly ascrip-
tive social structure with little social mobility; has a decentralized
political structure with localized leadership based on patriarchal
status; has an inflexible body of tradition and custom which
governs everyday behaviour; has a predominance of mysticism
and religion and in general is characterized by permanence rather
than change. By contrast, 'modern' society is overwhelmingly
urban and industrial; has a money economy based on factory
mass production; has an ever-expanding division of labour in
which positions are determined mainly by achievement; has
relatively high levels of social mobility, both within and between
generations; has a centralized state whose influence pervades
most areas of life; has formalized sets of rules and procedures
governing public affairs rather than tradition and custom; has
materialism and rationality as the dominant forms of thought
and is characterized by an ever-increasing pace of social and
economic change.

There are, of course, many other contrasting features which
could be listed as well as differences of emphasis, as we shall see.
What is more important though, rather than agreement on this
or that feature, is a shared acceptance of the methodological
assumptions of the great transition thesis. The assumptions of
holism and contrast frame the debate and anchor the programme

of investigation. Sociology has found this programme compulsive.

The Classical Debate

How did the programme come about? The short answer is that it was bequeathed to sociology by philosophy. At the heart of sociology lies the idea that human behaviour is conditioned by social environment. The actions, beliefs and dispositions persons display are not always the same but vary with their social circumstances. This commonplace idea, as it now seems, captured the imagination of social thinkers in the eighteenth and nineteenth centuries. It seemed to provide the key to the scientific understanding of man and history. Armed with such an understanding mankind would no longer be at the mercy of blind historical processes. It would be possible to control the course of history by reconstructing society in accordance with the laws of human behaviour. By perfecting man's social environment one could perfect man himself.

This, in essence, was the vision shared by the Enlightenment philosophers; by Utilitarians such as Bentham and Mill, by Marx and Engels, by Comte, Spencer and Durkheim, and many more. They differed, of course, in what they understood 'scientific understanding' of human behaviour to be and, therefore, also in the kind of social reconstruction it would promote. But what they agreed upon is much more profound and significant, as far as the development of sociology is concerned. They were in agreement that the path to scientific knowledge lay in understanding how the social changes which were happening around them were transforming society. For example, the image of a 'new society' obsessed philosophers of the Enlightenment in the eighteenth century (see Zeitlin, 1968, ch. 1). Though the versions they held of it differed considerably, the notion of *reason* as the proper basis of social life was common to them all. No social or political arrangements should continue simply because they had existed in the past. No claim to authority or position would be allowed which failed to meet the test of rational inquiry. The new society would involve a complete break with the past. Tradition, custom and religion would all be swept away. Political authority would be based on consent granted by free individuals or (in Rousseau's version) on a General Will distilled from the moral consciousness of all members of the society.

The emphasis upon reason in the Enlightenment conception of society was clearly influenced by the new scientific ideas of the seventeenth century and the materialist philosophies of men like Hobbes, Descartes and Leibniz. The materialist conception of the natural world as a mechanical order governed by immutable laws lay behind the Enlightenment vision. This influence is even more sharply apparent in the writings of the nineteenth-century Utilitarians. For them the new society would be constructed like a clock. Each of its parts would have a specific function and would fit harmoniously and effectively with other parts. Each individual would make a particular contribution to the whole and the whole would be no more than the sum of its interconnected parts (see Parsons, 1937, pt I). Social relationships would be wholly instrumental and would be guided only by rational calculations of common interests. Persons would co-operate because they needed one another, not out of considerations of sentiment, values or blind obedience. The result would be an ordered society in which the maximum distribution of happiness could be attained. Like the thinkers of the Enlightenment, Utilitarians like Bentham and Mill believed that they were merely bringing out and giving explicit formulation to possibilities that were present in the society of their time. They were proposing programmes not pipe dreams. The new society was being created around them. Their task was to act as its voice, to show to their fellow men what these social and intellectual changes signified.

Thus the 'founding fathers' of sociology inherited from philosophy the vision of a new society rising out of the old. They inherited not just the idea of societal transformation but crucial ideas about the key differences between the new and the old. The new society would be characterized by individualism, instrumentalism, rationality, secularism and impersonal market relationships. In the old society the group predominated over the individual, custom over decision, religion over rationality and personal ties over impersonal ones. The theories of the nineteenth-century sociologists were attempts to show how such features fitted together and to describe the mechanisms by which one societal 'type' was transformed into another.

Two of the most influential conceptions of societal transformation are those of Marx and Tönnies. For Marx the new and old societies, capitalism and feudalism, are in stark contrast. Industrial capitalism is dominated by the market. In the production of goods for the market their intrinsic worth plays little part; the worth of any commodity is its exchange value. Everything in society is dominated by the 'cash nexus', including labour which becomes another commodity to be bought and sold.

The organization of labour is determined solely by considerations of efficiency and the pursuit of profit. Mass production involves meaningless, repetitive tasks dictated by the requirements of the machine. It also necessitates the concentration of workers into huge factories. Differences between workers, skills, trades, experience and so on, are obliterated. On the other hand, the gap between the propertyless workers and the property-owning bourgeois increases dramatically. Differences of wealth and lifestyles become progressively more extreme as the insatiable appetites of capitalist production undermine all intermediate economic groups: shopkeepers, independent craftsmen and such.

These economic features of capitalist society are reflected in social and political conditions. The depersonalized values of the market pervade social relationships. Family ties are broken down as workers are crowded into cities, traditional family roles are destroyed as women and children are forced into the factories. Relationships based on personal bonds of status and custom disappear, to be replaced by formally defined relationships enforced through contract and law. The centralized state emerges as the administrator of these formal ties. Political life is declared formally independent of social and economic status and all citizens defined as 'equal before the law'. The appearance of equality or democracy is illusory, however. Their real purpose is to free social and economic relationships from the constraints of tradition. They reinforce the ideology of individualism which pervades capitalist society. In intellectual life, philosophical conceptions of the individual as the source of rationality and morality reflect the practical economic interests of the bourgeoisie and serve to justify the institution of private property. The focus in religion has changed from doctrines emphasizing the divine ordination of the social order to doctrines of individual sin and personal salvation.

All this is in marked contrast to the economic and social structures of feudal society. The class system of lords and peasants is based upon cultivation of the land in small-scale rural communities. These communities are organized into feudal manors, ruled over by a lord. The relationship between lord and peasant is quite different to that between capitalist and worker. The worker in capitalist society is formally free; in principle he can sell his labour to whomsoever he wishes. The feudal peasant has no independent status. He is tied to the manor of his birth. Such rights as he has are not legally enforceable but are defined solely by custom. His obligations far outweigh his privileges. His precarious livelihood from the land is hedged around with a multitude of taxes, rents and other payments to his lord and to the church. His lord is not simply his ruler and leader, but also his patriarch.

Just as the peasant differs from the worker, so also the feudal lord differs from the capitalist. The lord does not stand in relation to the land as its owner, in the way in which the capitalist owns his factories or mines. Land is not a market commodity, since feudalism is not a market society. The lord cannot dispose of his possessions at will. He also is tied to them, for they constitute an inherited seigniory which conveys title and position in society upon himself and his family.

In feudal society, additionally, there is no equivalent to capitalist notions of profit and efficiency. Production is not governed by rational calculations of output maximization but by rules of custom and practice. In the towns, the craft guilds exist to enforce customary methods and standards. The master craftsman organizes his workshop as an extension of his family. His journeymen and apprentices form an extension of his household. Payment in money is secondary to the rewards in kind they receive.

The particularism of feudal social relations finds expression in magic and superstition. Lacking objective knowledge of causal connections, the peasant invests the natural world with mystical powers and dangers. The land especially is regarded with a mystical sense of awe. In this intellectual climate religion is little more than a set of recipes for attaining some sense of security and control. The doctrines of the church pronounce the divine necessity of the fixed and unchangeable order of society. The peasant finds massive confirmation of this sense of permanence in his daily experience. Trapped within 'the idiocy of rural life', he cannot raise his vision beyond the horizons set by village and church.

Missing from this summary of Marx's conception of feudal society is his explanation of the forces of change which arise within it and eventually bring about its collapse. However, for the purpose of showing the connections between Marx's ideas and those of other nineteenth-century social theorists, Marx's explanation of the specific causes of the transformation are less important than his conception of its overall character. A brief look at Tönnies will illustrate this.

Tönnies's account of the transition from *Gemeinschaft* to *Gesellschaft* has strong similarities with Marx. The typologies Tönnies provides of these two forms of social life contain many of the same characteristics as Marx's models of feudalism and capitalism. There are, however, some crucial differences of approach. The most important is that *Gemeinschaft* and *Gesellschaft* essentially refer to abstract types of social relationship, rather than to historically specific forms of society. The basis of *Gemeinschaft* is 'natural' social relationships. These are typified by relationships in the family. A *Gemeinschaft* community, for Tönnies, is in essential ways like one large family group. The closeness and mutual dependence of family life involve strongly shared sentiments based on natural instincts and emotions. These sentiments are continually reinforced through shared activities and experiences. The family live together, work together and share a common fate. As a result, shared expectations and attitudes develop which are so deeply rooted that they take on a 'natural' status among the members. They experience their environment in the same ways and therefore, despite biological and psychological differences, they produce similar responses. These family-like ties extend across non-family relationships. In a *Gemeinschaft* society structures of neighbourhood, work and hierarchy are governed by customs and traditions which express time-honoured values. The holistic mentality predominates in every sphere of life. In law, for example, the needs of the group take precedence. Individuals have no legal status other than as members of a family or community group. Positions of authority are inherited and rulers are constrained by the rituals and traditions which express community identity.

Gesellschaft, by contrast, is characterized by 'artificial' social relationships. The model here is the contractual transactions of the marketplace. Individuals enter into relationships with others on the basis of calculations of self-interest. There need be no agreement between them beyond that which is necessary for the transaction. Each is an autonomous agent, motivated by his own goals and desires. The individual experiences his environment not in ways dictated by tradition and custom but through the filter of means–ends rationality. In *Gesellschaft* the principles of marketplace relationships pervade the whole social structure. Rules and laws are established through legislation and enforced by formally appointed officials. Political authority is based on franchise not inheritance. In all spheres of society, even down to family life, individual choice and decision is more important than shared sentiments and obligations. Society as a whole is a network of self-consciously created and formally regulated 'associations'.

Although *Gemeinschaft* and *Gesellschaft* are abstract models of two opposing types of social relationship, Tönnies is insistent that they have an historical reference. *Gesellschaft* characterizes modern industrial society, *Gemeinschaft* typifies to a greater or lesser extent all societies in the pre-industrial period. *Gemeinschaft* relationships cannot survive the shift from field and village to factory and city. Urban life with its crowding together of persons of different social types gradually destroys all 'natural' social bonds. It exacerbates social differences and promotes conflict and competition. Like Marx, Tönnies emphasizes the inequalities generated by modern capitalism. *Gesellschaft* is a class society, with an increasing gulf between a property-owning elite and propertyless masses. It is a society in which exploitation and moral hypocrisy predominate. Tönnies, no less than Marx, believes modern society to be destructive of the human spirit and man's potential for happiness. But this condemnation is contrasted with a rosy and positive view of life in pre-industrial society. Where Marx speaks of serfdom and rural 'idiocy', Tönnies stresses community and the stability of tradition. Although both emphasize the collectivism and immobility of rural society, what is repression and domination for the one is respect for established forms for the other.

Underlying this difference is a different conception of culture. For Marx, culture is synonymous with man's achievements. Capitalism is to be welcomed in preference to feudalism because despite its social evils it harnesses new forces of human productivity and creates the potential for a higher level of human existence. While he is no proponent of patient acquiescence, Marx regards the miseries of capitalist society, on one level at least, as the inevitable price of change. In this respect he is in the tradition of nineteenth-century apostles of progress. For Tönnies culture is conceived in terms of harmony, the fitting together of men and ideas in a unified whole. Whereas in Marx's view the goal of history is the liberation of mankind from oppressive social forces, in Tönnies view the issue is not liberation but unification. Because modern society has destroyed the basis of unity, history is on an inexorable downward path.

More important than these metaphysical differences between Marx and Tönnies, however, is a key theoretical similarity. Each in their own way proposes the idea that different forms of society are characterized by different types of social relationship. Therefore the transition from one kind of society to another involves a fundamental change in the kinds of relationships that members of society have with one another. Both reject the notion of a fixed, universal 'human nature'. In its place they put the idea of a socially created mentality which is specific to and characteristic of a form of society. The transformation of society is not just a transformation of its institutions. It also involves basic changes in the ways in which members of society think and act. Ways of thinking and behaving which are 'natural' in one type of society would be regarded as 'unnatural' in the other. Characteristic ideas and attitudes arise which are shaped by the social and economic context.

This 'sociology of knowledge' aspect of the great transition thesis is highlighted in the work of Max Weber. Weber emphasized that the modern capitalist economic system was built upon a foundation of 'rationality'. The social and economic changes which brought about this system were accompanied, even antedated, by a new attitude towards behaviour in general and economic activity in particular. This new attitude made possible the creation of new 'rational' social and economic practices:

In the last resort the factors which produced capitalism are the
rational permanent enterprise, rational accounting, rational technology and rational law, but again not these alone. Necessary
complementary factors were the rational spirit, the rationalisation
of the conduct of life in general, and a rationalistic economic ethic
                                (Weber, quoted in Eldridge, 1972, p. 279)

As is well known, Weber traces this rationalistic 'spirit of
capitalism' to the Protestant Reformation and the religious
doctrines of Calvinism. This explanation of the capitalist ethic has
been the subject of long and heated debate in sociology: a debate
largely conducted within the framework of the great transition
thesis. The main issue of debate has been over whether the
'rational' ethic is a cause or an effect of economic change and just
how necessary it is to the creation of capitalistic structures. As we
shall see later in the chapter, critics of the great transition thesis
have now questioned the assumptions upon which this debate
rests.

The Weberian concern with attitudes and ideas has come to
occupy centre stage in much recent theorizing about the great
transition. A central interest in much recent historical sociology
is the investigation of changes in beliefs and values, interpersonal
relations and everyday attitudes as related to larger scale changes
in the organization of economic life, the structure of the family
and the nature of community. It is to the contemporary state of
the 'great transition' thesis that we now turn.

Testing the Thesis

In recent sociological and historical discussions of the great
transition thesis the history of England has special significance as
a test case. Marx believed Britain to be the forerunner among
European societies. Britain was the first country to experience
industrial transformation. It was the society in which the central
components of capitalism, the free market economy, the factory
system and the urban proletariat, were most developed. It was
also the society in which the forces which brought about the
decline and disappearance of feudal institutions could most
clearly be seen. England in particular, for Marx, was both the
model for his conception of capitalist society and the test case of

his theories. To this day, the history of Britain from the sixteenth to the nineteenth centuries has continued to be viewed as the archetypal case of the feudalism to capitalism transition. Therefore, not surprisingly, it is over aspects of English history that the debate between supporters and critics of the great transition thesis has been joined.

We shall focus upon three areas of inquiry which form cornerstones of the great transition approach – economic change, change in family life and intellectual change. In each of these areas the dominant theories among sociologists and social historians have been shaped by, indeed built around, the great transition idea. And in each of them important new studies have been written in the last few years which seriously challenge orthodox views. To begin with, then, let us look at some debates over intellectual change.

Intellectual Change in Seventeenth-Century England

It is widely held that the seventeenth century was a key period in the intellectual history of England (see Webster, 1974). During this century new ideas developed which created new fields of knowledge or changed existing ones in fundamental and irrevocable ways. Two of the most important of these fields were political theory and natural science. In both, the seventeenth century produced thinkers whose work and ideas have remained enormously influential to the present day – people like Hobbes and Locke in political philosophy and Boyle and Newton in science. According to the great transition viewpoint, these thinkers were part of a single, unified 'intellectual revolution'. It was no accident that so many fields of knowledge experienced profound changes during this century. These developments co-occurred because they had the same underlying causes. They were intellectual responses to fundamental social, economic and political changes involving the collapse of the main elements of the 'old' socioeconomic structure and the emergence of 'new' social forces. As the intellectual manifestation of these new forces, the 'intellectual revolution' consisted of a related and coherent set of ideas across different areas of knowledge. The same set of principles lay behind major developments in political

theory and natural science, for example. Those principles were
rationalism, empiricism and humanism. The intellectual developments brought about were more than just an effect of social
and economic change, however. The relationship between ideas
and institutions was a reciprocal one. The 'new philosophies'
themselves promoted change. They did this in a practical way,
through the creation of new technologies, and also, more importantly, by establishing new attitudes towards social and political
life. They constituted the intellectual foundation of the massive
social and economic transformation of English society in the
eighteenth and nineteenth centuries which we know as the
Industrial Revolution.

So much for the broad outline of the orthodox conception of
intellectual change in the seventeenth century. But does the
historical evidence support this interpretation? To assess this it is
necessary to examine individual cases. Therefore we shall briefly
review the debates surrounding two modern classics of the great
transition approach, C. B. MacPherson's *The Political Theory of
Possessive Individualism* (1962) and Robert Merton's *Science, Technology and Society in Seventeenth Century England* (1939). Both
attempt to relate intellectual developments to their wider societal
context and, more specifically, to explain political philosophies
(MacPherson) and scientific discoveries (Merton) in terms of the
process of transformation towards a capitalist economic system.

MacPherson begins with the proposal that modern 'liberal-
democratic' theory (e.g. the idea that the authority of the state
derives from consent freely given by individual members of
society) originated in and emerges out of seventeenth-century
thinking about the relationship between the individual and the
state and how to reconcile authority with liberty. MacPherson
proposes that all major seventeenth-century thinkers framed this
problem in much the same way. He calls this conception 'possessive individualism'.

> Its possessive quality is found in its conception of the individual as
> essentially the proprietor of his own person or capacities, owing
> nothing to society for them. The individual was seen neither as a
> moral whole, nor as part of a larger social whole, but as an owner of
> himself. The relation of ownership, having become for more and
> more men the critically important relation determining their actual
> freedom and actual prospect of realising their full potentialities, was
> read back into the nature of the individual ... Society becomes a lot

of free equal individuals related to each other as proprietors of their own capacities and of what they have acquired by their exercise . . . Political society becomes a calculated device for the protection of this property and for the maintenance of an orderly relation of exchange.

(MacPherson, 1962, p. 3)

In MacPherson's view, then, a consistent vision of society underpins seventeenth-century thinking about politics. Relationships between individuals, and between the individual and the state, are modelled after economic relationships between owners of property in a free market. The pervasive influence of this model is demonstrated through a detailed analysis of the writings of Hobbes, Locke and Harrington whose views on individual freedom, rights, obligations and justice are shown to be powerfully shaped by it.

MacPherson's explanation of sevententh-century political thought is essentially a 'reflection' theory. It involves showing that England 'approximated closely to a possessive market society in the seventeenth-century' and that the image of a free and just society contained in the writings of political theorists corresponds to and presupposes the basic elements of such a system. Of course one obvious explanation for this correspondence, if it can be successfully demonstrated, is that Hobbes, *et al.*, consciously and explicitly modelled their thinking about political life on the economic structure of the society in which they lived. However, MacPherson proposes a more 'unintended' connection than this, essentially a 'sociology of knowledge' one. In seventeenth-century society, property, as a marketable phenomenon, had become so central to economic life, especially among the gentried classes from whose ranks Hobbes and Harrington came, that the assumptions of the possessive market system were *unwittingly* adopted as the framework for thinking about political liberty and authority. The problem of the relationship between authority and liberty has its roots in the new economic circumstances created by the emergence of the possessive market economy. It is an intellectual, 'superstructural' reflection of an 'infrastructural' phenomenon.

A number of writers on seventeenth-century political thought have challenged MacPherson's analysis. Much of the argument turns on textual interpretation. Does MacPherson's interpretation fit the bulk of a thinker's writings or has he concentrated upon those selections which give most support to his theory? On this point a persistent critic, J. G. A. Pocock, says of the analysis of Harrington:

> MacPherson's attempt to show that Harrington's system will not work unless entrepreneurial behaviour in landowners is presumed to be at its basis really comes down to his interpretation of a single passage ... But assuming MacPherson's interpretation to be correct here – I am not sure of this – there is still a great deal of Harrington's thought which he has not shown to be grounded on assumptions of entrepreneurial behaviour, and has more or less conceded not to be so grounded.
>
> (Pocock, 1972, p. 111)

On this level the very success of the MacPherson thesis in stimulating interest in the relationship between seventeenth-century political thought and its social and economic context has had the effect of making simple connections more difficult to defend. Hobbes and Locke may have been highly systematic thinkers, but their ideas are complex and resist distillation into a simple formula. The price of doing this may be to leave out all that is most distinctive and interesting about them.

From a sociological point of view, however, the more significant question is whether MacPherson's theory demonstrates the value of a holistic, social determinist approach to philosophy. Does it justify the assumption that

> The ideas of the ruling class are in every epoch the ruling ideas ... The ruling ideas are nothing more than the ideal expression of the dominant material relationships grasped as ideas; hence of the relationships which make one class the ruling one, therefore, the ideas of its dominance.
>
> (Marx and Engels, 1969, p. 64)

Assuming that England did change from a 'status society' to a 'market society' around the seventeenth century, does MacPherson show that liberal political philosophy was the necessary ideological partner to this transformation? Pocock believes not. Not only is the general relevance of conceptions of property to theories of political obligation problematic, but even where this relevance can clearly be seen, property is often an intellectual tool for the exploration of political dilemmas rather than political problems being symbolic versions of economic ones. Outlining an alternative conception of seventeenth-century philosophy as a reworking of classical concerns with questions of authority and justice, rather than a complete break with them, Pocock says

> In this scenario we can, of course, find highly systematic liberal philosophies occurring from time to time; but they always appeared in response to problems which they did not persuade everybody they had succeeded in solving, and they can be made to look as much like incidents as like turning points in the history of social consciousness. I am not calling into question the historical reality of 'liberalism' or 'possessive individualism', so much as those 'liberal', or rather antiliberal, interpretations of history, in which everything leads up to and away from a monolithic domination of 'liberal' ideas somewhere in the nineteenth century.
>
> (Pocock, 1980, p. 350)

Puritanism, Capitalism and Science

Important though it is, the debate over seventeenth-century political thought generated by MacPherson's work pales into relative insignificance when placed alongside the controversy over seventeenth-century science which surrounds 'the Merton thesis'. Merton's *Science, Technology and Society in Seventeenth Century England* was published in the mid-1930s, yet its arguments remain central to sociological and historical discussions of the origins of modern science (see the chapters by Merton, Hall and Kemsley in Russell, 1973).

Merton's basic aim was to show the influence of Puritanism in promoting the rapid expansion of science in England during the seventeenth century. Puritanism acted as a 'spur' to science in a number of ways, some of them 'direct' influences and others 'indirect'. The main direct influence involves the motivation to do science. Following Weber's lead Merton argues that the religious ethic of Puritanism created an outlook on the world which fostered the scientific attitude: an outlook that was a combination of two perspectives engendered by Puritanism. The first was an anti-mystical conception of the universe. In contrast to the medieval religious outlook, which presupposed an absolute distinction between the chaotic and impure world of man and the orderly, divine realm of the heavens, Puritanism conceived the mundane and the divine as dimensions of a single, unified reality. The whole universe was ordered and controlled by God; no matter how small and insignificant it might appear, there was nothing in the universe that did not display His presence and purpose. The Puritan deity was an orderly and methodical God, not a capricious and incalculable one. While men could not know Him directly, they could and should use the powers of perception and reason with which He endowed them to understand and appreciate His creation. From this point of view, then, inquiries into the inner workings of nature serve to *glorify* God, not question Him. Merton shows, using extracts from their writings, that many pioneers of science in seventeenth-century England, espoused religious sentiments like these to justify their investigations.

The second aspect of the Puritan ethic which acted as a motivation towards science was the importance it placed upon individual purpose and social welfare. As Weber argued, the doctrines of Puritanism produced a 'this-worldly asceticism' in which the worth of an individual was seen to be expressed in his commitment to a disciplined life of service to God and therefore to others. Merton suggests that science came to be seen as an activity which combined discipline of thought and material benefit to society. Therefore it was a proper field in which pious men could display their 'calling'. Merton argues that in the period before the institutionalization of science it was this kind of religious motivation that led men to treat science as a career. Individuals like Robert Boyle pursued their researches persistently and systematically, not for gain or fame but out of a sense of mission.

Puritanism also promoted the development of science in more indirect ways. Merton argues that the general impact of Puritan attitudes in English society created a climate of openness towards new ideas and a widespread belief in the capacity of human powers of reason and observation to solve mankind's problems. The overthrowing of traditional religious dogma led to a general humanism in society, even among those who were not themselves Puritans. This change in cultural values had the effect of making science publicly acceptable in a way it had not been before. Many people, especially among the educated and well-to-do classes, 'dabbled' in science in one form or another. Many more, while not engaging in science themselves, were interested enough to provide moral and financial support to those who were. In addition, the spirit of inquiry fostered by Puritanism, together with its emphasis on work and discipline, encouraged a search for new technologies to solve practical problems. New approaches in physics and astronomy required new instruments and more sophisticated forms of mathematical calculation. These developments had practical spin-offs. But also, the spirit of 'free inquiry' recognized no sharp distinction between pure and applied research. Therefore in fields as diverse as medicine, navigation, mining and land surveying the new attitude towards systematic investigation led to major technical developments, often by the very same individuals who were also grappling with fundamental issues of 'pure science'. The 'scientific revolution', Merton argues, was not just a transformation on an intellectual plane. It was linked with, and made important contributions to, the creation of new social and economic arrangements.

This aspect of the Merton thesis has been strongly emphasized by its principal proponent among contemporary social historians, Christopher Hill. Hill describes the social, political and economic framework of the seventeenth-century scientific revolution in more stark and simple (his critics say 'simplistic') terms than Merton. For him, science was a further manifestation of the emergence of new social forces in English society. It was strongly linked with the emerging 'bourgeois' class. The economic and political aspirations of this class were the foundations of the parliamentary opposition to royal authority which led to the Civil War of 1642–6 (or the 'English Revolution', as Hill prefers to call it). The two sides in the Civil War represented not just different political philosophies but also different social and economic interests. Not only that, they also represented different *scientific* mentalities: 'The civil war was fought between rival schools of astronomy, between Parliamentarian heliocentrics and Royalist Ptolemaics' (Hill, quoted in Webster, 1974, p. 222).

Hill has presented his version of the Merton thesis in a series of books and articles (e.g. Hill, 1965). It has attracted criticism from those who believe that the connections between Puritanism, science, political conflict and economic change in seventeenth-century England are more complex and problematic than Hill allows (see Webster, 1974, chs. 17–23). Many of the points of debate between Hill and his critics concern particular items of historical evidence for the Puritanism–science–capitalism link. For example, Kearney contests Hill's claim that interest in and support for science came mainly from the growing merchant and artisan classes through their support for 'dissenting academies' like Gresham College (Kearney, in Webster, 1974, ch. 17). Kearney argues that much scientific work was sponsored by landowning aristocrats rather than the urban bourgeoisie, and that the traditional universities were at least as important as sources of new scientific ideas.

A more general issue, though, is the question of how the term 'Puritanism' should be used. Both Hill and Merton use it to refer to a broad religious movement characterized by opposition to Catholicism and commitment to the values of 'ascetic Protestantism'. But as his critics argue, and as Hill himself recognizes, there was a wide range of beliefs in mid-seventeenth-century Protestantism, from, at one extreme, the high church 'Laudians', who advocated a hierarchical church on the Roman model, to, at the other, the radical 'enthusiast' groups like the Levellers, who were opposed to all forms of hierarchy. Despite this ideological spread, Hill maintains that there was a 'main stream of Puritan thought', at least in the period 1600–40. Kearney questions this (see Webster, 1974, ch. 19). However, terminology aside, the Merton thesis would lead one to expect that the majority of those active in science might come from, or be sympathetic to, the Nonconformist sects who rejected the established Anglican church. Recent studies have shown that this is far from the case. A key figure in the argument is Robert Boyle. Merton cited Boyle as a clear example of a man motivated to science out of strong 'Puritan' beliefs. The works of J. R. and M. C. Jacob show that Boyle was a 'latitudinarian' in theological matters, an Anglican who opposed both the authoritarianism of the high churchmen and the millenarianism of the 'enthusiasts'. He stood for the tie of church with state, but wanted a moderate and liberal church within which doctrinal differences were subordinated to a shared sense of moral purpose. J. R. Jacob (1978) accepts that Boyle's Christian faith was intimately linked with his scientific ideas. Boyle was committed to a 'mechanical' philosophy of nature. The universe was composed of 'matter in motion'; matter possessed an atomic structure and the atoms collided in empty space. But motion is not a 'natural power' that matter possesses.

Left to itself, matter is inert, and is imbued with motion from 'outside'. The dimension from which the power of motion originates is the spiritual realm of God. Boyle draws a sharp distinction between the material (atomistic) and immaterial (spiritual) realms. Man, for example, is biologically a material being, but also possesses a soul which is purely spiritual. Any attempt to conflate these realms leads to 'naturalism' – the idea that spirit is 'natural' to matter itself. This was unacceptable to Boyle, not so much because it was incompatible with experimental results (Boyle was a pioneer of experimental methodology) but because it denied the separation of God from the mundane world. If matter is inherently spiritual, there is no need to enforce Divine Law upon it, therefore no role for the established church to play.

On one level, Jacobs's study of Boyle gives support to Merton's conception of the religious origins of modern science. But the links it identifies are between a specific theological viewpoint and a particular scientific vision, rather than between 'Puritanism' and 'science' in general. Given that the seventeenth century was a highly religious time, a time when science was neither institutionally nor intellectually separated from other spheres of life, it is hardly surprising that men sought to integrate or reconcile their scientific and religious ideas. Boyle was no different to Descartes or Pascal in this respect. But whether this shows that Puritanism and science were aspects of a single 'intellectual revolution' must remain an open question, the more so since Descartes and Pascal were staunch Catholics.

Family Life and Social Change in England

The great transition thesis has shaped sociological thinking about the family even more profoundly than it has in relation to science or philosophy. Just how profoundly is indicated by the similarities between the conceptions of family life and social change contained in the writings of figures as diverse as Engels (1978), Weber (1961) and Parsons and Bales (1955, chapter 1). The view they share is that the transition from pre-industrial to industrial society was accompanied by a transformation in the structure of the family and the nature of family relationships. The result of this transformation is the creation of the 'modern family'.

The modern family is nuclear in form; the household consists of the married couple and their immature children. The relationships within this 'small face-to-face group' are far more intense than with other relatives. Family life is 'home and child centred', characterized by the values of domesticity and privacy. It is also dominated by notions of individual emotional satisfaction or 'personal happiness'. Conjugal roles are flexible and shared. Spouses select one another freely and equally and enter into marriage as a contract between individuals. If the emotional bond breaks down then the marriage can legally be terminated on the basis of mutual consent. Therefore divorce is an integral (and increasingly common) feature of family life. By contrast, the pre-industrial family is the economic basis of society. In the 'domestic mode of production' which characterizes pre-industrial society (of which more later) both production and consumption are organized through the family group. The household consists of a large number of kin, usually spanning three or more generations and with unmarried, and sometimes married, adult siblings living together under one roof. Authority is patriarchal, all the property and rights of the family are vested in the male head of the household. Children are an economic asset, therefore families are large. With high rates of infant mortality the pressure is upon women to bear many children, therefore regular and continual pregnancy is the norm. Marriage is subject to patriarchal authority, either directly through arrangement or indirectly through vetting of prospective spouses. This long-established conception of the pre-industrial family is nicely summarized by Brown and Harrison:

> the family provided a total form of security for its members, with an ordered accepted progression from one status to the next. The fusion of economic and familial activities and the close relationship to the land tended to combat feelings of alienation from work because they led to a natural harmony of interests between individuals and their environments. The pre-industrial family, thus, comprised an ordered society in which the problems of the various age-groups were catered for and the uncertainties of life were minimised.
>
> (Brown and Harrison, 1978, p. 72)

In the orthodox sociological view, then, there is a powerful connection between family types and types of society. The transition from pre-industrial to industrial society involves the destruction of the patriarchal, collectivist family pattern and its replacement by a nuclear, individualistic form of family. In the course of this change the family becomes a more narrow and limited institution while at the same time family members come to value the quality of their relationships in an entirely new way.

If this is the general outline of family change, what is the specific shape which the family took in England during the period of its transition to an industrial society? The major contemporary study here is Lawrence Stone's *The Family, Sex and Marriage in England, 1500–1800* (1977). In this book, Stone modifies and elaborates the family transition thesis. He argues that there were three main stages in the evolution of the modern English family. Up to the mid-sixteenth century, roughly, the predominant form was the 'Open Lineage Family'. From the mid-sixteenth to the early eighteenth centuries, this was replaced by the 'Restricted Patriarchal Nuclear Family'. Then, from the early eighteenth century onwards, there gradually emerged the 'Closed Domesticated Nuclear Family', containing all the main elements of modern family life. In all these changes it is the upper classes in English society who lead the way. Stone depicts the transitions in family life as filtering down from the 'top' of society towards the 'bottom'. He clearly believes that it is the upper strata of society who are most immediately and noticeably affected by social and economic change.

Another important feature of Stone's work is his claim that the changes in English family life involve not just demographic and organizational factors but also fundamental transformations in the way family members feel, think and act towards one another. Stone's description of the Open Lineage Family corresponds fairly closely to the sociological consensus about the pre-industrial, agricultural family (Stone, 1977, p. 6). Stone emphasizes the contrast between personal relationships in this period and those which characterize modern family life. Up to the seventeenth century the dominant fact of family life was the uncertainties created by economic instability and high mortality rates which made deep personal relationships 'very imprudent'. Therefore relationships between husbands and wives and between parents and children were lacking in affection. The typical sixteenth-century parent was, by modern standards, 'cold, suspicious, distrustful and cruel'. Like some previous

writers, Stone maintains that the modern conception of child-
hood was alien to pre-industrial thinking. Children were not
innocent, immature beings to be loved and guided, but necessary
burdens who only justified their existence by contributing to the
family economy. Stone complements this image of loveless
impersonal family life with an equally unpleasant depiction of the
pre-industrial village community:

> Overwhelming evidence of the lack of warmth and tolerance in
> interpersonal relations at the village level is provided by the
> extra-ordinary amount of back-biting, malicious slander, marital
> discord and unfaithfulness, and petty spying and delation which
> characterised life in the villages of Essex in the late 16th Century . . .
> The Elizabethan village was a place filled with malice and hatred, its
> only unifying bond being the occasional outbreak of mass hysteria,
> which temporarily bound together the majority in order to harry
> and prosecute the local witch.
>
> (Stone, 1977, p. 93)

This nasty, brutish society became, in some respects, even
worse with the advent of the Restricted Patriarchal Nuclear
Family. During the sixteenth century, especially among the
upper and emerging middle classes, social life became less
communalistic. Kinship and clientage declined in importance and
family life became more 'closed'. The effect of this was to make
relationships within the family more patriarchal and authoritarian. With the removal of communal controls and increasing
emphasis on individualism, wives became subordinated to their
husbands. Protestantism stressed the husband and father as the
spiritual head of the household, thus providing a religious
underpinning to domestic patriarchy. It also promulgated a rigid
code of morality in which children were seen as especially
vulnerable to sin and corruption. Therefore parents', particularly
fathers', relationships with their children became extremely
repressive. Concern with property placed importance on inheritance and succession. Thus marriage became a form of social and
financial investment and was even more rigidly controlled by
parents.

However, during the late seventeenth and early eighteenth
centuries, the trend towards increasingly authoritarian and patriarchal family relationships was reversed with the rise of 'affective
individualism'. Under this heading Stone seeks to connect a
number of developments. One is a growth in 'self-awareness'

and in the idea of 'individual autonomy'. Another is a relaxation in moral attitudes. There developed an 'increasingly open recognition and acceptance of sensuality'. For a time this new secular, sensual 'world view' was checked by the dominant ascetic Puritanism. But by the mid-eighteenth century its influence was widespread. The combined effect of these developments was to undermine patriarchalism and encourage a new conception of marriage as a sexual and emotional bond between equals, 'companionate marriage'. In the course of this change the idea of romantic love emerged, eventually to become the dominant theme of nineteenth-century writing about marriage and family life (Stone, 1977, p. 9).

But how acceptable is Stone's account of the history of the English family? His analysis is strongly challenged by MacFarlane (1979) and Laslett (1983). On the demographic aspects of the case, Laslett rejects the claim that family households were significantly larger in the pre-industrial period, once the data are adjusted to allow for infant mortality and adult life expectancy. Records for 100 parishes in the seventeenth century show that the extended family household was *not* the norm. The majority of elderly or widowed parents lived alone or with adult unmarried children (usually daughters). Rather than the extended household being a general phenomenon, it was only characteristic of the wealthy classes, who had larger families and servants living in. Also the notion that high infant mortality and low life expectancy are characteristic of the pre-industrial era is hard to reconcile with the fact that these rates remained stable during the sixteenth century and reached their highest and lowest points, respectively, during the eighteenth and early nineteenth centuries. For his part, MacFarlane denies that arranged marriage was the predominant pattern in rural communities. He emphasizes the distinction between parental *consent* and parental *selection* of spouses. On the question of the patriarchal structure of the family, MacFarlane's researches on land sales and inheritance (MacFarlane, 1978) show that, whilst the majority of land-holders were men, it was not unusual for a woman to succeed to the title of a piece of land upon the death of a husband or parent. Also there are several cases in the records he examined of women who increased their holdings through judicious buying and selling until they became substantial landlords. At least some women in pre-industrial

England, it would appear, were far from being disentitled chattels.

The thrust of these criticisms concern matters of interpretation as much as, if not more than, historical facts. Stone's conception of the pre-industrial family reads into the 'facts', even the correct ones, interpretations which are highly questionable. The cold, cruel, loveless family is little more than an inference from demographic and economic factors to the quality of interpersonal relationships. Even if the demographic and economic analysis was correct (which in MacFarlane's view, it is not), mortality rates and income statistics do not determine cultural definitions or moral values. Even if villagers' lives were brutish and short, that in itself does not necessarily make them nasty. Also, as MacFarlane points out, the claim that romantic love is an invention of modern society is contradicted by much medieval and Elizabethan literature. Stone acknowledges the existence of romantic love in sixteenth-century literature, but argues that it was viewed as fantasy, unrelated to 'real life'. One might ask how this differs from contemporary readers of romantic fiction. Again, Stone's image of the hostile and unpleasant social life of the pre-industrial village is highly dubious; as questionable in its way as the idyllic portrayal of the harmonious 'folk' community in the work of writers like Robert Redfield (see Redfield, 1968).

In his most recent book (MacFarlane, 1986), Alan MacFarlane has put forward a conception of marriage in pre-industrial England which differs utterly from Stone's. MacFarlane's conceptual starting point is the distinction between 'modern' and 'traditional' marriage patterns. This distinction, as we saw earlier, proposes that the entire character of marriage and family life differs between 'traditional' (i.e. pre-industrial) and 'modern' society. MacFarlane associates the 'modern' system of marriage with the ideas of Thomas Malthus. In this 'Malthusian marriage system' marital decisions are individualized. Whether, when and whom to marry is up to individuals themselves to decide, with few if any rules restricting the choice of spouse. The bearing of children is not mandatory – couples consider the question of children in rational, calculative terms, weighing up the economic and personal advantages and disadvantages and planning their families fairly precisely. These decisions are made jointly and the marital relationship is egalitarian. The key idea, which is implicit in the writings of Malthus, is that family life is constituted by rational decisions and thus the pattern of marriage and child-rearing in society is responsive to shifting economic and social circumstances. Thus in times of shortage individuals will delay marriage, or not get married at all, because they recognize that it is in their own individual interest to do so. This fact constituted, for Malthus, the main check against the tendency for population levels to expand at a faster rate than the resources required to support them.

MacFarlane points out that Malthus, writing in the early nineteenth century, can be interpreted from the point of view of the orthodox sociological approach to be a pioneer spokesman for a 'new' marriage system emerging out of the great transition. Prior to this, the theory goes, marriage had been a quite different phenomenon, governed by traditional, collectivist rules and constraints. In fact, MacFarlane claims, the rational, individualistic conception of marriage is not a 'new' phenomenon at all. Using a range of different kinds of evidence, including legal records and personal diaries as well as secondary sources, he examines attitudes towards courtship and spouse selection, the purposes of marriage, child-rearing, economic arrangements in marriage and marital breakdown, as far back as AD 1300. He finds little evidence for the kinship-dominated 'traditional' marriage patterns. For example:

> No substantial evidence has yet been produced to show that there were ever strong kinship rules, any form of 'elementary structure', concerning whom one *should* marry. Certainly by the thirteenth and fourteenth centuries such a structure, if it had ever existed, was gone. Likewise, evidence of rules forbidding marriage between different ranks in the social hierarchy is difficult to find from early on, and is certainly absent by the fourteenth century.
>
> (MacFarlane, 1986, p. 329)

MacFarlane concludes that the 'Malthusian' marriage system has its roots deep in the history of English society. But in the orthodox view, this system is tied to an economic system characterized by market forces and aquisitive individualism. If this functional link is accepted, one implication of MacFarlane's evidence is to suggest that rational economic individualism may not be a 'new' historical phenomenon either. MacFarlane is convinced that it is not. He first argued this in an earlier book,

The Origins of English Individualism (1978). In that work he attacked ideas which, for many sociologists and social historians, comprise the 'core' of the great transition thesis. While intellectual and family changes were involved, the great transition is for them first and foremost a transformation of economic life, centred around new economic groupings and structures.

The Economic Dimension:
The Individual and the Market

The great transition thesis posits two distinct economic systems in England over the past millennium. The modern system, industrial capitalism, arose out of the ruins of its predecessor, manorial feudalism. In the widely accepted view, there were three central components to the socioeconomic formation of manorial feudalism: (1) a domestic mode of agricultural production based on the family, (2) the politicoeconomic structure of the manorial estate, which was in turn based upon (3) a rigid social hierarchy involving legal and customary rights and obligations between lord and peasant, the institution of serfdom. When and why did this system break down? On the question of when, Marx is fairly specific. Although some aspects of feudalism began to decline as early as the fourteenth century, the period of its demise in England is between the mid-fifteenth and early seventeenth centuries.

As to why feudalism broke down, theories differ between those, like Maurice Dobb, who emphasize the inefficiency and 'internal contradictions' of the feudal mode of production (see Dobb, 1963, ch. 2) and others, like Paul Sweezy (see Sweezy in Hilton, 1978) and Marx himself, who locate the forces of change in 'external' factors like the growth of trade and the removal of restrictions on manufacture in the towns. Whatever the immediate causes of the decline of feudalism, the symptoms of this decline are clearly to be seen in the changing attitude towards the land in sixteenth-century England. According to Barrington Moore:

> Men ceased to see the agrarian problem as a question of finding the best method of supporting people on the land and began to perceive it as the best way of investing capital in the land. They began to

treat land more and more as something that could be bought and sold, used and abused, in a word like modern capitalist private property. Under feudalism too there had been, of course, private property in land. But in all parts of the world where feudalism grew up, the ownership of land was always burdened and hedged with a great variety of obligations to other persons. The way in which these obligations disappeared, and who was to win or lose by the change, became crucial political issues in every country that knew feudalism.

(Moore, 1967, p. 8)

The change from a feudal to a 'market' orientation towards the land in the sixteenth century was reflected in an upsurge in land sales and a great increase in rental revenues. The domestic form of production declined as manorial lands were converted to cash crops. Labour rent, such as working on the lord's desmesne, was replaced by money rent. The self-sufficient manorial economy was destroyed and in its place emerged a money economy. Landowners who could adapt to the new commercial environment accumulated great wealth. Those who could not were forced to sell, often to members of the expanding merchant middle class who spread into the countryside from the towns. Former serfs who had gained their freedom and managed their land efficiently rose from the ranks of the peasantry. They became yeoman farmers and some of their descendants continued the upward climb to eventually form part of the new rural middle class, the gentry. The tied peasantry as a whole gradually disappeared, to be replaced by a new class of agricultural wage labourers. The sixteenth century saw the beginnings of a mobile army of ex-peasants who were expelled from the land by enclosures and new farming methods. They were drawn to the towns and formed the basis of a new class of urban labourers. Their existence made possible the large-scale development of manufacturing and commerce.

This is the story of the English economy from the fifteenth to the eighteenth centuries which was told in outline by Marx (see Bottomore and Rubel, 1963, pp. 137–54), modified by Weber (1961), elaborated by Tawney (1912) and Dobb (1963) and summarized by Barrington Moore (1969). It no longer holds the stage unchallenged (see, West, in Kamenka and Kneale, 1975). But the most far-reaching critique of the orthodox story is MacFarlane's *The Origins of English Individualism* which questions whether England was ever, at any time, a collectivistic, family dominated, rigidly hierarchical 'peasant' society.

MacFarlane's argument centres around the nature of property in pre-industrial England, especially land. In the orthodox view the disposition of property in pre-industrial society is hedged around with traditional restrictions and obligations. Under the manorial system, as we have seen, the servile peasantry had rights of occupation but no rights of ownership. But even for 'free' peasants the dependence on the land was such that the hereditary family holding was a fundamental principle. It is not surprising, therefore, that sale of land was the exception rather than the norm (Hilton, 1973, p. 39).

This argument, that land sales and the 'alienation' of family holdings were highly exceptional in pre-industrial England is directly opposed by MacFarlane. He examines evidence drawn from two rural parishes, Earls Colne in Essex and Kirkby Lonsdale in Lancashire. He looks first at the records for the sixteenth and seventeenth centuries. During this period neither parish corresponds to the classic picture of an immobile population of family households, each settled on a parcel of land which is passed down from one generation to the next. In Earls Colne the land rental records show that of 111 pieces of land listed in 1549, only thirty-one were owned by the same family a mere forty years later. The parish register indicates considerable movement of population. A sample for the period 1560–1750 shows that only one-third of those entered were both baptized and buried in the parish, and the majority of these were infants and small children. In Kirkby Lonsdale hardly one farm is held consistently by the same family throughout the period 1642–1800. Therefore in both a relatively wealthy southern parish and a poorer northern one there is an absence of the sort of evidence one might expect for England as a peasant society.

It might be, however, that the sixteenth and seventeenth centuries are too late a period to look for that evidence. By that time in the parish of Earls Colne the pattern was of large manorial estates run as commercial agricultural enterprises. A large proportion of the workforce were agricultural wage labourers, not peasant farmers. There were a few large landowners and a multitude of small producers, and a significant amount of rural industry. From the standpoint of the great transition thesis, therefore, the evidence for peasant feudalism needs to be sought well before the sixteenth century. MacFarlane proceeds to examine the records for earlier periods. The further back one goes, of course, the fewer documentary sources are available. For example, court land rolls only began to be kept systematically in the second half of the thirteenth century. But studies of various parishes in different parts of England show that there was flourishing trade in land in many places right from the time records began. Indeed, in some parishes there appears to have been a bigger volume of land transactions in the thirteenth and fourteenth centuries than in later periods. The parish registers for Earls Colne suggest that there was as much geographical mobility there in the thirteenth century as in the seventeenth! MacFarlane argues that this evidence cannot easily be explained away as a temporary phenomenon created by exceptional circumstances. It is consistent with a different view: that land was a market commodity across much of England throughout the supposed heyday of manorial feudalism.

MacFarlane's analysis extends beyond the issues of land sales and population movement, however. In the orthodox view, these factors are connected with other basic characteristics of pre-industrial social structure, in particular the domestic form of production and the attitude towards the land which it engenders. In a 'peasant' society, land is possessed by the family group as a whole. Individual heads of households act as custodians of the family's right to occupy the land. Therefore patriarchalism does not equate with individualism. The land cannot be treated as the personal possession of the family head who happens, at this point in time, to control it. 'Possessive individualism' has no part to play in a feudal society. But how, then, are we to explain MacFarlane's findings on land sales, property accumulation and social mobility? As we saw earlier, MacFarlane is equally critical of the model of the English family as patriarchal, kin-dominated and collectivist. Therefore in his work the entire conception of pre-industrial England as a traditionalistic, rigidly hierarchical, non-market society is thrown into question. But such a rethinking presents a further problem.

In the orthodox account, the decline of feudal social relations and the rise of individualism, rationalism and commercialism constitute prerequisites for the sudden and rapid transformation of economic life which we call the industrial revolution. Between 1760 and 1840 manufacturing in Britain was revolutionized by the rise of factories and the invention of new technologies using new forms of power. As Polanyi says:

> The story has been told innumerable times: how the expansion of markets, the presence of iron and coal as well as a humid climate favourable to the cotton industry, the multitude of people dispossessed by the new 18th century enclosures, the existence of free institutions, the invention of the machines, and other causes interacted in such a manner as to bring about the Industrial Revolution.
>
> (Polanyi, 1957, p. 40)

For Polanyi, as for many others, social, moral and intellectual changes between the sixteenth and eighteenth centuries were the forerunners of the process of industrialization. With these foundations laid, industrialization could occur within an amazingly brief period of time. In little more than eighty years Britain was transformed from a predominantly agricultural economy to an industrial one. This change is epitomized in the development of the Lancashire cotton industry. In a few years cotton went from being an insignificant cottage industry to the major British manufacturing industry, utilizing remarkable technological innovations to employ thousands of workers in 'dark satanic mills'.

But what if the story of the rise of the cotton industry is not typical of the economy as a whole in the period 1760–1840? And what if the proportion of the British workforce employed in factories in 1840 was only between 10 per cent and 12 per cent of the whole? Add the further fact that the largest proportions of workers in the first half of the nineteenth century were employed in agriculture and in domestic service and the picture of sudden industrial transformation begins to require substantial modification. Fores (Fores, 1981), argues that the industrialization of the British economy was a far more gradual process than many writers who have focused upon the cotton industry lead us to believe. The rise of cotton manufacturing was untypical in several ways. It employed a much higher proportion of women than other manufacturing industries. The application of radically new technologies to the manufacturing process was a feature almost unique to cotton. In other industries there was relatively little connection between the growth of factory production and technological innovation. In some other ways, however, cotton was typical. Cotton manufacturing was located in the countryside not in the cities. This was true also for other textile production and other industries associated with the 'Industrial Revolution'. Fores rejects the usual association which is posited between industrialization and urbanization:

> The use of new techniques and the opening up of new types of employment, took people out of the towns into factories, mines and canal construction in the countryside; the process of urbanisation . . . took them the other way.
>
> (Fores, 1981, p. 196)

Fores's principal criticism of the classic account of the Industrial Revolution is that the image of rapid and total transformation has blinded many sociologists and historians to the complexities of a widely differing set of social and economic changes. Some of these were relatively sudden and dramatic, but many others were not. More significantly, perhaps, he points out that the concept of revolutionary transformation directs one's attention to things which changed to the exclusion of things which did not. In particular, it is often assumed that, because the factory system sometimes involved technological innovation and because new technologies sometimes utilized new scientific knowledge (though not often), industrialization transforms manufacturing from a pre-scientific to a scientifically based activity. But the use of machinery, Fores argues, does not make production 'rational' in any generalized sense. If rationality is defined, as it frequently is, as the application of scientific knowledge to practical tasks, then no general comparison is possible between rationality in 'modern' and 'pre-modern' society, for the obvious reason that science itself is an historically specific institution. If, on the other hand, it is claimed that technical activities in the present day are characterized by the mechanical application of formalized procedures, Fores maintains that this view is quite simply mistaken. Formalized procedures play a part, but only a part, in technical work, just as they *always* have done:

> Problems of construction – a machine, an institution, a legal or administrative judgement – are inevitably underspecified, in the way argued previously for the technical specialism, and even the most knowledgeable individual can rarely hope to be able to

demonstrate to others whether one, or another, solution is the best one possible. In a world which could be characterised as that of homo faber, rather than homo sapiens, it is important to grasp 'the rational fallacy': culture and the individual's experience in a special- ism inform the *faber* – constructor – about how to perform his work, far more than logic, reason and the written-down know- ledge of science can inform him. What, then, is discussion of the British 'industrial revolution' about?

(Fores, 1981, pp. 194–5)

The 'rational fallacy' is to suppose that the growth of formal knowledge transforms practical life into something quite differ- ent to what it was before. In Fores's view, it is this fallacy to which sociological theorizing about 'modern society' is obsti- nately and mistakenly committed.

Conclusion

What is at stake in the debate over the great transition? That some- thing important and fundamental is involved can be gauged by the reactions provoked by some of the studies described above. Mac- Farlane's *The Origins of English Individualism* was met with an out- burst of protest and opposition, some of it closely argued (for example, White and Vann, 1983), but in other cases stronger on outrage than argument. Fores's paper was condemned as a shallow terminological quibble over the word 'revolution', a criti- cism which missed the main point pretty spectacularly.

Another criticism wide of the mark is that critics of the great transition thesis are committed to the view that there have been no significant social changes in English society since the eleventh century: a bizarre charge which indicates the stranglehold with which the great transition thesis continues to grip much socio- logical and historical thinking. For example, MacFarlane does not deny social change, rather he denies that changes often cited as the fulcrum of the great transition of English society are well supported by historical evidence. It is important to recognize that in rejecting one general theory of social change writers like MacFarlane and Fores are not thereby committing themselves to some other general theory. The great transition debate is better conceived not as a dispute between two competing theories, but as a methodological argument between those who are committed to an holistic approach to social change and an historicist conception of history and those who reject such a commitment.

If we think about it in this way, the importance of the debate does not turn upon the detailed historical arguments. Since these involve questions of interpretation and significance as much, if not more, than matters of fact, there will always be room for disagreements. But the methodological implications of the great transition debate go to the very heart of sociological theorizing.

It is not simply that much of the conventional view of modern industrial society as a type, characterized by features such as rationality, individualism and materialism which take their significance from the contrast with 'pre-modern' societal types, may have to be rethought. Even more fundamentally, it can no longer simply be assumed that the methodological framework which enables the sociologist to conceive of societies as 'types' is the only or the best one for understanding social change. This framework, which is the bedrock of sociology's leading theories of change, requires justification. Such justification is not easily to be found in the knowledge it generates. If the critics are only half right, this now looks to be a collection of more or less plausible speculations at best.

References and Further Reading

Anderson, M. (1980), *Approaches to the History of the Western Family, 1500–1914* (London: Macmillan).

Bottomore, T. B., and Rubel, M. (1963), *Karl Marx: Selected Writings in Sociology and Philosophy* (Harmondsworth: Penguin).

Brown, D. and Harrison, M. J. (1978), *A Sociology of Industrialisation* (London: Macmillan).

Davis, K. (1948), *Human Society* (New York: Macmillan).

Dobb, M. (1963), *Studies in the Development of Capitalism* (London: Routledge & Kegan Paul).

Eldridge, J. E. T. (ed.), (1972), *Max Weber: The Interpretation of Social Reality* (London: Nelson).

Engels, F. (1978), *The Origin of the Family, Private Property and the State* (Peking: Foreign Languages Press).

Fores, M. (1981), 'The Myth of a British Industrial Revolution', *History*, vol. 66, pp. 181–98.

Hexter, J. H. (1961), *Reappraisals of History* (Chicago, Ill.: Chicago University Press).

Hill, C. (1965), *Intellectual Origins of the English Revolution* (Oxford: Clarendon Press).

34 *Classic Disputes in Sociology*

Hilton, R. (1973), *Bond Men Made Free* (London: Methuen).

Hilton, R. (1978), *The Transition from Feudalism to Capitalism* (London: Verso).

Jacob, J. R. (1978), 'Boyle's Atomism and the Restoration Assault on Pagan Naturalism', *Social Studies of Science*, vol. 8, pp. 211–34.

Jacob, M. S. (1976), *The Newtonians and the English Revolution, 1689–1720* (Brighton: Harvester Press).

Kamenka, E. and Kneale, R. S. (1975), *Feudalism, Capitalism and Beyond* (London: Edward Arnold).

Laslett, P. (1983), *The World We Have Lost: Further Explored* (London: Methuen).

MacFarlane, A. (1978), *The Origins of English Individualism* (Oxford: Blackwell).

MacFarlane, A. (1979), 'Review of *The Family, Sex and Marriage in English Society, 1500–1800*, by Lawrence Stone', *History and Theory*, vol. 18, pp. 103–26.

MacFarlane A. (1986), *Marriage and Love in England: Modes of Reproduction 1300–1840* (Oxford: Blackwell).

MacPherson, C. B. (1962), *The Political Theory of Possessive Individualism* (Oxford: Oxford University Press).

Marx, K. and Engels, F. (1969), The German Ideology (London: Lawrence & Wishart).

Merton, R. (1939), *Science, Technology and Society in Seventeenth Century England* (New York: Harper & Row).

Moore, B. Jr (1967), *The Social Origins of Dictatorship and Democracy* (Harmondsworth: Penguin).

Moore, B. Jr (1969), *Social Origins of Dictatorship and Democracy*, (Harmondsworth: Penguin).

Parsons, T. (1937), *The Structure of Social Action* (Glencoe, Ill.: Free Press).

Parsons, T. and Bales, R. (1955), *Family, Socialization and Interaction Process* (Glencoe, Ill.: Free Press).

Pocock, J. G. A. (1972), *Politics, Language and Time* (London: Methuen).

Pocock, J. G. A. (1980), 'Authority and Property: The Question of Liberal Origins' in B. Malamet (ed.), *After the Reformation: Essays in Honour of J. H. Hexter* (Manchester: Manchester University Press), pp. 331–54.

Polanyi, K. (1957), *The Great Transformation* (Boston, Mass.: Beacon Press).

Redfield, R. (1968), *The Primitive World and Its Transformations* (Harmondsworth: Penguin).

Russell, C. A. (ed.), (1973), *Science and Religious Belief* (London: Open University Press).

Stone, L. (1977), *The Family, Sex and Marriage in England, 1500–1800* (New York: Harper & Row).

Tawney, R. H. (1912), *The Agrarian Problem in Sixteenth Century England* (London: Longman, Green and Co.).

Tawney, R. H. (1938), *Religion and the Rise of Capitalism* (Harmondsworth: Penguin).

Tönnies, F. (1955), *Community and Association* (London: Routledge & Kegan Paul).

Weber, M. (1930), *The Protestant Ethic and the Rise of Capitalism* (London: Allen & Unwin).

Weber, M. (1961), *General Economic History* (New York: Collier).

Webster, C. (ed.), (1974), *The Intellectual Revolution of the Seventeenth Century* (London: Routledge & Kegan Paul).

White, S. and Vann, R. (1983), 'The Invention of English Individualism: Alan MacFarlane and the Modernisation of Pre-modern England', *Social History*, vol. 8, pp. 345–63.

Zeitlin, I. (1968), *Ideology and the Development of Sociological Theory* (Englewood Cliffs, NJ: Prentice-Hall).

Chapter 2

The Future of Capitalism

BOB JESSOP

Introduction

Theories and forecasts about the future of capitalism are among the most important and most contentious topics in the history of sociology. Disputes over this question can be regarded as 'classic' in three different ways. First, the future of capitalism provided a topic which was discussed directly or indirectly by many of the founding fathers of sociology. The genesis of sociology itself is closely connected with the rise of industrial capitalism and reflections on its origins, nature, dynamic, effects, and future were central issues for most sociologists. Secondly, the future of capitalism has been continually reappraised during the development of sociology. For capitalism has survived and expanded, changed in some respects and remained the same in others, experienced both boom and slump, been overturned in some parts of the globe and prospered elsewhere. Thus earlier theories have been tested as the future became the present and new ideas and forecasts have continually been proposed to reaffirm or correct past arguments. In this sense the future of capitalism has provoked disputes both *in* the classics and *about* their continued relevance.

It is also the focus of a classic dispute in a third sense. For the scientific status and/or political relevance of sociology have always been controversial and the present theme has obvious political implications as well as scientific pretensions. This is particularly clear in the recurrent claim that the growth of sociology represents a bourgeois reaction to Marxist and/or socialist interpretations of the origins, nature, and future of capitalism. More generally different sociological approaches towards capitalism and capitalist societies involve different expectations about the survival of capitalism. This holds both for theories which are merely concerned to predict what type of social organization will emerge next after capitalism and for those which aim to conserve, reform, or overthrow it. In this sense the classical views have also involved important political and ideological disputes.

In short we can approach the future of capitalism as a classic dispute in three different senses: as it occurs in the classic texts of sociology, as it has shaped sociology's subsequent development, and as it illustrates the fundamental political issues raised by sociological inquiry. We begin by briefly defining capitalism, then consider some problems involved in forecasting its future, discuss the key points at issue in the classic sociological approaches to this question, note how these points have been taken up in more recent work, and finally conclude with some general comments on the future of capitalism.

WHAT IS CAPITALISM?

Not all the theories discussed here are explicitly concerned with the capitalist economy or capitalist societies. But their inclusion is justified in so far as they focus on key aspects of capitalism as understood by Marx and/or Weber, its two most important theorists. In these terms capitalism can be defined as an economic system in which goods and services are produced for sale (with the intention of making a profit) in a large number of separate firms using privately owned capital goods and wage labour (Bowles and Edwards, 1985, p. 394). In turn a capitalist society is one whose economic system is predominantly organized along capitalist lines. This does not mean that the economy determines all other features of a capitalist society nor that political and cultural institutions have no effects of their own. It does mean that the class relations in such societies are largely shaped by the relation between capital and wage labour and that many economic problems confronting the political and ideological systems will be shaped by their insertion into a capitalist economic system.

Thus Durkheim can be included because he examined the capitalist division of labour and its implications for other spheres of society. Likewise theorists of post-industrialism can be included because they discuss the impact of the shift from a capitalist economy specialized in goods production to one which produces mainly services. But theorists who are chiefly concerned with say, urbanization, mass politics, or family patterns can be safely excluded.

FORECASTING THE FUTURE

In discussing the future of capitalism one is not (or should not be) engaged in detailed, long-range prediction of specific events. Instead one's task is to forecast how major trends will develop on the basis of existing tendencies, regularities, and recurrences which seem sufficiently marked to justify such projections. Sometimes this involves nothing more than the simple extrapolation of short-term statistical trends. But such trends can be misleading when taken out of context so that the constraints imposed by the overall structure and dynamic of the capitalist system are ignored. Two other approaches which often occur in the classic texts and in more recent work are those of extrapolating from the institutional logic of particular systems (rather than from specific statistical series) and/or from past cycles of development which can be observed over a long period of time. Thus some theorists have tried to identify the inherent dynamic of particular institutional systems (such as technology, the division of labour, mechanisms of economic exploitation, rationalization, or bureaucratization) and their implications for other systems and the overall organization of societies. Others have tried to identify long-term patterns or cycles of capitalist development and the events which typically trigger them off (such as changes in how production is organized, new military technologies, waves of entrepreneurial innovation, or wars). Even in these cases, however, forecasts become less specific as their time-horizon stretches further into the future. The problems involved in these different approaches will become clearer as we proceed.

Early Sociology and the Future
of Capitalism

Sociology first emerged as a distinct discipline within the social sciences after the French Revolution and it was eventually consolidated as such during the last quarter of the nineteenth century (Therborn, 1977). What made sociology distinctive was its evolutionary view of social development and its argument that a decisively new type of social order had recently emerged. Early sociologists such as Comte, Saint-Simon and Spencer drew a contrast, each in their different ways, between (1) the new, peaceful order based on modern industrial production, trade, and science and (2) earlier, war-like societies based on economic coercion, military conflict, and religious ideologies. From this they drew fairly optimistic conclusions about the peaceful development of industrial (or capitalist) society and emphasized that political life should also be reorganized so that it no longer reflected the old parasitic and feudal–military state systems. They differed on how this should be achieved – through a new industrial-scientific priesthood, socialist co-operation and technical administration, or through a liberal, nightwatchman state with minimal functions. But they were all convinced that this was feasible and that the evils of industrial society could be eliminated.

This early optimism about the peaceful future of industrial capitalism was shattered, however, by the growth of imperialism, the development of military rivalries and the intensifying conflicts between capital and organized labour. In turn this encouraged two different trends in sociology. Some sociologists turned to an analysis of politics. In different ways they emphasized the inevitability of rule by elites, of political and ideological manipulation of the masses, of racial and ethnic antagonisms, of conflicts between national interests and so forth. Among these theorists we should mention the continuing influence of such theorists of elites as Pareto, Mosca and Michels. But here we focus on the second trend. This involved an increasing concern with the political economy of industrial capitalism and its implications for the developing social order of modern societies. In this way the dispute with Marxist and socialist interpretations became a decisive element in the growth of classical sociology. Before turning to the founding fathers of classical (as opposed to early) sociology, therefore, we should briefly review the arguments advanced by Marx and Engels.

Marx and Engels on the Future
of Capitalism

The close ties between the analysis of capitalist societies and political attitudes emerge in a different way in the work of Marx and Engels. Like the early sociologists they lived during the crucial transitional period when competitive capitalism based on industrial production was establishing itself in Europe and North America and its influence was spreading throughout the world.

Marx and Engels provided their most general and accessible statement about capitalism and its future in the *The Communist Manifesto* (1848). They described capitalism as a revolutionary mode of production which was fundamentally changing the course of civilization. It introduced market relations and the cash nexus into all spheres of society and throughout the world, so overturning traditional social bonds. By continually modernizing the forces of production and promoting the division of labour, capitalism prepared the material conditions necessary for social co-operation and planning in economic life. But, despite the ever-increasing *social* character of production (often termed the socialization of the forces of production), the capitalist economy operated in an anarchic, uncoordinated manner determined by the *private* interests of individual capitalists concerned only with their own profits. The search for private profit imposed fetters on the further development of production. Wealth accumulated in the hands of capitalists whereas its direct producers were impoverished. This was reflected in the co-existence of unsold goods and unmet needs which produced ever-worsening economic crises. The dynamic of capitalism was one of self-destruction.

In particular, capitalism was creating its own gravediggers through the continued expansion of the so-called proletariat. This comprised workers whose only economic property was their labour-power and whose only alternative to starvation was to sell this to one or another capitalist. As capitalism destroyed pre-capitalist modes of production at home and abroad, other classes were eliminated and the proletariat expanded. It was also concentrated in ever-larger numbers as factories grew and the division of labour became more complex. As individual workers, then groups of workers in a factory or trade, and, eventually, all workers in a nation-state (or even the world economy) mobilized to resist capitalist exploitation, they would grow more conscious of their shared class position and their common interest in the overthrow of capitalism. Their economic struggles would also encounter the resistance of the state as well as individual capitalists and groups of employers. In this way the working classes would develop a revolutionary consciousness and move from trade unionism to party political organization. With economic conditions worsening and the proletariat gaining in strength (helped in part, according to Marx and Engels, by the Communist Party), the revolution would eventually break out. When the working class had conquered political power, it would take over the means of production and subject the economy to social control.

Marx presented a more developed account of the capitalist mode of production in the three volumes of *Capital* (1959). This was less concerned to forecast how capitalism would be overthrown (although he still believed this would occur) than to consider how it had developed, how it functioned, and how it expanded. Here we only consider Marx's analyis of the course of its expansion and not his views on how capitalism originated.

Capital describes several fundamental laws which were typical of capitalism and would shape its future development. Although Marx conceded that most of his evidence came from Britain, he also insisted that other countries would undergo the same experiences of capitalism. Some of these laws shape the recurrent rhythms of the capitalist system and others determine how it changes over longer periods of time. Here we concentrate on Marx's views on the long-term changes in capitalism before its contradictions became so acute that it either collapsed or was overthrown through revolutionary class struggle.

The most important general law was the so-called 'law of value'. This describes how capitalists allocate resources to different fields of production according to their expectations of profit. Although this law is mediated through market forces, it ultimately depends on the sphere of production. For only here can the surplus-value (added value) which finances profits be produced. Marx also described certain developmental tendencies of capitalist economies. These include: the growing *concentration* of capital, that is, the accumulation of capitalist assets by single firms through the reinvestment of past profits; the increased importance of *productivity* gains ('relative surplus-value') as opposed to longer working hours and greater effort ('absolute surplus-value') in the creation of surplus; the increasing urgency of overcoming the obstacles to capitalist expansion involved in the *tendency of the rate of profit to fall* – a general tendency which emerges in so far as all enterprises seek a competitive edge by substituting labour-saving machinery for wage labour even though the latter is, according to Marx, the sole source of profit on the total capital advanced to buy production goods, materials, and labour-power; the growth of the *reserve army of labour* (the unemployed) as productivity gains outstrip wages; the growing *centralization* of capital, that is, the management of assets owned by different individuals or firms by one enterprise (e.g. through joint-stock companies or banks); the growing *separation of legal ownership and effective control* of the means of production through the development of joint-stock companies and related forms of business organization; the growing importance of *credit* in the functioning of the capitalist system; and so forth.

It should be noted that Marx did not treat these developmental tendencies as 'iron laws' which operated with unbending necessity. Instead he always considered how they were mediated through capitalist competition and the struggle between capital and labour. In addition, *Capital* also modified Marx's earlier predictions about the growing polarization of class relations. For Marx indicated (somewhat imprecisely) that as capitalism developed it would require a growing middle class of clerks, engineers, managers, accountants and so forth. The implications of this developmental tendency for his analysis of how the working class would overthrow capitalism was not brought out.

Such complexities make it unclear exactly how Marx foresaw the final crisis, if any, of the capitalist economy. Sometimes he implied that it would occur through the collapse of profits owing to the tendency of the rate of profit to fall, sometimes that it would be through lack of demand owing to the growing impoverishment of the proletariat, sometimes to the disproportions between different branches of the capitalist economy, and, sometimes, that the class struggle – and not some automatic mechanism – would bring about the overthrow of capitalism. But he did insist that capitalism had a stricly limited future and would eventually be superseded by a new form of economic and political organization. This would involve collective ownership and control of the economy and the abolition of the political division of labour between people and delegates, delegates and bureaucrats.

In most respects Engels shared Marx's views on the future of capitalism as an economic system and, indeed, it was Engels who edited the last two volumes of *Capital*. But one point which Engels emphasized is that there would also be a tendency towards increased *state intervention* in the capitalist economy. He argued that the fundamental contradiction between the socialization of the forces of production and the anarchy of the market would become more acute. In turn this would encourage efforts to eliminate the anarchy of production. Initially this would involve joint-stock companies and other ways of co-ordinating different capitals; and then, as even monopolistic forms of capitalism encountered difficulties, there would be a move towards state production, planning, and intervention. In this way the state would become the 'ideal collective capitalist' and thereby prepare the ground for the management of all the productive forces by society itself (Engels, 1954).

Marxist Theories after Marx

As both Marx and Engels recognized, capitalism is a dynamic system which changes constantly. Indeed, important changes have occurred both in the most general features of capitalism and in the relations among different national economies. Not all these changes were anticipated by Marx and some of them he could not possibly have foreseen. Later Marxists have attempted to integrate these changes into Marxist political economy and to provide fresh forecasts about capitalist development and the prospects for revolution. Three classical revisions are examined here and some neo-Marxist accounts are discussed later.

Marxist theory suffered a certain sclerosis after Marx's death in 1883. This can be seen most clearly in the rigid orthodoxy which came to dominate the Second International. In part the views of the Second International are interesting in themselves but they are also important on other grounds. For they provided both the context in which disputes over the future of capitalism developed in Marxist thought and the foil against which those classical sociologists interested in a debate with Marxism developed their own ideas on industrial capitalism.

The most noticeable features of orthodox Marxism were its rigid economic determinism, its emphasis on the class struggle, and its faith in the revolutionary nature of the proletariat. Its economic determinism was often expressed in the view that the iron laws of capitalist development would sooner or later produce an economic catastrophe so devastating that it would spark the latent revolutionary consciousness of the workers and other oppressed classes and thus provoke the final overthrow of the capitalist system. This 'catastrophist' view was coupled with two further articles of faith. The revolution would break out in the most advanced capitalist societies – where the contradictions of capitalism and the socialization of the forces of production had most prepared for the transition to socialism. And it was the class struggle (more specifically, the struggles of the working class) which would bring about the revolution. Classes were the privileged agents of historical transformation.

Within the mainstream Marxist movement these articles of faith were challenged above all by Eduard Bernstein, a prominent German social democrat. Bernstein argued that capitalism was not developing as Marxist orthodoxy suggested (Bernstein, 1961). Indeed actual economic trends appeared to contradict its economic catastrophism. He noted that standards of living were rising, that shares were more widely distributed through the development of joint-stock companies, that there was no polarization of classes, that the peasantry had not been eliminated, that small and medium capital survived, that the middle class was expanding (especially with the growth of what we now call the white-collar groups), that the economic crisis tendencies of capitalism seemed to be moderating, and that it seemed possible to plan capitalism to avoid crisis. Although some of these developments were anticipated by Marx himself in *Capital*, orthodox Marxism had been less concerned to follow these arguments. For Bernstein all of this implied that contrary to the orthodox Marxists capitalism would not collapse. Instead it could be gradually adapted and transformed into socialism with the support of the middle classes and peasantry as well as the working class. Class alliances and democratic politics were the key to such a peaceful and gradual transition. In this way Bernstein helped to prepare the theoretical and intellectual ground for social democratic reformism and seemed to re-assert the early sociologists' belief in the peaceful, productive future of industrial society.

Somewhat different but equally influential views were developed by Rudolf Hilferding, a leading Austro-Marxist theorist and a prominent politician. In various studies during the first forty years of the present century, Hilferding described and tried to explain the principal changes in modern capitalism. He noted the growing dominance of large firms and the emergence of cartels and trusts, all of which try to restrict competition; the major expansion of the credit system in mediating the development of capitalism; closer links between banks and industry, amounting to their fusion in a form of finance capitalism; and growing state intervention in the economy. In particular he emphasized two main trends: imperialism and organization. Imperialism involved the competition for international economic and political domination among different finance capital groups and was pursued with the support of strong nation-states. Equally important was the growing trend towards the organization of capitalist production and markets through economic planning conducted by banks and the state. Indeed Hilferding claimed that a new stage, organized capitalism, had been reached. Like Engels, who anticipated such arguments in discussing the state's role as an ideal collective capitalist, Hilferding believed that the growing concentration of economic power in the hands of a few monopolies and the state would make it easier to seize power and to engage in democratic socialist planning.

Lenin substantially modified orthodox Marxism by focusing on the implications of monopoly capitalism and the imperialist rivalries among different national economies. Although he was influenced by Hilferding and Bukharin (another Marxist theorist of imperialism), Lenin drew quite different political lessons. He described imperialism as the highest, last stage of a moribund, decaying, monopoly capitalism. He identified five fundamental traits of imperialism: (1) the rise of monopolies, (2) the fusion of banking and industrial capital to form a financial capitalist oligarchy, (3) the export of capital in an attempt to counteract the tendency of the rate of profit to fall on the home market, (4) the development of international cartels and trusts, and (5) the territorial division of the world among the great capitalist powers (Lenin, 1982). He stressed that the rise of imperialism fundamentally changed the prospects and dynamic of revolution.

As monopolies struggled for extra profits and markets at home and abroad, political repression and wars became the order of the day. Although imperialist profits enabled the monopolies to buy off key sectors of the working class (the labour aristocracy), other workers were still oppressed, the intermediate classes and even non-monopoly capital were subject to monopoly domination, and capitalist powers contended with each other for control of markets. All this meant that the state became increasingly repressive and militaristic. This ruled out a peaceful, democratic road to socialism. The rise of imperialism also changed the likely site of the first revolutionary rupture in capitalism. It was no longer the most advanced capitalist societies which were most likely to experience revolution but those undergoing the most severe social disruptions. Lenin himself believed that Russia was especially vulnerable in this sense and that the Russian proletariat (with support from the peasantry) would instigate a revolution which would then spread abroad.

Even this short review has shown, first, that classical Marxists were seriously concerned with the changing character of capitalism and its political implications and, secondly, that they engaged in disputes about it. These concerns were maintained throughout the vicissitudes of capitalism and the changing fortunes of the working–class movement. The changing character of imperialism and state intervention has rendered many of the original arguments redundant but the themes advanced by Bernstein and Hilferding are still significant for contemporary Marxism. But we must now consider how classical sociology treated the future of capitalism.

Classical Sociology and the Future of Capitalism

The development of classical sociology was closely related to the consolidation of industrial capitalism and its impact on contemporary social institutions and relations. Here we consider Durkheim's work and then concentrate on Max Weber. This means neglecting such key German theorists as Tönnies, Simmel, and Sombart as well as leading American classical sociologists, but this can be justified by Weber's absolutely central role in sociological thinking about capitalism.

DURKHEIM AND THE CAPITALIST DIVISION OF LABOUR

Emile Durkheim was a French sociologist and moral philosopher. He was less interested than the classical German sociologists in capitalism as such but he was intensely concerned about the social pathology of contemporary industrial society. In certain respects his arguments take issue with those of Comte and Saint-Simon on the future of capitalism and, more generally, they develop key themes from the liberal republican tradition of the French Revolution. This can be seen most clearly in his critical analysis of the evolution of the division of labour and the specific forms it assumed in modern capitalism.

Durkheim argued that primitive societies were characterized by a mechanical division of labour. All individuals performed similar tasks and social solidarity was based on shared values. Then, for reasons which need not concern us here, there was a gradual move towards an organic division of labour. Individuals performed different tasks and social solidarity was based on moral individualism and cultural pluralism (Durkheim, 1962). In defining the modern division of labour in these terms Durkheim took issue with both Comte and Saint-Simon (Giddens, 1977). Thus he rejected both Comte's plan to impose a shared morality under the authority of an industrial-scientific priesthood as a return to mechanical solidarity, and the Saint-Simonian belief that routine co-operation based on economic interdependence could in itself secure social solidarity since any society must also have a fundamental moral dimension. None the less Durkheim did believe that the organic division of labour could provide the basis for individual freedom and social co-operation if the pathological features of contemporary society were eliminated.

In particular Durkheim criticized three aspects of the capitalist division of labour: its forced character, its excessive character, and its anomic character. It was forced because class relations and the inheritance of private property meant that individuals were not free to find the work most suited to their skills and talents; it was excessive because workers often had insufficient work to keep them occupied in a way that produced job satisfaction; and it was anomic because it was unregulated by a coherent value system (Durkheim, 1962).

It was these unhealthy features of the modern division of labour and not industrial society as such which engendered class conflict. Class struggles should disappear once this division of labour was properly regulated. This could be achieved through economic co-operation among modern guild associations and through the overall political and moral guidance of a liberal republican state whose power could be checked as necessary through these same guilds. In this way the future of capitalist society could be assured and its full potential for individual freedom and moral order could be realized.

MAX WEBER ON THE IRON CAGE OF CAPITALISM

Weber's work is often treated as *the* sociological counterpart of Marx's economic analyses and Weber himself as the bourgeois Marx. This suggests that we have here a classic dispute over the future of capitalism and not simply a difference of opinion. But, whilst subsequent commentators have certainly tried to construct such a dispute between Marx and Weber, their attempts are in many ways misleading. As the claim that Weber debated with the ghost of Marx implies, there was no direct confrontation between them. Even less could one argue, as is sometimes suggested, that Weber deliberately stressed the leading role of ideological as opposed to economic factors in historical development. Instead he addressed quite different methodological and theoretical issues. In addition, Weber was writing when the transition from competitive to monopoly capitalism was already well under way in Germany and elswhere and imperialist rivalries were becoming sharper. Thus the capitalism confronting Weber differed from that which Marx studied. None the less, Weber's approach to capitalism and its future did differ markedly from that of Marx. And he did side with the liberal bourgeoisie and Germany's national interests rather than with the international working-class movement. Thus, even if there was no open dispute between Marx and Weber, much can be gained from comparing their analyses.

Weber was concerned above all to understand the development of modern, Western civilization and its historically unique character. He focused both on its cultural values and its core institutional order. He considered that its value system was unique because it was dominated by formal rationality. This involved an emphasis on precise calculation of the relations among various means and ends in terms of abstract principles which are universally applied. This type of rationality could be found in spheres as diverse as technology, musical harmony, economic organization, the administration of government, the secularization of religion, the development of mathematics and science and so forth. Its growing predominance in the modern world was reflected in the latter's loss of ultimate values and mystery (disenchantment).

Weber also considered that two key institutions in the organization of Western civilization were bureaucratic administration and the capitalist enterprise. Bureaucracy involved the rational organization of administration not only in government but in many other types of association. It was characterized above all by close adherence to administrative codes and formal regulations. Likewise the modern capitalist firm engaged in rational calculation about the various opportunities for monetary profit on the market that would follow from different patterns of economic activity and directed its activities to securing the maximum profit (Weber, 1968, p. 85).

For Weber there were two crucial characteristics of modern capitalism: firstly, the institutional conditions which permitted a rational calculation of opportunities for profit *on the market* (as opposed to profits from plunder, war, political corruption, organized crime, etc.) and, secondly, the role of entrepreneurs in setting economic enterprises in motion after such profit opportunities. The importance of entrepreneurship received much emphasis in Weber's famous study of *The Protestant Ethic and the Spirit of Capitalism* but Weber also examined the institutional conditions of capitalism in *Economy and Society* and *General Economic History*.

For Weber modern capitalism was significant because it spread rational economic calculation into everyday life and was involved in satisfying ever-more needs. Among other things this spread of capitalist relations involved: (1) the appropriation by private enterprise of all physical means of production; (2) the freedom of the market from irrational restrictions on trade or labour, for example, laws on Sunday trading or trade union monopolies; (3) rational technology, permitting calculation, typically based on mechanization; (4) calculable law so that enterprises could foresee the legal consequences of their actions; (5) free labour – involving legally free but economically dependent workers who were free to sell their labour-power on the market; and (6) the commercialization of economic life, that is, the use of financial instruments to represent share rights in enterprise and property ownership (Weber, 1981, pp. 208–9; Weber 1968, pp. 92–3). The rise of the money economy and double-entry book-keeping were also important in permitting rational capitalist calculation both during the planning stage and when preparing profit-and-loss accounts. Indeed Weber stressed how the abstract norm of monetary profit came to dominate all aspects of the deployment of economic resources under capitalism. Thus a rational firm would reject the mechanically most-efficient technology if other techniques were more profitable (Weber, 1968, pp. 65–7). This calculation is undertaken within individual firms and is only later validated by the market (Cohen, 1981, pp. xxxii–xxxvi; and Collins, 1980).

Weber believed that rationalization rather than class struggle defined the main developmental axis of modern societies. This was reflected in his criticisms of both capitalism and socialism. He criticized capitalism on the grounds that the spread of formal rationality subordinates the original ends of rational action to its means. Capitalist economic activity becomes obsessed with making money rather than goods; and making money rather than satisfying human needs becomes the criterion of economic success. Thus the initial purposive rationality of capitalism is destroyed by the growth of instrumental reason. But Weber also criticized socialism. He suggested that technological rationalization and bureaucratic domination were essentially irreversible and implied that calls for their abolition were either retrogressive or utopian. They were retrogressive because other modes of economic and political organization could not sustain the material prosperity which had been secured through capitalism. They were utopian because the nationalization of capitalist enterprises would actually reinforce bureaucratic domination. Implementing the socialist programme would merely substitute public for private bureaucracy in economic management – thereby fusing the state and the economy into a single bureaucratic despotism.

Lacking the Marxist's faith in the self-destruction of capitalism or the revolutionary potential of the working class, Weber looked elsewhere for the solution to the pathology of modern capitalist societies. In particular he stressed the role of national power politics in providing both ultimate meaning and the means to temper purely technical domination. Everyone could strive, to be sure, for some measure of individual autonomy and responsibility in the face of increasing economic interdependence and political dependency. But the basic solution was to be found at the level of the nation-state and internal politics. A sense of purpose could be established by pursuing the interests of the national community and by advancing the economic and social welfare of all classes at home. In turn this would require vigorous political direction from charismatic leaders able to define and defend national interests and to mobilize popular support under a system of plebiscitary, parliamentary democracy (Beetham, 1985).

Locating Weber's arguments in this way reveals their significance for the development of classical sociology. For Weber was not only interested in the political economy of capitalism in the age of imperialism but also discussed the limits of democratic participation and emphasized the importance of elites through his account of political charisma and the entrepreneurial spirit. An account of his views which ignores their political as well as theoretical implications would be as deeply misleading as an account of Marxist political economy which ignored Marx's political alignment with the working-class movement. This does not mean that Weber developed his approach in direct opposition to Marxism. But it does help us to compare the ideas of Marx and Weber on the future of capitalism.

Some Interwar Developments

The formation of classical sociology between the 1870s and the First World War shaped theoretical developments for the next fifty years. Certainly few theoretical initiatives occurred during the interwar years in either sociology or Marxism which are still regarded as significant contributions to the classic disputes which concern us here. In part this reflects the shift of the sociological centre of gravity to the United States (where capitalism as such was not a major issue for most sociologists) and the stagnation in Marxist thought occasioned by the rise of Stalinism. None the less, one should mention the growing interest both in the expansion of the middle classes and in the consolidation of managerial capitalism with its apparent separation between capitalist ownership and managerial control. The emergence of a new welfare capitalism in some countries during the interwar years also received attention but this issue only became significant for sociology during the 1950s. For our purposes the most notable developments were Schumpeter's studies of capitalism and the emergence of the Frankfurt School. Schumpeter and the Critical Theorists both drew on Marx as well as Weber in discussing capitalism. Moreover, whilst Critical Theory has always been significant for debates over the future of capitalism, there has been a resurgence of interest in Schumpeter's work on this topic.

SCHUMPETER ON CAPITALISM AND SOCIALISM

Joseph Schumpeter, a conservative Austrian economist, affirmed Marx's analysis of the dynamism of capitalism, its cyclical character, the increasing concentration and centralization of capital, and its self-destructive tendencies. But he also affirmed Weber's emphasis on the crucial role of entrepreneurs in capitalist development. Schumpeter argued that the vitality of capitalism depended on innovations (especially in production) and that these in turn rested on the rise of new firms, the availability of credit, and the entrepreneurial activities of the captains of industry.

Sometimes Schumpeter approached these issues as an economist, but in *Capitalism, Socialism and Democracy* (1976) he offered a more sociological account. Here he identified certain tendencies towards the self-destruction of capitalism and forecast its decline in favour of socialism. Three developments were mainly responsible for this. First, the rise of managerial capitalism had routinized innovation and was making entrepreneurs redundant; the decline of the individual entrepreneur weakened the commitment of the dominant economic class to private capitalism. Secondly, the spread of capitalist relations was undermining the protective strata (e.g. the English aristocracy) and traditional institutions which provided political leadership and support for the bourgeois class in its struggle with labour. Thirdly, although the bourgeois revolution had thrived on the development of critical liberal thought and capitalism still encouraged critical reasoning, modern intellectuals had begun to call capitalism itself into question. Together these changes would result in capitalism losing its dynamism and the bourgeoisie losing its capacity and will to defend the capitalist system. At the same time the pressure for socialism would increase.

CRITICAL THEORY AND THE FUTURE OF CAPITALISM

The arguments of the Frankfurt School were strongly influenced by the history of the Weimar Republic and Nazism and its members were generally pessimistic about the future of capitalism. Like Schumpeter and many other contemporary theorists, they confirmed that modern capitalism has become managerial, bureaucratic, and routinized. What particularly distinguishes the Frankfurt School for our purposes, however, is its argument that modern capitalism actually destroys critical reason.

Thus theorists such as Neumann, Marcuse, and Kircheimer argued that monopoly capitalism was compatible with, sustained, and, indeed, required an authoritarian, if not a fascist, form of state. They believed that modern capitalism was prone to stagnation (giant firms would use their monopoly power to inhibit innovation), to growing rigidity (because of the increasing interdependence of a concentrated, cartellized, and trustified economy), and to predatory expansion (in the search for export markets and for secure access to raw materials). In turn this implied a growing need for state intervention to secure economic and political stability in the face of shocks such as unemployment, raw-material shortages and political struggles. Other members of the Frankfurt School, such as Horkheimer, Adorno and Pollock, agreed that an authoritarian state was inevitable but denied that it was essentially capitalist, since it undermined competition and market forces which were key elements in any orthodox definition of capitalism. Instead one could see the emergence of a so-called 'state capitalism' or else a much more general system of authoritarian, bureaucratic domination.

Although these arguments seemed less relevant after the defeat of fascism, postwar developments encouraged a second line of attack. For the Critical Theorists had also emphasized the dominance of instrumental reason in capitalism and how it deformed modern society. There was said to be a reciprocal link between the rise of instrumental reason (or technological rationality) and the spread of commodity relations throughout capitalist societies. Thus people had become separated and atomized and easily dominated by a bureaucratic despotism centred in private capitalist organizations and the state system. Even opposition to this system could be integrated and absorbed because it accepted instrumental modes of reasoning. For example, trade unions were only concerned with improving wages and working conditions *within* capitalism and not with developing a real, substantive critique *against* capitalism and modern societies. As the capacity for critical thought (critical rationality) declines, technological rationality becomes even more entrenched.

These arguments were further developed in the postwar years and extended to the question of whether opposition to capitalism was still possible. The conclusion was that it could no longer be expected in the core of capitalist society – least of all from the traditional working class. Instead it would be conducted by the marginal groups and strata (such as ethnic minorities, the poor, or Third World nations) who lose out in this system and/or by privileged groups (such as students) who can break through the one-dimensional, instrumental reason which dominates modern society. These forces should act as the catalysts of revolutionary change but would also need to mobilize the working classes. Thus the Frankfurt School overturned traditional Marxist expectations about the revolutionary process and also developed Weber's views on the impact of rationalization in a more critical and pessimistic direction.

The Postwar Boom and the Future of Capitalism

After the Second World War widespread worries that a serious economic crisis would develop were soon forgotten. Capitalism enjoyed a long period of rising prosperity which finally slowed in the 1970s. During the postwar boom various theories suggested that a new, crisis-free form of capitalism had developed or, indeed, that a post-capitalist era had arrived. Different approaches to the future of capitalism were developed in different countries. In the United States studies of the logic of industrialism was followed by work on post-industrialism. In Britain the Keynesian welfare state and the affluent society led to theories about state-managed capitalism and/or about the growth of a working class with middle-class incomes and values which were used to justify social democratic reformism. On the Continent some sociologists influenced by Marx focused on new technology, the rise of a new working class, and the expansion of the middle class; and some sociologists influenced by Weber explored technocracy, bureaucratic domination, and the decline of critical reason associated with the end of ideology. Critical Theorists continued to develop their ideas both in Germany and the United States. And in the Soviet bloc and among orthodox Marxists in Western Europe the dominant theories revolved around the scientific and technical revolution and the growth of state monopoly capitalism and economic crisis management. We cannot discuss all these themes here and focus instead on those which are most relevant to classic disputes over the future of capitalism.

THE LOGIC OF INDUSTRIALISM

During the postwar boom there was increasing interest in the more general dynamic of *industrialism* and *industrial societies* as opposed to that of capitalism and capitalist societies as such. Capitalism was often said to have been superseded and the class struggle and class ideologies were supposed to have come to an end. Attention shifted to the basic forces of industrial technology and economic rationality and to the role of elites and mass politics. The institutional logic of industrialism was held to be more fundamental than that of capitalism (which was merely one form which industrialism could take) and some sociologists argued that capitalist and communist societies would become alike under the impact of the technological constraints involved in industrialism. Clark Kerr predicted a bilateral convergence, for example, in which increasing state intervention in the West and growing decentralization and political liberalization under communism would produce a new, 'pluralist industrialism' in both systems (Kerr *et al.*, 1973).

We are not concerned here with why communist societies have not moved consistently (if at all) in the expected directions. But we should note that, while state intervention and economic planning did increase in capitalist societies (at least during the 1960s and early 1970s), other changes deduced from the logic of industrialism were not realized. In a recent critique John Goldthorpe identified three such expected changes and considered how far they had occurred. First, a more open and equal society was expected because industrialism requires an educated, mobile and efficient labour force. Secondly, class differences and subcultural particularisms were expected to break down because industrialism encourages the emergence of a 'middle-mass' society. And, thirdly, industrialism was expected to undermine the tendency towards a polarized class conflict between capital and labour and to encourage more particularistic, decentralized forms of bargaining. These predictions have been disappointed. For, while living standards have generally improved, major class-based inequalities in life-chances still exist. Indeed there is a growing tendency for the working class to be self-recruiting and for its members to belong to it for life. At the same time the rise of consumerism, the breakdown of traditional working-class communities, the essentially limitless demands involved in the concept of citizenship rights, and the growth of trade unions and trade associations have generated fundamental conflicts over income levels, welfare standards, and managerial prerogatives. Thus conflicts over distributional questions have been heightened rather than reduced. This could be seen in the rise of more militant trade union bargaining at plant and industry level and in the growing interest of unions in macroeconomic policy (Goldthorpe, 1984, pp. 318–22).

More problematic still was the changing character of the forces of production whose logic supposedly induced these convergences towards a shared pluralist industrialism, open society, and end of ideology. For, as the proponents of the institutional logic of *post*-industrial society noted, the very forces of production themselves were changing. This theme was first advanced by Daniel Bell in the 1960s, became popular in the 1970s, and is arguably even more relevant today.

THE POST-INDUSTRIAL SOCIETY

Bell forecast that the future of capitalist society was that of a post-industrial, information society. Basing his views on the current position in the United States, he argued that a post-industrial society would emerge in the last quarter of the twentieth century. Five major changes would occur in the social structure of advanced industrial societies and would pose problems for the political and cultural systems. These changes were as follows.

First, in the economic sector, there would be a change from a goods-producing to a service economy in which jobs in health, education, research and government became increasingly important. Secondly, the occupational distribution would witness a decisive shift in favour of the professional and technical class – especially those in science and engineering. Thirdly, whereas industrial society is organized around the co-ordination of machines and men for the production of goods, it will be the mastery of theoretical knowledge for social control and purposive innovation and change which will be the central organizational principle and the key strategic resource of the post-industrial society. Fourthly, with the increased importance of theoretical knowledge, the post-industrial society may be able to assess its technological needs and then plan and control its technological growth. Finally, in the realm of decision-making, post-industrial societies would witness the creation of a new 'intellectual technology', that is, the development of sophisticated models for rational decision-making in complex situations (Bell, 1973, pp. 14–33).

Much of the initial reaction to Bell's predictions focused on his empirical evidence to see whether he had over-stated the rise of the post-industrial service sector. Two key criticisms were that he had ignored how multinationals transfer industrial jobs abroad and how industrial companies often transfer 'in-house' services to specialized service enterprises. Both these trends led Bell to over-estimate the current shift to post-industrialism in the United States. In the longer term, however, his emphasis on the information revolution is less easy to criticize. Whether he took sufficient account of parallel changes in the organization of *industrial* production or drew the right conclusions about capitalism from this *post*-industrial trend are different matters. In this context it is interesting to compare Bell's views with Marxist analyses of the scientific and technical revolution.

THE SCIENTIFIC AND TECHNICAL REVOLUTION

Various Marxist theorists have argued that the development of the productive forces typical of capitalism has leapt significantly forward due to the so-called 'scientific and technical revolution' (or STR). This refers to the increasing importance of both fundamental and applied scientific and technical research in reorganizing the labour process, creating new products, and managing the economy. In turn this has considerably advanced the social character of the productive forces and has created much closer ties between the economic and non-economic spheres of society. There is now increasing interdependence among all branches of production, between industry and education, between capitalist management and the flow of information, and between the economy and the state.

These changes have not only transformed the economy but have also reorganized the class structure. The traditional industrial proletariat has declined in significance and could lose (or has already done so) its vanguard role as the leading force for socialist revolution. On some views this requires a class alliance between the old proletariat and the new technical intelligentsia under the latter's intellectual leadership. On other views it implies that there is a new working class made up of skilled, technical workers who could (or would) become the revolutionary vanguard. In all cases a revolution is still considered necessary, however, because people cannot realize the full benefits of the STR under capitalism itself.

This could only occur when the socialization of the productive forces which is involved in the STR is matched by social control over all aspects of the economy. Until this occurs it will be the profit motive which determines the development and application of science and technology. In turn this implies that some of the tendencies which Bell forecast (such as expanded provision of health and education or social planning of technological growth) might only be realized when capitalism itself is superseded in a post-industrial society. On this Bell himself had little to say.

HABERMAS ON LATE CAPITALISM

Jürgen Habermas has built on the Frankfurt School tradition of mixing themes from Marx and Weber whilst also going beyond them in key respects. His significance for the classic dispute which concerns us here is found in two lines of criticism of late capitalism. The first concerns its recent development as a specific economic and social order; the second concerns the possibilities of rational public debate over the purposes of man and the goals of modern society.

On the first theme, Habermas argues that state intervention has transformed competitive capitalism so that it is increasingly organized, subject to instrumental reason and bureaucratized. Among the most significant changes which have occurred are the growth of monopoly capital; the increasing interdependence of science, technology and industry (so that science has become a fundamental productive force and an independent source of surplus-value); increasing state intervention to stabilize the economy; and the key role of technocratic arguments in legitimizing the social order. Indeed Habermas once argued that economic crises can now be avoided and the economic conflicts between capital and labour contained. But this did not mean the end of crisis and conflict in late capitalist societies. Instead, new types of crisis (involving planning problems and/or legitimation deficits) would emerge and other forms of conflict would predominate. In particular, late capitalism would suffer from a decline in mass loyalty. This legitimation crisis would occur because social life has lost its mystery, all spheres of life are politicized, government is overloaded with demands it cannot meet, and the state's actions in support of capital become increasingly transparent.

On the second theme, Habermas argues that the growth of bureaucracy and instrumental rationality undermines the public sphere in which ordered, rational political discussion can take place. In advanced capitalism this sphere is restricted and distorted. For it has become a sphere for interest-group lobbying directed at influencing specific actions by the interventionist state and is no longer a sphere of general public discussion aimed at shaping the broad principles of the liberal state. At the same time the public and private spheres have become more closely intertwined. The state system has assumed a new 'feudal' form because large organizations and groups share power with the administration and try to exclude the broader public from political life. In turn the private sphere has become increasingly politicized because the state intervenes in ever-more areas of social life. All this is accompanied by changes in the sphere of public opinion and the formation of a general will. Instead of open, informed, and critical discussion, there is only publicity, public relations and public-opinion research. And, instead of public participation in decision-making, we find only a plebiscitary democracy in which alternative sets of political leaders compete for the chance to preside over the state's administrative personnel.

LONG WAVES, FORDISM AND POST-FORDISM

The collapse of the postwar boom forced a reappraisal of the more optimistic theories of capitalism similar to that which occurred in the movement from early to classical sociology. Among other trends there has been renewed interest in the view that capitalism experiences repeated long waves of boom and slump. It is in this context that economists and sociologists have turned to Schumpeter's work on the role of entrepreneurs in capitalist innovation. There has been a parallel movement in Marxism with fresh interest in the technological, political and social bases of the transition from one wave to another. The latter concerns can be illustrated from recent discussions of Fordism and post-Fordism.

The last long wave has often been labelled 'Fordism' after one of its foremost pioneers and spokesmen: Henry Ford. This emerged in the 1920s with the rise of mass production techniques but was only consolidated after the Second World War with the rise of mass consumption and the interventionist welfare state. It is the general crisis of Fordism together with America's declining influence in the world economy which is reckoned to have brought the last long wave to a close. Fordism allegedly broke down for two main reasons. Its dynamizing impact became exhausted once it had been adopted in all advanced capitalist countries and this was reflected in declining profit rates and declining investment. And it also encountered growing working-class resistance in the form of absenteeism, labour turnover and strikes. In turn this prompted a search for new ways to organize capitalist production to overcome the rigidities of Fordism and to counteract working-class resistance. Crucial in both respects has been the growing trend towards greater flexibility in production (made possible by automation, robots and information technology) and towards a polarization of the labour force into a technologically skilled, full-time core and a peripheral, unskilled labour force often engaged part-time or irregularly: changes not confined to industrial production but which also occur in the service sector.

There is considerable discussion about what the transition to post-Fordism implies for the reorganization of capitalist societies. Since the transition is still under way, however, forecasts have proved difficult. In part this is because the transition is not driven by some inevitable technological imperative but depends on the outcome of political conflicts. In this context most Marxist commentators and many sociologists seem to agree that one of the most important issues at stake is what post-Fordist flexibility implies for the labour force. Some predict that there will be a new class polarization between a 'functionally flexible' core of skilled workers with permanent jobs and a 'numerically flexible' periphery of unskilled workers who will serve as a 'reserve army' of labour. Others argue that there could be a more flexible use of work- and leisure-time for all workers and that this could lead to a more open and equal society. Which of these outcomes occurs will also influence the nature of the state, education, welfare systems, the class structure and so forth.

Conclusions

The issues raised by Marx and Weber still dominate sociological inquiry on the future of capitalism. In many ways their work was complementary rather than contradictory. Although Marx wrote extensively on contemporary social and political questions, his main theoretical interest was in capitalism as a mode of production, its laws of motion, and its implications for class struggle. Thus he sought to understand capitalist societies in terms of the anatomy of the capitalist economic system. Weber emphasized the extra-economic institutional preconditions for capitalist production (most notably in the fields of law, the nation-state and bureaucracy), the form of rational capitalist accounting, and the role of entrepreneurs. Although he developed important points about capitalist enterprises and market forces, Weber was interested in the whole field of social relations in industrial capitalist societies. Thus he placed less emphasis on the causal role of economic factors and did not accept that class struggle is the motor force of history. Through skilful reinterpretation of Marxist and Weberian concepts one could probably develop a synthesis which did not overly betray their key arguments. None the less, Marx and Weber clearly had different expectations about the future of capitalism and also adopted different positions in the conflict between capital and labour. These differences, together with the controversies over the role of economic institutions and class struggle in societal development, have fuelled long-running disputes in sociology.

In reviewing developments since Marx and Weber wrote on capitalism and its future, we have emphasized how social and political theorists have taken up and modified themes from their work. Some theorists have been more concerned with the logic of capital accumulation (such as Bernstein, Hilferding, Lenin and Schumpeter) and others with the impact of rationalization in all spheres of society (such as the Frankfurt School). Yet other theorists have given less emphasis to a specifically capitalist logic than to the implications of more general changes in the forces of production. Included here would be such theorists as Kerr and Bell and, to a certain extent, writers on post-Fordism. Finally, there are many social and political theorists who have developed more general moral critiques of industrial societies or their specific capitalist forms.

In discussing these approaches we have interpreted 'classic disputes in sociology' in a specific way. For, although the classic sociological theorists certainly devoted much time and effort to discussing the future of capitalism, the three main founding fathers of the discipline (Marx, Durkheim and Weber) did not directly confront each other on the topic. Within the Marxist tradition, however, there have been many disputes over the future of capitalism. In addition, the theoretical traditions which these founding fathers helped to develop have been debated ever since. This is particularly clear in the recurrent attempts to confront the Marxist and Weberian traditions. Thus we are dealing with a highly mediated dispute but one which is none the less significant. It should also be clear that these traditions have their roots not only in different scientific perspectives on socio-logical inquiry but also in different political positions. This too is an illustration of the classic nature of the debate over capitalism and its future.

What conclusions can be drawn from this brief review? The most obvious is that predicting the future of capitalism is fraught with methodological and theoretical difficulties. For any such attempt must confront three problems rooted in the nature of capitalism itself. Capitalism is a complex, dynamic and open system. Thus theorists run the risk, first, that capitalism will be treated in a one-sided manner at the expense of more rounded, multi-dimensional accounts; secondly, that temporary features and tendencies will capture attention at the expense of longer-term aspects; and, thirdly, that the many and varied ways in which factors outside the capitalist system affect its operation will be ignored. Some of these problems should be evident from the theories reviewed above.

Five further conclusions also recommend themselves. First, there is no single, unambiguous and inevitable logic which predetermines the future of capitalism or capitalist societies. No such logic exists either technologically (such as industrialism), economically (capital accumulation), or societally (rationaliza-tion). Obviously particular systems can have specific develop-mental logics but these are always mediated through social agents and are qualified by their interaction with other systems. Even those Marxist theories which are strongly committed to economic determinism generally allow for a contingent, subjec-tive element which introduces indeterminacy into the future of capitalism. Likewise Weber stressed the key historical role of entrepreneurs and political leaders in shaping the future of industrial societies.

Secondly, although the future of capitalism is open, it is not fully open. Two reasons can be cited for this. There is an accumulation of past technical and institutional systems which provide the initial conditions from which capitalist economies and societies must respond to new challenges; and the continuing vitality of competition and market forces means that there are always pressures to adapt to developments elsewhere. How successfully different economies and societies adapt to (or resist) such pressures will depend on many factors.

Thirdly, not all the developments which occur in capitalist societies are immediately attributable to the capitalist economic system. How conflicts among nation-states, the proliferation of nuclear weapons, the activities of new social movements, the dynamic of racial antagonisms, regional problems and gender cleavages, for example, will shape the development of capitalist societies is not fully determined by the logic of capitalism. This both complicates predictions about the future of capitalism and makes the future more open.

Fourthly, at different times different countries have been cited as the model for future capitalist development: Britain, the USA, Germany, Sweden and Japan. Indeed the existence of many nation-states within the capitalist world system means that there is a wide variety of social structures and economic and political strategies which have proved able to sustain capitalist expansion and/or to alleviate its worst effects. The advantages which some societies have can, however, be overturned; and other economies and societies may become more competitive. Indeed, as the problems confronting capitalist societies change, there is a tendency to look abroad for new ways of responding to the challenges. Thus the fact that capitalism has not yet created a homogeneous global village could be considered an advantage from the viewpoint of its continuing vitality and adaptability.

Finally, capitalist development seems to move in long waves. There is still much debate over the reasons, timing and rhythm behind this movement but nowadays its existence is rarely questioned. Whatever the ultimate future of capitalism, its short-term future appears to involve a transition to a post-industrial, post-Fordist society. But precisely because we are living through a transition period, it is not yet clear what the dominant form of this society will be. The USA and Japan are important models for this but there will no doubt be other variants. Indeed the very flexibility permitted by information technology and automated production suggests that the range of societal forms compatible with the next long wave of capitalism will still be large.

References and Further Reading

Andreski, S. (19971), *The Essential Comte* (London: Croom Helm).

Badham, R. (1984), 'The Sociology of Industrial and Post-Industrial Societies', *Current Sociology*, vol. 32, pp. 1–141.

Beetham, D. (1985), *Max Weber and the Theory of Politics* (Oxford: Polity Press).

Bell, D. (1973), *The Coming of Post-Industrial Society* (New York: Basic Books).

Bernstein, E. (1961), *Evolutionary Socialism* (New York: Schocken).

Bowles, S. and Edwards, R. (1985), *Contemporary Capitalism* (New York: Harper Row).

Bukharin, N. (1972), *Imperialism and World Economy* (London: Merlin).

Cohen, I. (1981), 'Introduction', in M. Weber, *General Economic History* (New York: Transaction Books).

Collins, R. (1980), 'Max Weber's Last Theory of Capitalism', *American Sociological Review*, vol. 45, pp. 925–42.

Durkheim, E. (1962), *Socialism* (New York: Collier).

Durkheim, E. (1964), *The Division of Labour in Society* (New York: Free Press).

Engels, F. (1954), *Anti-Duehring: Herr Eugen Duehring's Revolution in Science* (Moscow: Foreign Languages Publishing House).

Freeman, C. (ed.) (1983), *Long Waves in the World Economy* (London: Butterworth).

Giddens, A. (1971), *Capitalism and Modern Social Theory* (Cambridge: Cambridge University Press).

Giddens, A. (1977), *Studies in Social and Political Theory* (London: Hutchinson).

Goldthorpe, J. H. (1971), 'Theories of Industrial Society: the Future of Futurology or the Recrudescence of Historicism?', *European Journal of Sociology*, vol. 12, pp. 263–88.

Goldthorpe, J. H. (ed.) (1984), *Order and Conflict in Contemporary Capitalism* (Oxford: Oxford University Press).

Habermas, J. (1976), *Legitimation Crisis* (London: Heinemann).

Held, D. (1980), *Introduction to Critical Theory* (London: Hutchinson).

Hilferding, R. (1981), *Finance Capital* (London: Routledge & Kegan Paul).

Kerr, C., Dunlop, J. T., Harbison, F. H. and Myers, C. A. (1973), *Industrialism and Industrial Man* (Harmondsworth: Penguin).

Lenin, V. (1982), *Imperialism: The Highest Stage of Capitalism*, in *Collected Works*, vol. 22 (Moscow: Progress Publishers).

Maddison, A. (1982), *Phases of Capitalist Development* (Oxford: Oxford University Press).

Marcuse, H. (1974), *One-Dimensional Man* (London: Abacus).

Marx, K. (1959), *Capital*, 3 vols (London: Lawrence & Wishart).

Marx, K. and Engels, F. (1969), *The Manifesto of the Communist Party, Selected Works, 1* (Moscow: Foreign Languages Publishing House).

McLellan, D. (1979), *Marxism after Marx* (London: Macmillan).

Piore, M. J. and Sabel, C. (1984), *The Second Industrial Divide* (New York: Basic Books).

Schumpeter, J. (1976), *Capitalism, Socialism and Democracy* (London: Allen & Unwin).

Shonfield, A. (1965), *Modern Capitalism* (Oxford: Oxford University Press).

Therborn, G. (1977), *Science, Class and Society* (London: New Left Books).

Touraine, A. (1974), *The Post-Industrial Society* (London: Wildwood House).

Weber, M. (1958), *The Protestant Ethic and the Spirit of Capitalism* (New York: Scribners).

Weber, M. (1968), *Economy and Society* (New York: Bedminster Press).

Weber, M. (1981), *General Economic History* (New York: Transaction Books).

Chapter 3

The Concept of Class

PETE MARTIN

The Vital Illusion

Commentators often remark on the extent to which British society is permeated by social class distinctions. In Japanese factories, it seems, managers and workers take their meals and recreation together, so that all are made aware of their common purpose. In Britain, by contrast, such social mixing is not only unusual but often unwelcome, with both 'sides' of industry preferring not to bridge the gulf between 'us' and 'them'. Indeed, the persistence in Britain of a stable pattern of class inequalities – at work, in education, housing, health and welfare and even leisure – has been seen as one of the main factors responsible for the country's relatively poor economic performance. Moreover, not only does a rigid pattern of class distinctions persist, but the British are often held to display an awareness of class factors in their everyday lives which strikes foreigners, especially Americans, as rather odd.

There can be little doubt, then, that the idea of class and the pattern of inequalities which it implies are simply taken for granted in everyday speech. We all know what terms like the 'working class', the 'middle class' or the 'upper class' mean, in the sense that we accept them as reasonable ways of describing an important aspect of society. Such terms tell us something about both the division of labour, and the division of rewards, whether these be wages, profits or inherited wealth. But two important points emerge as soon as we reflect for a moment on the use of such familiar terms. First, it is clear that 'class' factors are not the only ones which we could use in order to make distinctions and discriminations within a population. In fact, in our everyday lives we habitually employ other criteria – sex, age, race, religion, for example, not to mention physical characteristics or people's beliefs. So when we decide to categorize people in terms of social classes, we are implicitly suggesting that some factors – in this case economic – are of particular importance for our understanding the pattern of social organization, and that others may be less fundamental. In other words we are recognizing, in a common-sense sort of way, one of the basic ways in which our society is structured.

Secondly, it soon becomes evident that the familiar terms used to divide society into classes are not as simple as they seem. We may have no trouble accepting the term 'working class' as a generalization, but we soon run into difficulties once we try to decide exactly who is in it and who is not. There are, for example, enormous differences in both skill levels and incomes amongst all those who perform manual work. Are they really a 'class', in the sense of a recognizable or coherent social group? Moreover, there are other people – dentists and clerical workers, for instance – whose work is 'manual', yet who are generally regarded as having middle-class occupations. It seems, then – and this is a point to which we will return – that in practice it is very hard to specify exactly where the boundaries of social classes lie. Of course, in everyday conversation we rarely need such a degree of precision. But for other purposes we do, as when the Registrar-General assigns each member of the population to one of five 'socioeconomic classes' when analysing the census returns. The resulting 'classes', while useful for the purposes of data analysis, may seem at odds with our experience of the social world, as when rather different sorts of people are grouped together. The point is that as soon as we try to move from the comfortable vagueness of everyday speech to a more precise specification of social classes, we run into difficulties which can only be over-come by a conscious decision to assign people to one category rather than another. The use of the term class in this sense, then, inevitably involves an active process of definition. Neither the census analyst nor the sociological researcher are simply reflect-ing social reality in a neutral or objective way when they draw up schemes of social classes. Rather, they are producing one of many possible representations of that reality, on the basis of their own assumptions, beliefs and theoretical inclinations.

This leads us to the third point. Just as researchers' own values and beliefs are involved in the process of defining social classes, so most people have their own ideas about the social hierarchy, and particularly their place in it. Obviously, the views of the researchers and those they study may not coincide: anyone who has ever done any survey work will be familiar with the wide range of perceptions and opinions which shape people's views of their own situation. The boss of a large company may very well describe himself as 'working class' because he works, and works hard, for his living. Similarly, many people in manual jobs with relatively low incomes are prone to describe their situation as somewhere 'in the middle'. It has become customary to refer to such perceptions as the 'subjective' aspect of social class, reflecting a person's own experience of life in a particular context. But in this sense the word 'subjective' is misleading. For such ideas, although they may be personal and even idiosyncratic, cannot simply be dismissed as 'wrong' or 'biased' in comparison with some correct or objective state of affairs. However strange, or inaccurate, or inconsistent a person's ideas may seem they are nevertheless of sociological significance, in the sense that they may influence the way in which that person chooses to act. Moreover, as I suggested above, all official accounts or academic research reports are ultimately based on the assumptions and theoretical choices of the researcher. In other words, there could never be some final, objective picture of the 'class structure' which everyone would accept. Moreover, the example of social class illustrates well the point that because there is a word for something, this does not necessarily mean that there is a corresponding 'thing' in the real world. No one has ever seen, or touched, far less measured the dimensions of, a social class. (And if you do try to define or measure them, you soon run into difficulties, as we have seen.) Class is a *concept*: a device through which we can order our perceptions so as to highlight some features of reality at the expense of others. When we use such concepts in everyday speech, we proceed *as if* their meaning is unambiguous, and *as if* they refer to real, tangible entities (even though these conditions do not obtain). In a sense, then, their use rests on an illusion – that something is real when it is not. Yet this does not mean that such concepts are unimportant, far less that they could be dispensed with. Class is not just, or only, or merely, a concept. Such concepts are the vital, essential building blocks of human communication.

The idea of social class is a 'vital illusion' in another sense. The concept has played a vital role in shaping our understanding of social stratification throughout the whole period of modern sociology. So much so that, notwithstanding the huge literature on stratification and inequality, discussions of the concept itself are relatively rare. Just as its use is taken for granted in everday speech, so sociologists, especially in Europe, have accepted it as one of the fundamental concepts of their discipline. The concept of class provides a powerful tool with which to examine the workings of whole societies: it seems to offer a means of establishing what the major social groups are which is far more systematic than the jumbled and inconsistent experience of everyday life. Moreover, it shows how these major social groups are related through the fundamental economic and political processes of society, and how patterns of inequality are generated in them. So it is hardly surprising that for most of the time sociologists do not ask, for example, whether there is or is not a working class, but concern themselves with such questions as who is in it, whether it is getting bigger or smaller, richer or poorer, and so on. In doing so, they implicitly accept a certain way of viewing reality which, as I have suggested, is not without its problems from a scientific point of view. But before considering some of these problems, it is useful to discuss briefly the way that the concept of class has developed over the years. For it is only in quite recent times that the 'vital illusion' has been taken for granted, either in sociological or everyday language.

The word class is derived from the Latin *classis*, which came to mean a division of the Roman citizens according to their wealth, and its use has been traced back to the time of the Emperor Servius Tullius, who 'classified' the Romans into six categories of property-owners. It continued to be used mainly in the context of Roman history, and only in the seventeenth century did the English form of the word come to be used 'as a general term for a group or division' (Williams, 1983, p. 60). One early usage, which survives to this day, was to refer to a group of school pupils or students. But throughout most of the seventeenth and eighteenth centuries other terms – notably rank, order, or estate – were mainly used to denote important divisions in the population, and not until the time of the Industrial Revolution in Britain did the word class become established in anything like its modern sense.

By the 1820s and 1830s, however, terms such as 'lower', 'middle', and 'upper' classes were increasingly familiar. But as Williams suggests, even in those days the concept was used in rather different, and sometimes confusing ways. The term 'middle class' was often used by the commercial and professional groups who had risen on the tide of the new industries and who referred to themselves in this way, often in a clearly self-congratulatory manner. The idea is conveyed of a new and dynamic social force, now established between the declining aristocracy of pre-industrial times, and the 'lower orders' or 'common' people. Increasingly, though, the term 'working class' came to have rather constrasting implications. Often used in an explicitly political context, it bore the idea that those directly engaged in productive work are the sole source of wealth in society. In this sense, the working class is seen as having interests which are clearly opposed to those of the other classes, which are essentially parasitic on those who carry out 'productive' or 'useful' work. There were two senses, then, which often overlapped (as when members of the 'middle class' described themselves as the truly 'useful' members of society): the notion of a simple hierarchy of social groups, and that of classes whose interests were basically antagonistic.

A similar, though more general, distinction has been made by Calvert (1982, chapters 2 and 3). Most authors of the eighteenth century, he suggests, reflected the view – which is expressed by both Greek philosophers and medieval Christian theorists – that the division of society into distinct groups is both 'natural and desirable'. The great medieval estates, too, had been regarded as a just and beneficial differentiation of the population, with the nobility, clergy and common people all playing a distinct but essential role in promoting the common good. The thinkers of the Enlightenment echoed many of these ideas: as when people carrying out different trades were each seen to be making a distinct, but useful, contribution to society. Moreover, Adam Smith suggested that the greater the degree of specialization and differentiation, the more productive, and thus wealthier, society would be. And there is a similar idea in the later political philosophy of Hegel: that there are, ideally, three different but complementary classes in society.

This long chain of social thought, then, expressed the idea which Calvert describes as 'class as balance': that the division of societies into distinctly different groups, each making a specialized contribution to the whole, would result in stability, harmony and prosperity. Of course, the emphases of the thinkers varied in significant respects. Some condoned a high degree of inequality, others argued that it should be minimized; some advocated a strong state to mediate between the claims of the various groups, others believed that regulation depended on obedience to God, and others again that self-discipline proceeded from the acknowledgement of universal moral principles. Several of these themes have been echoed in the development of modern sociological theory, particularly in the structural-functionalist school of thought.

The idea of 'class as balance', therefore, has a long pedigree and continues to have a pervasive influence on both social thought and political ideologies. Since the eighteenth century, however, there has developed an altogether less benign view of social divisions. In general, there has been an increasing tendency to adopt dichotomous, conflictual models of the social order, with social divisions seen as inherently exploitative. Such ideas were influential in shaping the forces that brought about the French Revolution, and were in turn stimulated by it: the French aristocracy was seen as an oppressor by *all* other elements of society.

Similarly, the period of the English Industrial Revolution brought massive, often calamitous upheavals, unprecedented social unrest and heavy political repression. Social thinkers of the day were preoccupied with attempts to defend or attack the political status quo, and simply to understand the nature of the social changes which were occurring. There was an increased awareness of conflict and the decline of the old order. As Williams has suggested, it is no mere coincidence that this was the period in which the terminology of class became prevalent in the English language (Williams, 1983). And it is this historical period, too, which provides the background to the thought of Karl Marx.

Karl Marx and the 'Error of Genius'

It is generally accepted that the three main influences on Marx's thought were French socialism, English political economy, and German philosophy. The last of these seems to have had a profound and permanent effect. The Germany of Marx's youth was dominated intellectually by the towering figure of G. W. F. Hegel and his complex system of idealist philosophy, and we know that Marx, in his student days, was closely involved with many of those who sought to develop and criticize Hegel's ideas. It is not surprising, then, that certain distinctively Hegelian themes became basic elements in Marx's own thinking – his dialectical method of analysis, for example, and his belief in historical change as a process of conflict. But in one crucial respect Marx rejected Hegel's perspective. Whereas idealists, then and now, believe that the source and the ultimate form of existence is a being without physical reality – God, for example, or Hegel's idea of Spirit – Marx came to see that real people and the physical environment which sustained them must be the starting point for any understanding of human societies.

For this reason, Marx has been described as a materialist, as opposed to an idealist, thinker: for him, human beings are essentially producers, who must work collectively on their physical environment in order to survive. Thus the economic activity of a society, or its 'mode of production', is its fundamental characteristic. The starting point of Marx's sociology, and one of his profoundest ideas, is the notion that any given mode of production exerts a definite influence on the pattern of social organization which develops around it. Though commonplace now, this idea was in Marx's day a vital clue to understanding the new societies being forged in the clamour of the Industrial Revolution. As Marx put it, 'the handmill gives you society with the feudal lord; the steam-mill, society with the industrial capitalist' (Marx, 1955). More generally, the development of the 'forces' of production (or what we might nowadays call technology) tend to bring about changes in the 'social relations of production'.

It is from this perspective that Marxists have analysed both the process of historical change, and the pattern of social stratification in societies. But changes in knowledge, technology or the methods of production do not automatically or inevitably transform societies. The actions of human beings are not determined like the fall of an apple or the motions of colliding billiard balls: social change can only come about through real people acting in pursuit of their needs and interests. Moreover, technological innovations are inevitably made in the context of a mode of production which is already established, and the new techniques may threaten to disrupt the pattern of social organization based on the old ones. In our own times we are confronted daily with examples of such conflicts between the new forces and the existing relations of production: the introduction of computers, for example, has created new jobs and a demand for new skills, but is simultaneously a threat to those who work in older industries or whose skills have become obsolete. And it goes without saying that the automation of factory and office work produces a huge loss of those jobs which have employed large numbers of people ever since the Industrial Revolution: after all, the main incentive in introducing the 'new technology' is to cut costs (particularly wages) and 'rationalize' the production process.

In Marx's analysis, then, it is at the level of the relations of production that the process of social change occurs. Moreover, the process is inherently conflictual: in any mode of production, the dominant *class* will consist of those people who own or control the fundamental forces of production. But gradually, inevitably, this established class will be challenged for supremacy by the class whose interests are tied to the new, developing forces of production. It was in this way that Marx explained the historical process by which European feudal societies, based on a system of agricultural production, were transformed into industrial capitalist ones, and it is in this context that we can understand the famous claim at the start of *The Communist Manifesto*: 'The history of all hitherto existing society is the history of class struggles'.

Marx's general perspective led him to conceive of every society in terms of a dominant and an exploited class, whose interests were inevitably opposed, and whose basis was the possession of or exclusion from, ownership of the means of production. Inherent in such a view is the idea that political power is ultimately derived from relations which obtain in the sphere of economic production. The aristocracy of feudal and medieval times was the dominant class because it could control the dominant factor of production, land. By contrast, increasing commercial and industrial activity meant that ownership of capital, and the ability to increase it by investment in the production process, became more and more important. From the sixteenth century on, the 'new' class of merchants, manufacturers and financiers – the 'bourgeoisie' – was inexorably rising to prominence, transforming and disrupting the 'old order' of social relations as it emerged. The colonization of overseas territories provided new sources of raw materials, new markets for manu-factured goods, and the pace of technological innovation was constantly accelerating. By the nineteenth century, the new bourgeoisie had replaced the old aristocracy as the dominant class in British society, and was involved in a struggle to convert its economic supremacy into political authority. The Reform Act of 1832 stands as a symbol of this transition.

It should already be apparent that we are now using the term 'class' in its specifically modern sense of a group of people who share a common economic situation, and whose interests inevitably conflict with those of others. Such a usage emerged primarily in the course of Marx's analysis of the process of social change; it would be virtually impossible, however, to underest-imate the influence which this conception of class has had on subsequent social and political thought.

In Marx's scheme of things, of course, the triumph of the bourgeoisie was not the end of the historical process. Indeed, he was particularly scathing about those economists and philoso-phers who believed that modern 'free market' capitalism was the highest stage in the development of humanity, or even the natural condition of mankind. Even in the very hour of its triumph, wrote Marx, the bourgeoisie was being undermined by the relentless process of class conflict, and capitalism was sowing the seeds of its own destruction. For its development had necessarily created another new class, of landless and propertyless wage workers, whose labour could be bought for less than the market value of the goods they produced: the proletariat.

As before, the proletarian class is a group with a common economic situation – the definitive criterion of the proletarians is their exclusion from either ownership or control of the means of production. Clearly, too, their interests are opposed to those of the bourgeoisie, since the dominance of the latter derives from its economic exploitation of the former. Marx's analysis, moreover, led him to conclude that the evolution of capitalism would itself generate the conditions for the development of the proletariat to the point where it could, in revolutionary action, overthrow the bourgeoisie. Just as the latter had grown from a position of insignificance to become the dynamic force which shattered the old order, so the historical destiny of the proletariat was the destruction of capitalism.

In *The Communist Manifesto*, published in 1848, Marx and Engels outlined the processes which they believed would ultimately bring about the destruction of capitalism. The spread of modern bourgeois capitalism, they suggest, has brought about a historically unique situation: instead of being confined to a small sector of the economy, as in previous societies, market capitalism is now the principle which dominates the organization of the entire system of production and consumption. Not only goods and materials, but labour too, has been reduced to the status of a 'commodity', the value of which is not established by need, custom, or tradition but determined by prevailing conditions of supply and demand. The religious and political beliefs which gave order and stability to the societies of the Middle Ages, and all considerations of morality and personal worth, have now been drowned 'in the icy water of egotistical calculation'. Increasingly, therefore, the organization of capitalist society reflects the underlying economic reality: there is an inherent conflict between owners and non-owners of the means of production, with the latter forced to sell their labour, and thus be exploited, by the former. Moreover, relationships between individuals are dominated, not by human needs and interests, but by money – the 'cash nexus'.

'Society as a whole', wrote Marx and Engles, 'is more and more splitting up into two great hostile camps, into two great classes directly facing each other: Bourgeoisie and Proletariat'

(Marx and Engels, 1968, p. 36). Moreover, they listed some of the reasons why this process was likely to lead to a final confrontation between the classes. So powerful are the new forces of production that periodic crises of 'overproduction' occur: the result is the bankruptcy of the less competitive capitalists and the concentration of the remaining means of production into fewer and fewer hands. Simultaneously, workers are concentrated into ever-larger factories, doing mindless and degrading work for only subsistence wages, and becoming increasingly embittered. The old 'petty bourgeoisie' of traders and craft workers can no longer compete with the big capitalists, and they too sink down into the ranks of the propertyless workers. As the process continues, the vast majority of the population come to form a huge class, defined by their common economic situation – impoverishment – and their opposition to the tiny capitalist class in whose hands economic and political power is overwhelmingly concentrated. The idea that social classes in capitalism would be increasingly dichotomized in this way has come to be known as the 'polarization' thesis.

But the fact that people share an identical economic situation does not make them a class in any sociological sense. For this to happen, says Marx, a class 'in itself' (i.e. those who can be defined as occupying similar economic positions) must become a class 'for itself' (i.e. people who are aware of their common situation and prepared to take collective political action). According to Marx and Engels, this process, the development of 'class consciousness', was indeed likely. The concentration of workers in factories, within great conurbations, would lead to a growing awareness of their common and collective subordination. Trade unions would be formed in the struggle to defend the workers, there would be conflicts with employers and occasional riots. Such events, said Marx and Engels, more and more take on 'the character of collisions between two classes' (Marx and Engels, 1968, p. 43). Gradually, and in spite of numerous setbacks, the workers' struggle becomes a coherent political movement, which will, when the 'decisive hour' arrives, bring about revolution on a global scale: the first step towards the establishment of the 'communist' society, in which truly human needs and values would dominate the system of production, rather than vice versa.

The belief that the conflict between the proletariat and the bourgeoisie would lead to a revolutionary transformation stems in part from Marx and Engels' observation that capitalistic social relations were coming to permeate, not just whole societies, but the whole world economy. Past class struggles, such as that between the bourgeoisie and the old aristocracy, 'were movements of minorities, or in the interests of minorities. The proletarian movement is the self-conscious, independent movement of the immense majority, in the interests of the immense majority' (Marx and Engels, 1968, p. 45). It cannot realize its emancipation, therefore, without, in the process, destroying the existing institutions which only serve to oppress it. Some commentators have been sceptical of the notion of revolution as it is embodied in these writings, suggesting either that a revolution is not the inevitable outcome of capitalist development, or that it would not necessarily lead to the 'communist' society envisaged by Marx. We shall return to the question of the revolution below; in the present context, however, it is interesting to note that it is in such a society that Marx envisages the end of social class divisions. Just as the origins of classes lie ultimately in the division of labour, which – by enabling humans to produce an economic surplus – allows some groups to appropriate the products of others' labour in the form of 'private property', so the abolition of private property will bring about the end of class divisions and the process of exploitation on which they are based. Marx was not, it should be emphasized, suggesting that property would be shared equally, as some political theorists did. Rather, the essential idea is that the whole concept of property – the idea that human products can be 'owned' by one person rather than another – would be irrelevant in a society where production was geared to the needs of the community as a whole, rather than making profits for a few. The ending of alienation, which develops as a result of the division of labour and is brought to its ultimate level in the capitalist mode of production, would mean the beginning of the classless society.

Capitalism and Classes

As I suggested above, it would be hard to exaggerate the extent to which Marx's ideas have influenced later writings about social class and stratification. In one respect this is odd, for Marx's specific discussions of class form a very small part of his work as a whole, and – as we shall see presently – a part which is by no means clear or unambiguous. In a more general sense, though, the fascination which Marx's ideas have had is readily understandable: what he offers is nothing less than a coherent account of how the institutional pattern of a society is formed, and how it changes. It is an account, moreover, which has an obvious appeal to those who are concerned to bring about changes in the existing economic and political order – which was, after all, Marx's primary purpose. In the present section, however, our main concern is with the ways in which some later authors have sought to use Marx's ideas as a basis for analysing the class structures of capitalist societies as these have developed in the century or so since his death.

First, however, it may be useful to deal with two themes which are central to Marx's own scheme of things, but which are of less immediate concern from the point of view of understanding social stratification: the revolution and the classless society. Marx's belief in the inevitability of revolution was derived partly, as we have seen, from his analysis of the internal dynamics of the capitalist system and the resulting polarization of the classes. But it was also a consequence of his commitment to a dialectical view of historical progress which he adapted from the philosophy of Hegel. In short, Marx saw in capitalism both the negation of all truly human qualities (the situation of the proletariat), and the development of alienation to the point where people had become the slaves, rather than the masters, of the production process. It followed that, in bringing down the capitalist system, the proletariat would be bringing about the emancipation of humanity as a whole, and ushering in the final stage in human development – the communist society – which would be a synthesis of both man's true social nature and the productive capacities which had developed during previous historical periods. For Marx, it must have seemed as if both economic logic and philosophical analysis had converged on the same inescapable conclusion: the coming of revolution. But while tracing the influence of Hegel's ideas helps to make Marx's beliefs intelligible to us, the fact remains that such ideas are no more and no less than philosophical speculations. While the concept of the liberated, communist society has proved to be a potent political symbol, it does not seem that the advent of such a society is a sociological necessity.

The ideas of revolution and the coming of classless society are, however, only two of the elements in Marx's theoretical thinking. One of the other ingredients has continued to generate a great deal of debate amongst both sociologists and Marxists: the idea that the development of capitalist societies will tend to produce a growing polarization between the dominant capitalist class and the mass of exploited wage workers. Such a perspective can be used to provide a coherent framework in which to understand the historical development of modern societies. But how valid is such an interpretation? For more than a century now, Marx's view has come under attack: some have regarded it as simply speculative, others have rejected what they saw as its determinism – history, they argue, does not conform to any clear pattern, nor can the actions of human beings be explained simply in terms of the play of class forces. In recent years, too, critics have pointed to what they took to be a fatal flaw – the apparent failure of polarization to occur, and the emergence of a 'new' middle class.

Far from splitting into two hostile classes, industrial societies are now increasingly 'middle class' in composition, or so runs the orthodox interpretation of liberal and conservative political theorists. In everyday life, too, we talk of the 'middle' and 'working' classes rather than the bourgeoisie and proletariat of Marxian analysis. And it has often been argued that this swelling of the middle ranks in the occupational structure is a direct result of the evolution of industrial capitalism.

Technology – the very 'forces of production' of which Marx spoke – has developed so that there is now an increasing demand for managerial, technical and administrative skills, rather than a mass of unskilled manual workers. In several of the advanced industrial countries manual workers now constitute less than half the employed population, and most experts are confident that the trend will continue, if anything intensified by the effects of microelectronic technology.

In the 1950s and 1960s, the growing evidence of such trends prompted many commentators to talk in terms of 'embourgeoisment', by which was meant the process by which an ever-growing proportion of the population were aspiring to, and achieving, styles of life and standards of living which were previously thought of as exclusively middle class. Welfare provisions, increasing educational opportunities and the constant expansion of 'white-collar' jobs, it was thought, would gradually bring about greater social equality and thus the decline of the old class-based political antagonisms. One of the most influential theorists of this period was the German sociologist, Ralf Dahrendorf.

Dahrendorf's study of *Class and Class Conflict in an Industrial Society* was published in 1959, and in part of it he attempted to examine Marx's ideas in the light of historical changes in the century or so since they were first developed. It is instructive to reconsider Dahrendorf's discussion in the present context, not so much because of the validity of its analysis – on the contrary, as we shall see it has proved seriously deficient – but because it systematically presents a series of ideas about patterns of class structure in modern industrial societies which have been widely accepted in these societies. Indeed, as I have suggested, such ideas have become fundamental elements in the thought of many liberal, conservative, and indeed some socialist theorists.

Dahrendorf's basic contention is that the capitalist society which Marx analysed in the nineteenth century was not the model for future social development, but rather a limited phase in the evolution of *industrial* societies. Whereas capitalist societies, such as Britain in the nineteenth century, displayed both an industrial mode of production and a pattern of economic organization based on highly competitive, entrepreneurial capitalism, the connection between industry and capitalism is not a necessary one and in fact the passage of time has brought about the decline of 'pure' capitalism. Thus, for Dahrendorf, modern industrial societies are now 'post-capitalist', and it follows that the pattern of class structure and conflict which Marx envisaged is no longer relevant. As Dahrendorf puts it, it is 'highly doubtful whether the concept of class is still applicable to the conflict groups of post-capitalist societies' (Dahrendorf, 1959, p. 57).

Marx's analysis, then, is treated by Dahrendorf as a series of predictions which have been 'falsified' by subsequent events. We may consider each of these, and then examine the contrasting analyses of some of those who claim that class, in Marx's sense of the term, is still a useful, indeed essential concept if we are to understand the workings of modern societies.

The Decomposition of Capital   Whereas the classic capitalist entrepreneur both owned and controlled his business, and directed it with the sole aim of producing personal profit, the typical modern organization is now owned by a large number of shareholders, who may in fact themselves be institutions such as pension funds. Moreover, the running of such businesses is now in the hands of managers, whose aims are very different from those of the classic entrepreneur: it is in their interests to pursue the long-term stability of the firm, and thus their own security, rather than to maximize profits in the short term. Dahrendorf thus emphasized the significance of the separation of ownership and control, which instead of increasing the homogeneity of the bourgeois class had in fact split it, and led to the decline of the profit motive. Managers and owners are held to have rather divergent interests, but these are unlikely to produce class conflict in Marx's sense.

This view has been widely challenged. Although managers may not be substantial capital owners themselves, the rational pursuit of profit remains their fundamental responsibility. Indeed, in a period of relatively high interest rates, there may be increased pressure on companies to produce profits: if shareholders' investments are to be attracted and retained, firms must be able to show a competitive return on money invested. To break even, or produce a small profit, are seldom enough. Moreover, some recent research indicates that it is still both possible and useful to identify a tiny economic elite whose members are 'involved in the process of business leadership in relation to these units of capital whose operations are central to the British economy' (Scott, 1982, p. 125). These people, suggests John Scott, constitute the 'business class'. They share a 'community of interest', and it is their aim to control the dominant sectors of the economy. In this they are assisted by 'subordinate managers' who are 'structurally distinct from top managers' but 'who do not differ from them in their orientation towards business'. Such conclusions, clearly, offer little support to Dahrendorf's view of the 'decomposition' of capital.

The Decomposition of Labour   Technological change, it has been claimed, far from reducing all workers to unskilled manual labourers, has in fact generated a complex hierarchy of skill levels within the so-called 'working class'. Indeed, the demand for simple manual labour has been steadily declining throughout the twentieth century. Differences of skill, authority, and income have thus led, in Dahrendorf's view, to a highly differentiated labour force rather than the proletariat of Marx's vision.

But Braverman, in particular, has argued that the basic thrust of Marx's argument is still powerful, since capitalist rationalization has led to 'deskilling'. It is true enough, says Braverman, that there has been a great increase in the numbers of scientific, technical and engineering specialists in the twentieth century. But such groups still only account for a relatively small proportion of the total labour force: the vast majority of workers are restricted to routine, boring, low-paid jobs which only seem 'skilled' or 'semi-skilled' as a result of various manipulations of the official occupational categories. Moreover, thousands of genuine craft skills have been wiped out by the spread of cheap, low-quality manufactured goods. It seems, too, that advanced industrial economies will no longer be able to provide 'full' employment, with the resulting pool of the unemployed forming what Marx called a 'reserve army' of labour. The implication, then, is that Marx's basic perspective retains its validity; or, as Braverman puts it, up to three-quarters of the labour force 'appears readily to conform to the dispossessed condition of the proletariat' (Braverman, 1974, p. 403).

The 'New' Middle Class   As we have seen, *The Communist Manifesto* talks of the formation of two great classes, and the progressive elimination of those which are a legacy of earlier historical periods (such as the peasantry) and those which stand between the forces of capital and labour. Clearly, few would dispute that the peasantry has dwindled in the manner which Marxian analysis suggests. But there is much less agreement about the fate of the intermediate classes, and Dahrendorf, in common with many recent authors, rejects the idea of the disappearance of the middle classes. While it may be true that the old 'petty bourgeoisie' has declined in face of the rise of big business, the group still persists in all industrial economies. And, of supreme importance, the progress of industrial societies has led, not to the decline of the middle classes, but on the contrary to the emergence of a huge new class of managers, administrative staff, technical specialists and professional groups. These have developed precisely because of the requirements of advanced industrial economies, with their sophisticated technologies and large-scale organizations.

For Dahrendorf, then, the rise of the new middle class has demonstrated the failure of the polarization thesis. Others, however, have suggested that much of this new middle class is in fact simply an extension of the old working class. Thus Westergaard and Resler pointed out that much of the apparent expansion of the middle class is in fact simply a result of the growth of administrative and clerical occupations, mostly performed by women, and misleadingly classified as 'non-manual'. Very many of these people have quite low earnings, and whatever job security they once had is now increasingly being threatened by the automation of office work (Westergaard and Resler, 1975, pp. 39–50). The attractions of a Marxist interpretation are once again evident: far from constituting a new middle class, much of the workforce seems to be experiencing 'proletarianization'.

Such an interpretation, however, in attempting to reconcile the basic elements of a Marxist interpretation with the changing occupational structure of the twentieth century, raises the problem of where the 'boundary' between the working and middle classes is to be drawn. As we have seen, Braverman takes the view that the great majority of working people are in a 'proletarian' situation, while another influential Marxist, Poulantzas, preferred to restrict the term to the 20 per cent or so whose labour is both 'manual' and 'productive' (using the terms in Marx's sense) (Poulantzas, 1975). A third possibility, of course, is to regard those in intermediate occupational positions as occupying 'contradictory' class locations – bourgeois in that their work is done on behalf of the capitalists (with whose interests they often identify), but proletarian in that they remain employees with little autonomy or significant capital (Wright, 1985, p. 45). Though they differ in their conclusions, it should be clear that each of these interpretations of modern class structures accepts the fundamental validity of Marx's insights into the dynamics of capitalist development.

Social Mobility   The rise of the new middle class also calls into question the idea, again derived from Marx's analysis, that as time passes the divisions between the social classes will become more rigid. If there has been an expansion of middle- and upper-middle-class places in the occupational structure, then it follows that there must have been a good deal of 'upward' social mobility as people were recruited from 'lower' class origins to fill vacancies higher up. And most studies of social mobility in industrial societies have suggested that, at least from the First World War to the 1970s, relatively high rates of upward mobility did in fact obtain. For our purposes, the significance of this is the further claim, advanced by Dahrendorf and restated by sociologists such as John Goldthorpe, that high rates of mobility into and out of class positions have the effect of reducing the homogeneity of social classes, thus rendering questionable the Marxian contention that they would tend to display increasing solidarity (Goldthorpe *et al.*, 1980, p. 276).

The occurrence of high rates of upward social mobility throughout much of the twentieth century is not in dispute; several studies, however, have raised doubts as to whether this is a general characteristic of such societies. The period from the First World War to the mid-1970s was the time of the great expansion of 'non-manual' work, but since then the 'room at the top' created by this process has diminished considerably, and with it the possibility of much upward mobility.

Equality   The polarization thesis clearly implies that the development of capitalist societies will generate ever-greater inequalities. But many recent commentators, including Dahrendorf, have questioned whether this process is in fact occurring. Rather than increasing inequality, he argues, industrial societies exhibit a general tendency to greater equality: 'As a tendency, the process of social levelling cannot be denied.' All members of such societies now have equal citizenship rights and entitlements to welfare; moreover Dahrendorf accepts the view that there is a trend towards the redistribution of incomes which is inevitably producing a greater degree of economic equality.

Recent empirical studies, though, have cast doubt on the idea that there is some inexorable trend leading to greater economic equality. Significant personal wealth, although it is now less concentrated at the very top of the economic hierarchy, is still overwhelmingly in the hands of a small elite, and is largely acquired through inheritance rather than individual effort (Noble, 1981, p. 245). Similarly, the overall shape of the income distribution does not display an inevitable trend to greater equality. Reporting on Britain, the Diamond Commission concluded that 'if the share of the top 1% is ignored, the shape of the distribution is not greatly different in 1976–77 from what it was in 1949'. Nor has poverty been progressively eliminated: on the contrary, rising unemployment and a higher proportion of old people in the population have tended to increase it (Atkinson, 1975).

Other studies have documented the persistence of stable patterns of inequality in such fields as education, housing and medical care – in other words, just those spheres in which Dahrendorf argued that citizenship rights would lead to greater equality. In general, then, the widespread belief that there is an inexorable trend towards greater equality is not supported by the available evidence.

The Institutionalization of Class Conflict   Whereas Marx saw class conflict as leading to eventual revolution, Dahrendorf argues that industrial societies have developed institutions which are able to contain the conflicts generated by the opposition of capital and labour. Representatives of each accept the rules of parliamentary democracy, as do employers and trade union officials when they engage in collective bargaining. In recent years, moreover, it has been argued that the balance of political power, and the distribution of incomes, reflects a process of accommodation between three 'corporate' groups: employers' organizations, trade unions and the state. Whilst negotiations amongst these bodies cannot eliminate the possibility of overt conflict, they do ensure that for most of the time bargains over wages and conditions are struck and adhered to, and thus that the potential for revolutionary conflict is diminished.

But while it is hard to deny that the major power blocs in modern societies are now large corporate bodies, many have disputed Dahrendorf's view that their collaboration leads to a stable process of reward distribution which is generally accepted as legitimate. Marx's claim that the contract between capitalists and workers is *inherently* exploitative has been reasserted, and it has been argued that those who hold economic power only make sufficient concessions to 'buy off' overt challenges. In this view, Marxists tend to regard the rituals of parliamentary democracy and collective bargaining as merely superficial appearances which conceal the realities of economic exploitation. Moreover, the relative absence of overt conflict, it is suggested, does not mean that the system is generally acceptable. By the term 'hegemony', Marxists refer to the processes by which the dominant economic class can impose its values and culture on the rest of the population; in recent years, for example, some studies have examined the role of the mass media in this respect while others stress the role of education as a 'state apparatus' which systematically inculcates the 'dominant ideology' into children and rewards those who accept it. And in the last resort, the coercive power of the state is seen to be available to discipline those who challenge established economic interests.

The discussion of the themes developed by Dahrendorf has suggested that however wide their currency ideas of the decline of capitalism and the advent of 'post-industrial' society are challenged by recent theoretical arguments and, more crucially, the results of many empirical studies. Such studies suggest that many of Marx's original insights remain compelling, even after a century of rapid social change. However, it is also difficult to sustain some of the conclusions which Marxists have drawn.

In the present context, the debate about the process of class polarization is of great importance. While it is true that there is little evidence of increasing equality, it is not apparent that modern societies are 'splitting into two great hostile camps, into two great classes' (Marx and Engels, 1968). Indeed, sociological investigators are frequently led to comment on the remarkable stability in the pattern of inequalities which their studies reveal. There is, too, the question of the rise of the new middle class, which as we have seen has caused Marxist theorists some considerable problems. In short, while Marx's analysis of the dynamics of capitalism as an economic system has much to commend it, it does not seem that the social consequences of capitalist development conform to the expectation of class polarization and ultimate revolution.

Marx himself, as an astute observer of contemporary events, was well aware of the burgeoning new middle class (Abercrombie and Urry, 1983, pp. 49–50). In the present context, it is useful to note that, in considering this group, he reminds us of his basic analytical method: in Victorian England, he wrote, 'the stratification of classes does not appear in its pure form. Middle and intermediate strata even here obliterate lines of demarcation everywhere ... However, this is immaterial for our analysis.' (1959, p. 885). Marx continues by stressing the *tendency* for the progress of capitalism to 'separate the means of production more and more from labour'; his prime object in *Capital* was to elucidate the underlying dynamics (or structural properties) of capitalism as an economic system. His analysis is thus no more intended as a description of any real society than are those of the 'classical' economists, with their theoretical assumptions of free markets, perfect competition, and 'economic man'. But Marx was concerned to show that their political economy was not the objective science to which they aspired: perhaps because of his intense preoccupation with economic matters he has often, and wrongly, been regarded as an economic determinist. Late in their careers, both Marx and Engels were at some pains to distance themselves from 'younger people [who] sometimes lay more stress on the economic side than is due to it. We had to emphasise the main principle vis-a-vis our adversaries, who denied it' (Engels, 1968). Given this clarification, it is somewhat surprising to find that Marx's views on the class structure often continue to be treated, by both friends and foes, *as if* they implied some kind of economic determinism (see Parkin, 1979; Cottrill, 1984). It may well be that, for all their influence, a greater burden of interpretation has been placed on Marx's fragmentary remarks about class than they can reasonably bear.

In general, then, while Marx's analysis of capitalism is far from invalidated by the development of modern economies, there remains the problem of establishing specific links between economic processes and the formation of real social groups. In his own discussions of particular historical events, Marx displays a great sensitivity to the effects of political intrigue, personalities, chance events and conflicting interests; while he seeks to relate such factors to the processes of class conflict, there is no simple reduction of the former to the latter. More generally, in the century or so since Marx's death the whole question of the relationship between economic processes and social structures has been extensively explored, and, as we have seen, considerable efforts have been made to identify the conditions governing the formation of social classes.

In sociology, much of this work has been inspired by the writings of Max Weber. Weber's view of the fundamentally economic nature of social classes is similar to that of Marx, but he was particularly concerned to emphasize the significance of group conflicts which could occur *within* the basic class categories (between 'finance' and 'industrial' capitalists, for example, or between 'skilled' and 'unskilled' workers). Moreover, Weber also emphasized the non-economic factors which can influence the formation of groups and political alignments in real societies; there are potentially an infinite number of such 'status' factors, but in practice religion, race, sex and age have been of particular importance in this respect. In addition, Weber argued that there is nothing necessary or inevitable about the process by which economic, or any other interests actually give rise to real social groups, or 'parties' which will pursue them. Thus, for example, while there may be a high degree of economic exploitation or inequality in a society it does not follow that antagonistic social classes will crystallize: on the contrary, the very 'status' factors mentioned above will tend to cut across, and possibly obscure, the basic economic divisions, while real political parties – if they are to receive mass support – must reflect a range of interests other than narrowly 'class' ones.

The picture of social dynamics which emerges from Weber's discussion thus differs in crucial respects from that of the 'polarization' thesis. In essence the social order is viewed as a perpetual struggle for advantage among a variety of groups, as they pursue interests of both economic and non-economic kinds. It is important to emphasize that, unlike some later theorists of political 'pluralism', there is no implication in Weber that such groups have equal access to power: on the contrary, much of the struggle concerns the quest for power and wealth, and the effort to defend it. Weber's general perspective on social stratification is discussed elsewhere (see Parkin, 1982); for present purposes, the essential point is that the emergence of social classes as real 'communities', in which people have both an awareness of their common interest and a prime commitment to pursuing it, is in reality unlikely, though of course it remains a theoretical possibility. Thus while Weber accepted much of Marx's analysis, he was unable to conclude that class polarization was a likely outcome. In retrospect, however, it seems clear that Weber was reacting, just as Engels had done, to the rather simplified version of Marxism which had gained currency in his own day, rather than to Marx's own work, much of which was still unpublished. Nevertheless, it should be apparent why Weber described the argument of *The Communist Manifesto* as an 'error of genius' (Weber, 1978).

Weber's own discussion has, in its turn, been considered unsatisfactory. Giddens, for example, while agreeing that the basic sociological problem is to specify the 'processes by which economic classes become social classes', argues that a Weberian approach leads us to identify 'a cumbersome plurality of classes'. Indeed, if class situations reflect differences in property-ownership, qualifications, and the skills which individuals bring to the labour market, then we could identify 'as many "classes" as there are concrete individuals participating in market relationships'. This is clearly pointless, the more so as Giddens claims that 'there are only, in any given society, a limited number of classes'. Giddens's own solution is to concentrate on the 'structuration' of classes – the way in which economic capacities generate identifiable social groups. Thus the three major economic resources in capitalist societies – property, educational qualifications and manual labour – tend to generate a 'basic three-class system', the familiar 'upper', 'middle', and 'working' classes of everyday speech (Giddens, 1981, p. 105). The strengths and weaknesses of Giddens's proposals are not our major concern here. What is important, though, is the recognition that in his efforts to reformulate the theory of class, Giddens has to confront the fundamental problem raised at the beginning of this chapter: the definition of social classes on the basis of a particular set of assumptions about the nature of the social world. In other words, ideas about class, class conflicts and class structures are not simply reflections of an objective social reality, but rather represent ways in which theorists choose to define that reality. And just as many sociologists have investigated the 'images' of society and class structure which they presume ordinary people have, so the concept of class structure is *itself* an image which the sociologists use to make sense of the social world. By way of conclusion, it is to this topic that we must now return.

Two Classic Disputes:
The Nature of Class and the Concept of Class

The issues raised in the discussion of the concept of class lead us to consider two distinct classic disputes. First, there is the extensive debate about the nature of the class structure in modern societies. As we have seen, the protagonists in these disputes – that is, the vast majority of authors who have considered the topic – tend to assume the validity of the concept of class, and are concerned with such matters as how many classes there are, their relative sizes and membership, where the boundaries between them lie, the extent to which people in them are 'class conscious' and so on. Even Dahrendorf's analysis, which dismisses much of Marxist thinking on the topic, retains the idea that class is a valid and useful concept; whereas the Marxists see class relations rooted in economic inequalities, Dahrendorf argues that they really derive from the unequal distribution of power.

Moreover, as I have suggested, the works of Marx and Engels remain, overwhelmingly, the dominant influence on these debates. It is no exaggeration to say that their ideas about the evolution of capitalism and its ultimate collapse has set the agenda for a century of research and theorizing, and that their vocabulary has defined the terms of the debate. In the 1950s and 1960s, there was much discussion of the possibility of 'embourgeoisment', while later authors, as we have seen, have preferred to talk in terms of 'proletarianization'.

We have also noted, however, some of the problems encountered by later authors who have tried to reformulate some of the basic Marxist concepts. Prominent among these difficulties is the 'boundary' problem, concerning where the 'middle' class ends and the 'working' class begins. As we have seen, Marxist theorists display a range of opinions about where the line should be drawn; indeed, one recent commentator was moved to comment on the 'conceptual gerrymandering' which some have employed in order to protect their favourite theory.

Among sociologists, there is also a wide spread of opinion

concerning the nature of class divisions in modern societies, although many now accept the model which was used by Goldthorpe and his colleagues in their analysis of the British Oxford Mobility Study data: the 'service class' consisting of those 'exercising power and expertise on behalf of corporate bodies' plus independent businessmen and professionals (about a quarter of the occupied male population), the 'intermediate classes' of white-collar workers, small proprietors, the self-employed, supervisory staff and technicians (about 30 per cent of occupied males) and the 'working class' of manual workers (about 45 per cent) (Goldthorpe *et al.*, 1980, pp. 39–42). The problem remains, however, of relating such 'classes' to observable social groups or collective action. There are crucial differences between the situation of the economic elite and those who perform the routine managerial and administrative tasks which are typical of the rest of the 'service class'. By their very definition, it is hard to envisage the 'intermediate classes' as a coherent body, and the political history of Britain in the mid-1980s has demonstrated how difficult it is to generate collective action of the working class, even when jobs and basic rights are at stake. Moreover, since many commentators have been concerned to emphasize the increasingly fragmented nature of the class structure, it might seem likely that the traditional concept of class itself would come in for critical scrutiny. To date, however, there are only a few signs of this, although it is apparent that 'Weberian' ideas are in the ascendent.

The second fundamental dispute, then, concerns the analytical validity of the concept of class itself. As I have suggested, this has not (yet) emerged as a major issue among students of social stratification, the majority of whom seem satisfied to take it for granted. But the problems faced by class theorists and empirical researchers serve to illustrate some of the most serious issues of sociological methodology in general.

One set of difficulties is encountered in efforts to 'operationalize' ideas about class and class structure – that is, to devise research procedures which will allow the collection of relevant data. Most of the studies which have been undertaken by sociologists are large-scale sample surveys, in which the occupations of randomly selected individuals (usually men) are taken as an indicator of their class position, so that a picture of the overall class structure is assembled. The procedure is not without its problems, however. By its very nature, the sample survey is not an efficient means of collecting data about the wealthy or powerful elites which may be expected to be of great significance in any system of class relations, and as we have seen no such groups are identified in the reports of the Oxford Mobility Study. Critics – particularly of a Marxist persuasion – may thus complain that the attempt to collect data objectively has in fact led to the exclusion of the most important 'class'. For their part, several influential Marxist authors have, as noted above, become preoccupied with reformulating class theory and they, in turn, have been criticized for engaging in complex speculations, remote from the realities of social life (Thompson, 1979).

The basic methodology of the sample survey also leads to problems. Since it is individuals who are sampled, it is hard to relate the resulting data to any pattern of family organization without making some rather gross assumptions about the links between kinship patterns and the distribution of economic rewards. A good deal of research has been condemned as 'male-centred', largely because it is based on the assumption that women's class position is ultimately dependent on the occupations of their husbands or fathers. It also involves the assumption that women's domestic labour is marginal to the system of production, and that women in occupations play an essentially secondary role in determining the shape of the class structure (Garnsey, 1978). It is thus understandable why much of the research on class and mobility has recently attracted hostile criticism; for our purposes, the important point is that, by excluding women and by its inability to incorporate families, survey research yields a picture of social life which is hard to relate to any real, or possible, society. In their pursuit of 'objectivity', the survey researchers ultimately end up with a set of atomized individuals, divorced from any cultural or institutional context, floating up and down through a class structure which is defined by the researcher.

A further difficulty in using occupation as an indicator of class position may be mentioned. In discussing the 'boundary' problem, many authors examine the situation of those in 'routine non-manual', often clerical, work. Are they 'really' middle class, or are they becoming 'proletarianized'? First, it should be said that most people in clerical work are women, and thus, as suggested above, hard to assimilate to existing class schemes. Secondly, what is known about male clerks indicates that it may not make much sense to seek an unambiguous class position for them. The majority of young men who enter clerical work subsequently move on to 'higher' administrative and managerial work, whereas older male clerks tend to have moved 'up' from manual work at later stages of their working lives. The point is that the occupation of 'clerk' at any one time does not constitute a homogeneous group as far as processes of social stratification are concerned (Stewart, *et al.* 1980, p. 191).

Once again, then, we encounter what is now becoming a familiar theme. The attempt to analyse societies in terms of social classes involves the imposition of some more-or-less arbitrary categories on the perpetual motion of social life. Class is itself an 'image' of society, a 'way of seeing' which alerts us to some aspects of our cultural environment to the exclusion of others. As such it is not an objective description of social life but a reflection of the interests and assumptions of those who use it. The point may be emphasized by a final reference to Marx, whose aim after all was not to 'interpret' the world 'but to change it'. Thus, in political polemics (such as *The Communist Manifesto*), it was natural that he and Engels should stress the simple, inspirational idea of the two great classes and the final, revolutionary, triumph of the proletariat. It does not follow, however, that such ideas should be taken as the basis for sophisticated sociological inquiry. Indeed, it could be argued that some of the recent sociological work has lost the great strength which even the simplest version of Marxism retains – the stress on change and dynamism in social relations. Progress in this field, as in others, may well depend on our ability to abandon such ideas as 'class structure', with all its rigid and static connotations, and think instead in terms of *processes*.

It is not self-evident, as Giddens asserts, that there are 'only a limited number of classes' in any given society. To abandon a line of inquiry because it implies 'a cumbersome plurality of classes' seems hardly a scientific attitude: there are surely a 'cumbersome plurality' of particles in atomic nuclei, but this did not lead the great theoretical physicists to stipulate the number that they would consider appropriate. On the contrary, the problem became that of dealing with very large numbers, uncertainty and continuous change in situations where conventional experiment-ation was impossible. In social life, what is undeniable is a pattern of inequality – of wealth, power, prestige, etc. – which is the outcome of the activities of individuals and groups as they pursue their perceived interests. It may be that our understanding of the processes of social stratification will be furthered by the direct investigation of these activities in the real world rather than the heavy-handed imposition of the concept of class.

We return, then, to a point with which we began: the idea of 'social class' is essentially a 'common-sense' one, as opposed to a 'scientific' concept (Schutz, 1962). This does not in any way diminish its importance, for such 'common-sense' ideas are indispensible in the process of linguistic communication – they are the building blocks, so to speak, with which we construct coherent and communicable meanings. But – and this is the general issue which our discussion leads us to con-front – such 'common-sense' concepts cannot simply be taken for granted as the basis of sociological analysis which aspires to be scientific, for the 'objective' research ends up simply reflecting the subjective preferences of the researcher. Such a conclusion is not welcomed either by Marxists or most sociol-ogists of stratification. But it is the stuff of which classic disputes are made.

References and Further Reading

Abercrombie, N. and Urry, J. (1983), *Capital, Labour and the Middle Classes* (London: Allen & Unwin).

Atkinson, A. B. (1975), *The Economics of Inequality* (Oxford: Oxford University Press).

Braverman, H. (1974), *Labor and Monopoly Capital* (New York: Monthly Review Press).

Calvert, P. (1982), *The Concept of Class* (London: Hutchinson).

Cottrill, A. (1984), *Social Classes in Marxist Theory* (London: Routledge & Kegan Paul).

Dahrendorf, R. (1959), *Class and Class Conflict in Industrial Society* (London: Routledge & Kegan Paul).

Engels, F. (1968), 'Letter to J. Bloch' in *Marx and Engels: Selected Works* (London: Lawrence & Wishart), pp. 682–3.

Garnsey, E. (1978), 'Women's work and theories of class and stratifi-cation', *Sociology*, vol. 12, pp. 223–43.

Giddens, A. (1981), *The Class Structure of the Advanced Societies*, 2nd edn (London: Hutchinson).

Goldthorpe, J. H., Llewellyn, C. and Payne, C. (1980), *Social Mobility and Class Structure in Modern Britain* (Oxford: Oxford University Press).

Marx, K. (1955), *The Poverty of Philosophy* (Moscow: Progress Publishers).

Marx, K. (1959), *Capital, Vol. III* (London: Lawrence & Wishart).

Marx, K. and Engels, F. (1968), 'The Communist Manifesto' in *Selected Works* (London: Lawrence & Wishart).

Noble, T. (1981), *Structure and Change in Modern Britain* (London: Batsford).

Parkin, F. (1979), *Marxism and Class Theory: A Bourgeois Critique* (London: Tavistock).

Parkin, F. (1982), *Max Weber* (London: Tavistock).

Poulantzas, N. (1975), *Classes in Contemporary Capitalism* (London: New Left Books).

Royal Commission on the Distribution of Income and Wealth (1979), *Report No. 7*, Cmnd 7595, (London: HMSO).

Schutz, A. (1962), *Collected Papers*, Vol. 1 (The Hague: Martinus Nijhoff).

Scott, J. (1982), *The Upper Classes: Property and Privilege in Britain* (London: Macmillan).

Stewart, A., Prandy, K. and Blackburn, R. H. (1980), *Social Stratification and Occupations* (London: Macmillan).

Thompson, E. P. (1979), *The Poverty of Theory* (London: Macmillan).

Weber, M. (1978), 'Socialism' in W. G. Runciman (ed.), *Weber: Selections in Translation* (Cambridge: Cambridge University Press).

Westergaard, J. and Resler, H. (1975), *Class in a Capitalist Society* (Harmondsworth: Penguin).

Williams, R. (1983), *Keywords*, 2nd edn (London: Fontana).

Wright. E. O. (1985), *Classes* (London: Verso).

Chapter 4

The Protestant Ethic Debate

LARRY RAY

Introduction

It is not difficult to see why Weber's thesis on the *Protestant Ethic and the Spirit of Capitalism* (*PESC*) has generated seven decades of debate. As a sociologist, writing about capitalism (which concerned economists), and Protestantism (which concerned theologians), in the seventeenth century (which concerned historians), with reference to anxieties and motivations (the province of psychologists), Weber was bound to tread on interdisciplinary toes. This is indeed what has happened, with the result that although Weber's arguments are widely known, they are often misunderstood. Sociologists, for example, tend to focus on the thesis in general terms, without giving too much attention to its empirical details; while historians, on the other hand, often allude to the 'Weber thesis' as untenable in details, without reference to his theoretical and methodological concerns. The result, as many commentators complain, has been a great deal of 'misunderstanding' amongst sociologists, historians, economists and theologians.

One aim of this chapter is to examine Weber's sociological intentions in the *PESC* in the context of his other work. The *PESC* was not a work of history, nor theology, nor economics, but was an exploration of sociological problems to do with rationality, values and the understanding of history. In particular, Weber developed here an important methodological device, namely the 'ideal type'. This he defines as, 'an analytical category which the content of an actual cross-section of history *approaches* by degrees' (Weber, 1978b). Ideal types are one-sided: they accentuate an aspect of social life that is relevant to the research at hand. They are analytical constructs that enable us to simplify a set of social relationships, to detail what is relevant and exclude misleading complexities. Underpinning Weber's use of ideal-type constructs lies a philosophy of history that identifies the central problem faced by the historian or sociologist to be that of reducing complexity. We highlight, for a particular purpose, or from a particular perspective, a corner of reality, amongst an infinite mass of possible relations.

That Weber intended to develop a methodology in the *PESC* does not mean, however, that one can escape from confronting the difficulties associated with the thesis. These in particular are: (1) there is more than one thesis in the *PESC*, and therefore Weber himself is partly responsible for other scholars' 'mis-readings'; (2) methodological it might have been on one level, but Weber does refer to historical realities, and one cannot shrug off questions of historical validity too lightly; (3) the aims of the *PESC* are not all clearly stated, and are generally inferred from Weber's other works, and this opens up a vast terrain of interpretation and counter-inference.

The strategy followed here is first to present a statement of the thesis, and its initial reception by historians. Secondly, to discuss the historical and substantive points that have been made for or against it. Thirdly, to examine the methodological and historiographical debate that is still underway, about history and causality, the usefulness of ideal types and models of historical explanation, that has arisen out of Weber's thesis. In this context the question of the relationship between the Weber thesis and Marxism will be discussed.

The Thesis

Nothing contributed more to Weber's fame than his essay, first published in 1905, on Protestant ethics and the spirit of capitalism, yet it is not characteristic of the bulk of the rest of his work. In his *Religionssoziologie* as a whole he discussed Hinduism, Judaism and the Chinese religions in such a way as to relate religious beliefs to social institutions, viewing culture and society as an integrated whole. The argument in *PESC* is much more specific but sociologically less integrated. After some general observations on religious affiliation and social stratification, he constructs an ideal type of the 'spirit of capitalism', drawn largely from the eighteenth-century Pennsylvanian moralist, Benjamin Franklin. This is followed by a brief discussion of the appearance of the concept of 'calling' (*Beruf*) in Luther's work. The bulk of the essay is an extensive discussion of the implications of four Protestant sects – Calvinism, Pietism, Methodism and Baptism – for economic life. Weber concludes with a slightly hasty account of 'Asceticism and the Spirit of Capitalism' that tries to pull the argument together.

The reader should be aware that the English edition, published first in 1930, was not taken from the 1905 original but from the expanded versions prepared by Weber for the *Religionssoziologie* in 1920. To the original essays Weber added 100 pages of notes that provided further evidence and responses to his critics. Further, the 'Authors' Introduction' that appears in the English edition was originally written for the *Religionssoziologie* series as a whole. This is not, as Marshall points out, mere pedantry, for it is through reading the 'Introduction' as an original part of the *PESC* that much confusion has arisen, (Marshall, 1982, p. 18). The 'Introduction' reflects on the diverse origins and social and cultural consequences of modern capitalism as an economic system, whilst the *PESC* essays are concerned with the origins of the *spirit* of capitalism. This distinction between the system and spirit of capitalism frequently becomes blurred in the debate.

With this point in mind, let us first ask why Weber was interested in religion and capitalism. In part Weber's interest in the origins of capitalism was related to the economic and social problems facing Germany at the turn of the century. Though a major imperial power by the end of the nineteenth century, Germany had followed a course of development fundamentally different from that in France, Britain and the USA. In Germany heavy industrialization had proceeded late in the nineteenth century under the direction of the aristocratic Prussian ruling class, and had failed to establish a politically independent bourgeoisie. The result was that Germany was governed by an authoritarian, militaristic state that regulated many aspects of social and economic life. The absence of a bourgeois revolution, as in America in 1776, France 1789, or Britain in 1642, was, Weber believed, partly responsible for Germany's problems: 'a nation that has never the nerve to behead the traditional powers that be will never . . . gain proud self-assurance' (Weber, letter to Keyserling, cited by Bendix and Roth, 1971, p. 19).

However, in seeking to understand the specificity of German development, Weber and his colleagues, such as Sombart, Simmel and Troeltsch, were determined to present a theoretical alternative to Marxism. First, they believed that Marx's law of value had been disproved by marginalist economics of the 1890s; and, secondly, they did not accept that there were necessary stages of economic development. Indeed, Werner Sombart had addressed the question of the origins of the 'spirit of capitalism' in *Modern Capitalism* in 1902, and it was this in particular that stimulated Weber's inquiry. Weber took issue with the details of Sombart's argument, but felt above all that the question of the origins of the capitalist spirit remained unanswered.

Weber looked to Protestant religions as a possible source of this spirit largely because of the well-documented observation that Protestants seemed to be economically more successful than Catholics. In fact, he tends to take this general association much for granted, opening his essay with the comment: 'A glance at the occupational statistics of any country of mixed religious composition brings to light . . . the fact that business leaders and owners of capital, as well as the higher grades of skilled labour, and even more the higher technically and commercially trained personnel of modern enterprises, are overwhelmingly Protestant' (Weber, 1974, p. 35). Moreover, capitalism had developed not in the Italian city-states of the fifteenth and sixteenth centuries, which had sophisticated banking systems, but in the less economically developed north of Europe, which was Protestant.

Sociologically, though, Weber was also concerned with the fact that it was not only the origins of capitalism that seemed peculiar to north-western Europe. As he says in the 'Author's Introduction', one can find here a more general process of 'rationalization', indications of which were evident elsewhere in the world, but which developed with full force only in the Occident. For example, 'only in the West does science exist at a stage of development which we recognise as valid', although

'Empirical knowledge, reflection on problems of the cosmos and of life, philosophical and theological wisdom ... are not confined to it' (i.e. to the West). Again, 'In architecture, pointed arches have been used elsewhere as a means of decoration in antiquity and Asia ... But the rational use of the Gothic vault as a means of distributing pressure ... does not occur elsewhere' (*ibid*, p. 15).

The importance of this is that we see here how Weber constructs his argument through a comparative approach to civilizations. Capitalism, as part of a broader phenomenon of progressive rationalization or disenchantment, appeared only in the West, during the sixteenth and seventeenth centuries. Yet China, India, or ancient antiquity, had at certain periods conditions that might have made capitalist development possible. What condition or conditions, then, were specific to the West? What existed there and not elsewhere, that can account for capitalist development?

Crucial to this question was the view that Weber shared with Marx, that capitalism was an historically specific economic form. Capitalism was not a ubiquitous human drive: 'The impulse to acquisition, pursuit of gain, of money, of the greatest possible amount of money, has in itself nothing to do with capitalism. This impulse exists and has existed among waiters, physicians, coachmen, artists, prostitutes, dishonest officials, soldiers, nobles, crusades, gamblers and beggers' (*ibid*., p. 17). What then, is capitalism? Again, not unlike Marx, Weber defines capitalistic activity as 'one which rests on the expectation of profit by the utilization of opportunities for exchange, that is on (formally) peaceful chances of profit ... and pursuit of profit and forever renewed profits through continuous, rational, capitalistic enterprise' (*ibid*., p. 17). It is rational rule-following behaviour that constrains the actions of the capitalist since: 'an individual capitalistic enterprise which did not take advantage of its opportunities for profit-making would be doomed to extinction' (*ibid*., p. 17). In other words, unlike the pursuit of gain, or forceable expropriation, capitalism as a system of rules and expectations, is organized around a central motivation – the continual accumulation of profit *as an end itself*. Similarly, in *Capital*, Marx said that 'The circulation of money as capital is ... an end in itself, for the expansion of value takes place only within this constantly renewed movement . . . The capitalist is a rational miser' (Marx *I*, 1974, p. 162).

So much for capitalism – but remember that the *PESC* is not supposed to be about capitalism *per se* but about the origin of one of the preconditions for capitalism – the spirit of capitalism. At this point let us look more closely at Weber's argument, and why he believed this 'spirit' to be of such crucial importance. In his *General Economic History*, Weber listed the circumstances that must exist for capitalist production to develop. These are (1) the existence of a mass of wage labourers who are formally 'free' to sell their labour yet are forced by necessity to do so; (2) the absence of restrictions on economic exchange on the market (removal of state monopolies, for example); (3) the use of technology through mechanization of the productive process; and (4) the separation of the productive enterprise from the household (Weber, 1978a). These economic conditions have been found to greater or lesser degrees outside of Europe, and the USA, but have not resulted in capitalist development. One reason for this, Weber thought, was the absence outside Europe and the USA of the 'rational-legal form of the state' which made possible the rational regulation of economic life. But also of crucial importance was the more illusive 'spirit of capitalism'.

Simply put, the 'spirit of capitalism' is a set of motivational dispositions that govern the constant accumulation of capital as an end in itself. It involves the following maxims for everyday conduct: be prudent, diligent and ever about your lawful business; do not idle, for time is money; cultivate your credit-worthiness and put it to good use, for credit is money; be punctual and just in the repayment of loans and debts, for to become a person of known credit-worthiness is to be a master of other people's purses; be vigilant in keeping accounts; be frugal in consumption and do not waste money on inessentials; and finally, do not let money lie idle, for the smallest sum soundly invested can earn a profit, and the profits reinvested soon multiply in ever increasing amounts (Weber, 1974, pp. 48–50).

There is in this notion though an interesting paradox. The spirit of capitalism stands opposed to all forms of traditionalistic behaviour. Traditionalistic attitudes, whether amongst producers or entrepreneurs, favour increased leisure over increased profit or wages. Such attitudes produced the well-known 'backward-sloping supply curve' for labour – the higher wages are, the less work will be done, so long as producers are satisfied with their conditions of life. However, the 'spirit of capitalism' supplants traditional economic values with the idea of hard work and increased income as ends in themselves, but here lies the paradox. Labour must be performed 'as if it were an absolute end in itself . . . But such an attitude is by no means a product of nature' (Weber, 1974, p. 62). Indeed, the modern capitalist 'gets nothing out of his wealth himself, except the irrational sense of having done his job well' (*ibid.*, p. 71). Capitalism appears to be a more rational system than traditional economies, but in fact is governed by an irrational drive (to accumulate more and more) that cannot be justified by appeal to any other criteria or values.

In this way, through highlighting this paradox, Weber defines a further objective of the *PESC*: 'If this essay makes any contribution at all, may it bring out the complexity of the only superficially simple concept of the rational' (*ibid.*, p. 193). Moreover, by highlighting the essentially irrational nature of the 'spirit of capitalism', Weber leads into his central thesis – 'that the chances of overcoming traditionalism are greatest on account of the religious upbringing', thus 'it is worthwhile to ask how this connection of adaptability to capitalism with religious factors occurred in the early days of capitalism' (*ibid.*, p. 63). The self-disciplined methodical life of the early capitalist merchant or workshop owner suggest to Weber the dedicated life in pursuit of a 'calling'.

The concept of 'calling' is the central link for Weber between the religious Protestant ethic and the secular spirit of capitalism. Again the pattern of motivation and belief involved is constructed as an ideal type especially through the English Puritan, Richard Baxter. The idea of 'calling', Weber argues appears first in Luther's work and has no precedent in earlier, Catholic, theology. However, Luther's concept involves a fulfilment of obligations imposed upon the individual by his position in the world (*ibid.*, p. 80). This ethic of resignation, of accepting one's place in life has little to do with the thrusting, competitive ethos of capitalism. Its significance, though, was in that it transposes 'calling' from the world of religious asceticism, that is, from the monastic life, to the everyday world of work, as the task set by God. Luther, despite his traditionalism, sanctified the mundane task of earning a living.

The real break with traditionalism, in Weber's view, came with Calvin, or rather with Calvinism, since Weber says almost nothing about Calvin himself. In his descriptions of Calvinism, Weber emphasizes the belief in predestination, which demonstrated a rigorous consistency. Since God was omnipotent and omniscient, He must have determined the whole pattern of Creation for eternity. To suggest otherwise was in effect to impose a limit to God's knowledge and power and to imply that the universe might in part be unknown to Him. The belief in predestination applied to personal salvation – only a part of humanity was saved, and this had been ordained for eternity. To suppose that as a mere mortal one could affect the predetermined plan of the universe was sinful arrogance. One might think that this was not a very promising ethic from which worldly activity could commence, but the meaning that this belief was to have for Calvinists became crucial for the development of a capitalist spirit.

A major consequence of the belief in predestination was an 'unprecedented inner loneliness' amongst believers. 'The question – am I one of the elect? – must sooner or later have arisen for every believer and have forced all other interests into the background' (*ibid.*, p. 110). One had a duty to consider oneself chosen, yet faith had to be proved by its objective results – by increasing the glory of God through a life of systematic self-control. In particular, Weber argues, the Calvinist, knowing that there was no hope of salvation through good works or through sacraments, sought evidence of salvation in worldly success. Calvinists were alone in the world and were forced to rely on their individual consciences for knowledge of grace. This provided a major incentive for worldly activity oriented towards proof of election, for one thing was certain: that the pursuit of *any* pleasure was contrary to God's law, and thus a dissolute, hedonistic or idle life was prima-facie evidence of damnation. Thus, 'Calvinism not only had a quite unique consistency, but . . . its psychological effect was extraordinarily powerful' (*ibid.*, p. 128).

What of other seventeenth-century Protestant sects? Weber proceeds to discuss Pietism, Methodism and Baptism, none of which shared the Calvinist belief in predestination, yet are still viewed as orienting action towards the world. Regarding

Pietism, Weber points to its rational and ascetic elements, but admits that 'vacillation makes it definitely weaker than the iron consistency of Calvinism ... [which] was more closely related to ... the active enterprise of bourgeois-capitalist entrepreneurs' (*ibid.*, p. 137). Methodism preached methodical, systematic conduct and an aspiration to higher life (*ibid.*, p. 143). The Baptists repudiated idolatry of the flesh, refused office in service of the state and therefore channelled activity into worldly callings. Overall then, there was a conception of a state of religious grace, common to all denominations, that could not be obtained by good works, confession, nor magical sacraments, but that promulgated rational planning of the whole of life in accordance with God's will. The Christian 'now strode in the marketplace of life' (*ibid.*, p. 154).

The direction of Weber's concluding analysis will now be clear. What had begun as a *religious* movement – with Luther a reaction to the laxity of a Church that sold indulgencies, and granted forgiveness through ritual and magic – developed implications for economic action that were *wholly unanticipated* amongst Reformation theologians. This is important because it reflects a methodological underpinning of the *PESC*, namely, to show how history, rather than follow a course determined by any single factor such as the economy, follows a logic of unintended consequences. Seventeenth-century Puritans could not possibly have known that their religious enthusiasm and dogmatism, in interaction with other preconditions for capitalism, might have given an impetus to an economic system that would probably have horrified them.

It was for religious motives that the Puritans turned with full force against the relaxed enjoyment of life and the pursuit of pleasure. 'If God shows one of this elect a chance of profit he must do it with purpose', said Richard Baxter (*ibid.*, p. 166). Yet the pursuit of profit combined with a denial of the pleasures of conspicuous consumption produced an economic spirit that had never before existed. This had the effect of freeing the acquisition of goods from traditionalistic ethics – it was no longer sinful, or of dubious morality, to make a profit in trade. What was sinful was the enjoyment of profit in conspicuous consumption. The result of these injunctions, then, was to promote the constant accumulation of capital through an ascetic compulsion to save (*ibid.*, p. 172). Thus, religious asceticism remodelled the world and gave material goods their inexorable power in history.

What Weber claims to have shown, then, is that the spirit of capitalism – a set of dispositions or motives encouraging an ascetic life style as an end in itself – was formed out of the Protestant ethic – especially in Calvinism's 'paradox of predestination'. This capitalist spirit, the unintended consequence of theological practices, acted with other preconditions to generate capitalist development. Weber has not claimed, not directly anyway, that Protestant Nonconformism 'caused' capitalism, and he continually protested that he was not attempting to posit 'ideas', in this case religious beliefs, as a cause of material processes. It is, however, in these two areas that much subsequent debate has dwelt.

The Initial Reception

In the above summary, one of Weber's theses has been spelt out in the *PESC*, although a second has not. He has attempted to specify the origin of an economic orientation in the religious concept of 'calling' but he has also implied that the new economic 'spirit' was a necessary, though not sufficient, condition for capitalism. It was on this basis that critics such as Fischer, Rachfahl, and later Tawney, accused Weber of arguing that 'the Protestant ethic caused modern capitalism'. Fischer accused him of offering nothing less than a version of Hegelianism with the Protestant ethic substituting for Hegel's Absolute Spirit. Weber responded with outrage to such charges of idealism, but this sort of debate arose in part from ambiguities in his own position.

Felix Rachfahl, for example, raised several of the issues that were to recur in subsequent debates. First, he argued, the traditional/capitalistic dichotomy had been overstretched. Capitalism did not require Calvin or the Reformation and Weber ignores more general motivations like power, honour, security that gave much greater impetus to capitalistic behaviour than did religion. Indeed for Rachfahl, religion's influence can be absorbed into the effects of wider social relations. Secondly, inner-worldly asceticism was not peculiar to Protestantism (a point also made by Sombart, Fanfani and Robertson). In fact it was common to the Catholic laity and was actually rejected by many Calvinists. Thirdly, he provides some specific examples: Dutch capitalism had little to do with Protestant sects, while in the USA in the seventeenth and eighteenth centuries many people practised worldly ascetisism but in the context of an agrarian, not capitalist economy. In England capitalism antedated Protestantism (a point developed by Tawney). Fourthly, the 'great' capitalists such as Jakob Fugger, whom Weber mentions, were hardly shy about ostentatious living; indeed many Puritans who became rich drifted towards established religion and did enjoy their wealth. Fifthly, what was most important for economic development in the Reformation was not the concept of 'calling' but its tolerance of economic activity. Again this is a point made by Tawney and others, though not neglected by Weber himself.

Amongst Weber's early critics, Sombart, whose *Modern Capitalism* had stimulated Weber's work, took issue with the alleged connection between Protestantism and capitalism. In *The Quintessence of Capitalism*, first published in 1913, he makes three main criticisms of the 'Weber thesis'. First, that in general Catholicism did not stand in the way of capitalist growth, but was often beneficial to it. He saw Franklin's ethics as a word-for-word repetition of writings of the Renaissance philosopher, Leon Albert (a suggestion that Weber flatly rejected, see 1974, p. 194). Sombart suggests that the fourteenth-century doctrines of the Catholic Church, formulated by Thomas Aquinas, preached the rationalization of life: reason governs the universe, and must regulate and control passions and appetites. It is here, rather than in Calvinism, that Sombart locates the transition from traditional to modern motivations: fourteenth-century religion up-rooted 'natural man with all his passions, to replace the primitive and original outlook by specifically rationalist habits of mind' (Sombart, 1967, pp. 236ff). Acquinian philosophy encouraged methodological economic activity and condemned both idleness and avarice. The prohibition of usury amongst the Italian School-men posed (*pace* Weber) no special obstacle to capitalism, because it discouraged only unproductive, not productive loans. Indeed, 'the more carefully I study the sources the more convinced I become that the prohibition of usury gave a mighty *impetus* to the capitalist spirit' (*ibid.*, p. 246, emphasis added).

Secondly, looking both at Luther and at Puritans such as

Baxter, Sombart argues that 'Protestantism has been all along the line a foe to capitalism' (*ibid.*, p. 254). This is because it directs man's gaze to the joys of existence here below, rather than on preparation for the life hereafter. The Puritans condemned riches as irrelevant to the soul's purity. Baxter himself preached the evils of love of money, since every moment spent not in the service of God is lost. Hudson, some years later, also quotes Baxter at length to demonstrate an anti-capitalist ethic in his work. The following passage is often used to indicate Baxter's sanction for capitalism: 'If God shows you a way in which you may lawfully get more than in another way . . . if you refuse this, and choose the less gainful way, you cross one of the ends of your calling, and you refuse to be God's steward'. Placed in context, argues Hudson, echoing Sombart, Robertson and others, this proves to be a distortion. Baxter's point in context was that if your calling makes you rich, then you must 'regretfully accept' it, but remember that this only increases responsibility and the risk of damnation (Hudson, 1949, p. 5).

The third criticism of the Weber thesis made by Sombart concerns the historical location of capitalism. 'It would be but a narrow conception of the capitalist spirit thus to see its various manifestations springing from Puritanism' (Sombart, 1967, p. 260). Rather, he identifies capitalism with the merchant adventurers, the Raleighs, the Cavendishes, the Drakes, the Fuggers, and more recently men like Cecil Rhodes, who were all 'immune from the abstruse stuff which a ghost like Mr. Baxter crammed into the *Christian Directory*'. Sombart concedes that there were some great capitalists among the Puritans, but doubts whether they owed their greatness to Puritan ethics. Rather, this was 'due to their racial qualities or to fortune's guiding hand'.

These sorts of arguments only damaged the Weber thesis if this was interpreted as positing a link between Protestantism and capitalism as an economic form. Weber himself repeatedly denied that this was his intention. For example, in response to Rachfahl he dismissed as idealist the idea that the 'capitalist spirit' created an economic system. Rather he had attempted to prove that the Reformation influenced the capitalist spirit by illustrating how maxims such as Franklin's differed from those of the Middle Ages. The link between religious and secular spirit, Weber reiterated, could be made through the notion of *Beruf*, that was *not* found in texts earlier than Luther's (*pace* Brentato, see Weber, 1974, pp. 204–10). The causal thesis therefore concerned spiritual attitudes, associated by affinity with the habits of the entrepreneur, through the idea of a practical–rational regulation of life (Weber, 1978b). Yet Weber does not, as Marshall points out, entirely lay to rest the suspicion that he was positing a stronger thesis – that the capitalist spirit was a necessary condition for the development of capitalism. Indeed he concedes that, '"The Protestant ethic and the spirit of capitalism" *presupposes* that the modern capitalist mentality had a definite influence on the development of modern capitalism', and that his strategy had been to show 'the general direction in which ... religious movements have influenced the development of material culture' (Weber, 1974, p. 91).

On the more general point made by Sombart and others that Protestantism, and Puritanism in particular, were anti-capitalist in orientation, Weber could agree. The whole point was that a secular capitalist spirit emerged, as an unintended and unforeseeable consequence of a religious ethic. A number of writers, including Sombart, pointed out that under Calvin's influence capitalism in Geneva was retarded, not encouraged. This, if true, did not affect Weber's argument, since he dwelt not so much on Calvin, but on the meaning that Calvinism had for believers, and the implications of the 'calling' for worldly activity long after Calvin's death. Hence Samuelsson's point that Weber was wrong to use Franklin as an example of the capitalist spirit because he was not a Calvinist falls. Franklin was used to illustrate the fully developed spirit of capitalism which it only attained in its secular phase (see Eldridge, 1972, pp. 37ff).

Not all immediate responses to Weber's thesis were hostile. Ernst Troeltsch, a colleague of Weber's at Heidelberg, was interested in developing a sociological explanation of the origins and modifications of Christianity. Troeltsch, described by Fischoff as the early commentator who best understood Weber's intention, defined the major problem not in terms of whether Calvinism facilitated capitalism, but in terms of what was Protestantism's influence, once its 'totalistic impulses' had failed. That is, the transposition of a purely religious doctrine into secular activity occurred after Calvinism had failed to create a new civilization totally regulated by religious precepts. Adherents then transformed their asceticism into worldly callings. This in a sense anticipates Hyma's point, moralisticly expressed, that many seventeenth-century Calvinists who become capitalists were guilty of apostasy – they were 'pseudo-Calvinists who will no doubt look for and find excuses for their behaviour ... in many cases after they have ceased to be Christians' (Hyma, 1955, p. 570).

Troeltsch reiterated Weber's view that there was an 'affinity' between Calvinism and the spirit of capitalism, and that the conjunction of these two phenomena in itself was an historical accident. Weber in return acknowledged his debt to Troeltsch for having provided historical detail in support of his thesis that he, 'not being a theologian, could not have done' (Weber, 1974, p. 284). Troeltsch emphasized, more than Weber, Calvinism's rejection of the canonical veto on usury. The affinity between Calvinism and the spirit of capitalism rested in former's 'calling' of work which declares that the earning of money is allowable and could give it intellectual and ethical backbone. From this point the pursuit of industry could be conducted with a 'clear conscience', provided it was conducted with an inner severance of feeling and enjoyment from all the objects of labour (Troeltsch, 1950, p. 812).

Subsequent Debates of Historical Substance

Thus far we have considered the debate that developed after publication of the original essays in 1905 until Weber's death in 1920. During the following two decades the debate spread to France and Britain and then to the USA, to the extent that in 1944 Ephraim Fischoff could write of 'The History of a Controversy'. This early phase of the debate was characterized by close picking over historical substance – of interpretations of religion, of economic change and the direction of causality. Although conducted mainly amongst historians, there were sociological aspects to this controversy – especially in Tawney and Sée, both of whom favoured a more materialist interpretation, that was later pursued by C. P. Hill and, in a way, by Robertson too.

Tawney's *Religion and the Rise of Capitalism*, first published in

1926, covers similar terrain to the *PESC*, but emphasizes the chronological priority of capitalism over Protestantism, and suggests that the latter was a religious adaptation to the former. Regarding Weber's thesis, Tawney identifies three points on which Weber's arguments appear to be 'one-sided and over-strained'. First, he says, Weber seems to explain by reference to moral and intellectual influences developments which have their principal explanation in another region altogether. Capitalism existed in fifteenth-century Venice and Florence, which were Catholic. The subsequent development of capitalism in Holland and England in the sixteenth and seventeenth centuries was due to 'discoveries and the results that followed from them'. It is artificial to talk as though capitalist enterprises could not appear until religious changes had produced a capitalist spirit.

Secondly, Tawney claims that Weber ignores political, as opposed to religious movements that were favourable to an individualistic attitude towards economic relations. Renaissance political thinkers like Machiavelli, or the speculation of economists on money, both contributed to a single-minded concentration on pecuniary gain; which is what Weber understands by the 'capitalist spirit'.

Thirdly, Weber oversimplifies Calvinism in ascribing to English Puritans the social ethics held by Calvin and his followers. The individualistic ethics of later Puritans would have horrified sixteenth-century Calvinists, for whom life had to be lived under rigorous discipline. However, Protestantism was not a unified movement, and different social doctrines were fought out within it (Tawney, 1975, pp. 312–13). Thus there was in Puritanism an element which was revolutionary, a collectivism which grasped at an iron discipline, and an individualism which spurned the savourlessness of human ordinances (*ibid.*, p. 211).

For Tawney the crucial transition was between a society in which economic activity was subordinated to religion, to one in which religious and economic life each followed separate rules and authorities – something that the medieval or Reformation theologians would have found morally reprehensible and intellectually absurd. The importance of this view is that if conflicts in the transition to capitalism were fought out *within* Protestantism, then the motivative force for not only the transition, but also religious controversy itself, might come from elsewhere: perhaps from the economy.

This is a point developed by Sée, a Marxist, who viewed the works of Weber and Troeltsch (and Sombart) as a 'counterpoise to the famous doctrine of historical materialism as it has been formulated by Karl Marx'. For the Weber thesis to hold, he argued, the 'spirit of capitalism' would necessarily have had to exist before the triumph of capitalism. It is more plausible though to look to the political and social context in which Puritans turned to capitalist activity. Calvinism spread chiefly in France, the Low Countries and in Britain, in the urban environments among the bourgeois and merchant classes who were naturally apt to become imbued with the capitalist spirit, even without submitting to the influence of reformers' doctrines. Thus the new ideas spread chiefly in the cities. Everywhere except in Holland, the Calvinists were in a religious minority and thus were barred from government positions and the liberal professions; thus 'naturally' they devoted themselves to business. As persecuted outcasts, scattered across the world, their religious bonds developed an international character. These bonds in turn (rather than religion itself) enhanced their economic relationships and contrasted with the economic nationalism of the different countries where they lived (Sée, 1959).

Sée further cites Tawney in support of his position, to the effect that the divisions within the Puritan movement reflected the varied class bases from which members were recruited. It is doubtless the case that Calvinism 'stimulated the energies and the individualism of its adherents', but it is also possible that it was already economically active individuals who embraced the Calvinist cause. The entanglement is difficult to unravel but Sée concludes, 'We can admit with Tawney that "the spirit of capitalism was not the offspring of Puritanism, but the latter was a tonic for it".'

This inversion, so to speak, of the Weber thesis in which the receptivity of incipient capitalists to Puritan doctrines is viewed as the central factor, appears in other histories. Christopher Hill, for example, argues that Protestant doctrines appealed to artisans and small merchants, while the old priestly magic gave no sense of control over the world of economic fluctuations. Only an assertive self-confidence – justification by faith and certainty of election – could do this. The sixteenth- and seventeenth-century businessman in Geneva, Amsterdam, or London 'found that God had planted in his heart a deep respect for the principle of private property'. This is the sort of ethic, Hill suggests, that flourishes in periods of rapid social change – the appeal to inner conviction and the rejection of the routine of ceremonies could have liberating effects. Like Tawney and Sée though, Hill recognizes the mutual interaction that might have occurred between Protestantism and capitalist development (Hill, 1961).

Tawney's thesis itself however, did not pass unchallenged. We have seen already how Hudson pointed to the anti-acquisitive nature of Baxter's notion of 'calling'. When read fully in context, he suggested, it subordinated economic activity to a religiously disciplined lifestyle. On this basis, Hudson accuses Tawney along with Weber, of having oversimplified and slanted his material. At the same time, though, Hudson shoots himself in the foot by conceding that, 'Emphasising as they did the economic virtues of diligence and thrift as religious duties, it was inevitable that Puritans should prosper and advance in economic status.' Moreover, 'the middle class was less bound by tradition than the other classes of society and thus was more receptive to new religious ideas' (Hudson, 1949, p. 10) – thereby acceding to both Weber and Tawney at the same time! In several places the Weber controversy became quite circular.

Actually, later, Tawney himself did a better demolition job on his own thesis than did other historians, by conceding that it was not Weber's intention to advance a 'comprehensive theory of the genesis and growth of Capitalism'. Thus Tawney was wrong, he says, to have regarded references to economic causes, and the political thought of the Renaissance, as *lacunae* in Weber's work. Indeed, he admits that he had 'overlooked' Weber's observations on the latter point. Rather, Tawney said, he should have stressed the parallels to the social theory of Calvinism that can be found in contemporary Catholic writers; and the changes through which Calvinism passed in the seventeenth century. For Marshall this retraction means that Tawney's position became 'in the final resort . . . an almost identical stance to Weber's' (Marshall, 1982, p. 202). This is not necessarily so. In his Forward to the English translation of *PESC* Tawney insists again on the centrality of the question of what caused the change *within* Calvinism from austere collectivist to individualist attitudes; especially since this change was 'so convenient to its votaries and so embarrassing to their pastors'.

From a rather different perspective than Hill or Tawney, Robertson's *Aspects of the Rise of Economic Individualism* developed a systematic critique of Weber, in order to defend Calvinism from any association with capitalism. He presented his critique as that of 'sound historical analysis' against the 'constructional [i.e. ideal-typical] method of the sociologist'. None the less, in the process, Robertson presents a view not unlike Tawney's, in which religion is seen as adapting to capitalism. He argues that both Protestantism and Catholicism were ambiguous regarding capitalism. Read correctly, he suggests like Hudson, that Baxter gave only highly qualified sanction to economic activity and this was in the context of the strict regulation of commerce by Calvinist churches. Further, the idea of 'calling' was not peculiar to Protestantism – rather it was 'nothing but a new expression of the old belief in the existence of divine and natural distributive justice, a belief that different men were "called" to their several occupations and estates by divine providence' (Robertson, 1933), p. 10). He goes to some lengths to show that amongst Catholic theologians, especially Jesuits, one could find sanction for capitalist attitudes. Indeed, the Jesuit doctrine of the direction of intention, by which the same contract might be lawful or usurious according to the intentions of the parties, made it impossible to distinguish lawful from unlawful dealings, and this in practice justified all payments on a loan.

If both Protestant and Catholic theologians were making concessions to capitalistic activity, argues Robertson, this was because both churches sought to find a place in their congregations for the new, hardworking, hard-headed type of bourgeois trader that had arisen independently of any religious influences. In the case of Protestantism, 'the course of events influenced Protestant ethics by making them ever more Protestant' and hence more favourable to the legitimation of the capitalist spirit. In the end though, the Reformed Churches, as much as the Catholics, failed, since by the eighteenth century, a secular bourgeoisie had developed an ethic of individualism and self-interest, in its fight against the monopolies. This was of profane, not religious origin.

Further, Robertson identified in Weber, as much as in Marx, 'a deep hatred of capitalism'. The *PESC* was he says, a heavy attack intended to 'undermine the basis of capitalist society' by portraying it as 'a massive and imposing superstructure on a foundation of shifting and out-of-date religious ideas' (*ibid.*, p. 207). Weber's preoccupation was to show that capitalism was not a 'natural' growth, but a 'crass construction of the Calvinist mind', of 'evil import and unreasonable origin'. There is no biographical or textual evidence for such a view yet it indicates how far from Weber's original concept the debate could at times stray.

So far, this chapter has focused on the debate over substantive and historical issues, in which the question of the direction of causality was central. That is, were religious motivations a necessary condition for capitalist development, or on the contrary, did theology adapt to the rise of new economic forces? Bendix, like many sociologists, regards such controversy as having missed the point, since Weber never tried to explain the rise of capitalism (Bendix, 1969, p. 72). It has been suggested here that while there are some grounds for this objection, there is also sufficient ambiguity in the *PESC* to make this controversy understandable. Now, though, we should turn to examine the other main branch of the controversy – that over methodological and theoretical issues.

Methodological Debates

The debate over substantive historical issues was conducted largely by historians, many of whom like Tawney, Hill and Robertson were seventeenth-century specialists. Sociologists, on the other hand, beginning with Parsons in the 1930s have paid less attention to the empirical details than to the theoretical and methodological importance of the thesis. An inevitable, and justified theme in this literature has been the implications of the *PESC* for our evaluation of Marxist accounts of history. Certainly one reason behind Parsons's enthusiasm for the thesis was what he saw as its potential role in constructing a systematic alternative to Marxist social theory. More generally though, this controversy between historians and sociologists has involved a great deal of talking past one another, of refusing to acknowledge each other's positions, which has perhaps raised questions about the most fruitful ways that the two disciplines might talk to one another.

WEBER AND MARX

Let us first take the Weber–Marx controversy. Weber frequently repeated that he was never suggesting anything so 'foolish and doctrinaire' as the idea that the spirit of capitalism was caused by the Reformation (e.g. Weber, 1974, p. 90). An often quoted disclaimer appears at the end of the *PESC*: 'of course it is not my aim to substitute for a one-sided materialistic an equally one-sided spiritualistic causal interpretation of culture and of history. Each is equally possible' (*ibid.*, p. 183). Weber thus escapes the accusation of idealism, or the interpretation that he was trying in a straightforward way to invert the materialistic account of history. Nonetheless, it is questionable whether Marshall is justified to claim that, 'Contrary to much popular opinion they [PE Essays] were not conceived as a critique of historical materialism and the account of the development of capitalism these proposed. Weber is debating, not with the ghost of Marx, but ... with that of Adam Smith' (Marshall, 1982, p. 33). How, then, would Marshall explain the fact that Weber presented much of the content of the *PESC* as a series of lectures at the University of Munich under the title 'A Positive Critique of the Marxist Theory of History' (Mommsen, 1977)? Moreover, Weber states clearly in the essay that 'the origin and history of such ideas (spirit of capitalism) is much more complex than the theorists of the superstructure suppose' Weber, 1974, (p. 56); or again that 'To speak here of a reflection of material conditions in the ideal superstructure would be patent nonsense' (*ibid.*, p. 75); since 'religious ideas themselves simply cannot be deduced from economic circumstances ... [they] contain a law of development and a compelling force entirely their own' (*ibid.*, p. 227, n. 84).

Such comments of Weber's should leave little doubt that it was one of his intentions to criticize what he took to be Marx's theory of history (although many commentators point out that Weber understated the complexity of Marx's and Engels's views). Further, in some of the omissions and assumptions in the *PESC*,

Weber's attitudes are apparent. Considering the motivations of labour, Weber identifies only one form of adaptation to be rational, namely that of increasing productivity by overcoming the 'immensely stubborn resistance of . . . pre-capitalist labour' to wage-incentives. A Marxist, or a writer more distanced from the point of view of German employers, might have acknowledged other forms of labour adaptation as being 'rational'. Eldridge points to solidaristic forms of behaviour of a political and economic character, whether revolutionary or instrumental, as types of worker-rationality not considered by Weber. Eldridge also points out that 'stubborn resistance' to the internalization of capitalist values would have provoked more direct systems of labour discipline and coercion (Eldridge, 1972, pp. 37ff). Again this is an aspect excluded from Weber's model of capitalism.

In addition to discernable intentions in the *PESC*, many of the implications of Weber's work, intended or not, have become the focus of discussions about the status of Marxism. There is in the *PESC* a distinct, though not always explicit, view of history that stands opposed to Marxism. Unlike Marxists and classical economists, Weber questioned whether there were laws of historical development, and certainly held that no *single* structure, such as the mode of production, could satisfactorily explain social evolution. Rather, an understanding of history required the recognition of a number of methodological tenets. First, development was a succession of unintended consequences, and is therefore inherently unpredictable. No sixteenth- or seventeenth-century Calvinist could possibly have known that these austere and authoritarian practices would contribute to the growth of mass, secular, consumer societies. If the consequences of mass social movements in the seventeenth century were unpredictable, then so equally are those of movements in the twentieth century. Socialists in the Sozialdemokratisch Partei Deutchland for example could have no prescience as to the 'inevitable' collapse of capitalism, and Weber was dismissive of such predictions. Secondly, historical explanation had to be multi-causal and had to take into account all those factors that made a particular event or probable outcome, as well as all those that made it improbable. Any particular explanation, then, took its place amongst a range of approaches that could each emphasize different sets of probabilities. Historical research was pluralistic with regard to 'competing' accounts. Remember the quote above – materialism and idealism are *equally* possible. Thirdly, ideas and economic processes have separate logics of development and only act upon one another at specific conjunctures. Weber was especially opposed to what he understood as the base/superstructure model. Rather than derive ideas, beliefs, or legal systems, from economic structures, ideas should be seen as 'switchmen' of history. At crucial junctures, such as in seventeenth-century Europe, ideas and economic forces shared an 'elective affinity'. Thus it was the complementarity or affinity between the Protestant ethic and the spirit of capitalism that allowed one to powerfully effect the other.

This view of history, underlying the *PESC*, has been subject to controversy that goes beyond the specific claims made in the thesis. Marshall claims that 'Marxists have, in fact, tended to be among the most lenient of Weber's critics' (Marshall, 1982, p. 141), perhaps because Weber and Marx agree in general about the economic preconditions for capitalist development. Further, their definitions of capitalism, whilst different, both stress the importance of the irrational compulsion to accumulate. Certainly some Marxists have regarded Weber's criticisms as applying only to the 'vulgar' economic determinism of the Second International and SPD and not to more sophisticated versions. Karl Löwith argues that both thinkers are concerned with the same central issue, namely, how humanity can be permanently preserved for people in industrial society. Weber was not aware, he points out, that Marx in the 1844 Manuscripts was deeply involved with the emancipation of the 'alienated man' (Löwith, 1960). Birnbaum (1953) argues that rather than see Marx and Weber as offering conflicting accounts of the rise of capitalism, Weber should be seen as providing an analysis of the motives behind capitalistic activity – an aspect not dealt with in Marx's economic explanation.

Many more Marxist writers, though, have been hostile to the thesis. Georg Lukács, for example, identified Weber's method, and his conception of capitalism as lying at the heart of the controversy. Weber's method, he says is to replace relations of causality by analogies and typologies that 'never get down to the fundamental questions of capitalism'. In this way, through the construction of ideal types, objective forms, the real movements of capital, are converted into a web of 'chances' and 'expect-ations'. His relativism and agnosticism in epistemology (i.e. that he doesn't believe in a single correct standpoint) degenerate into irrationalism – there are no valid means for deciding between competing accounts of history. Theory becomes a question of subjective value-commitment, and is always one-sided. Further, for Lukács, Weber's view of the capitalist rationalizing process as the 'workings of destiny' renders capitalism necessary and inevitable. Indeed, like Sombart, Weber's concept of capitalism is 'spiritualized' – rational book-keeping and asceticism rather than exploitation and value are its defining characteristics (Lukács, 1972; 1980, pp. 607ff).

Lukács expressed some of the aspects of Weber's thesis that challenge Marxism on a theoretical level. Clearly the thesis is incompatible with the standpoint of structural determination. Ted Benton argues that multi-causality and elective affinity 'do not pose the question of historical causality in a theoretical way' (Benton, 1977, p. 136), that is, they offer a method that is necessarily tentative and pluralistic and therefore provides no basis for a unified account of history. Bryan Turner characterizes this pluralism in the *PESC* in the following way: 'Explanation is seen to be a sort of democratic competition between conflicting approaches in which that explanation which is most able to account for the complexity and richness of historical phenom-enon will be accepted as provisionally valid' (Turner, 1977). There is, in other words, an absence of any integrating theory – each phenomenon, movement, institution, event, can be explained in terms of its specific development, the motives of the social actors involved and their consequences. This gives rise to an extremely formalistic approach, such that as Lukács says, Weber could (in *Religionssoziologie*) equate ancient Egyptian bureaucracy with socialism (Lukács, 1980, p. 607ff).

Further, the emphasis in *PESC* on the motives and beliefs of social actors has been seen as teleological and 'subjectivist'. Hindess and Hirst (1975, p. 288) argue that Weber's view of a struggle between two ethical systems – traditionalism and the spirit of capitalism – simply reflects the bourgeois myth of primitive accumulation. In this way the exploitative process of establishing capitalist social relations appears as the rational progress of modernization.

Thus on account of his methodological pluralism, Weber was accused of irrationalism and of reducing material processes to clashes of values. Similarly, Poulantzas argued that to present the global structure of capitalism as a product of a 'society-subject' (i.e. of meaningful action), is teleological – it presupposes that purposes and intentions (rather than structures) create social formations (Poulantzas, 1973, pp. 145ff). Remember though that many people would respond that Weber had suggested no such thesis, and Turner himself sees Weber as 'sliding uncertainly' between subjectivism and structuralism (Turner, 1977).

Weber himself saw a role for Marxist accounts of history but this does not resolve the controversy because the role that he offered was highly circumscribed. For Weber, Marxism was acceptable in two forms: first, as a political theory that did not pretend to be founded on scientific truths but that, on the basis of fundamental ethical convictions, advocated revolutionary action. Secondly, as a brilliant system of ideal-type hypotheses that deserves utmost attention by all sociologists, for it is capable of intensifying our knowledge of modern societies (see Mommsen, 1977, for further discussion of these points). Marxism is acceptable, then, as another interpretation of the infinite complexity of historical data, alongside other interpretations, but is not acceptable as a scientific theory of history. As Aron says, this is not a thesis *opposite* to that of Marx, but it is contradicting Marx (Aron, 1967, p. 224)

Historians and Sociologists

If we move finally to look at more general methodological discussions of *PESC*, we find that Weber's view of explanation and value-relevance has again been central. Sociologists have tended to counter the objections of historians by emphasizing the methodological significance of the study. A few examples will illustrate this. Robert Moore argues that the importance of the *PESC* was as an exercise in the use of *empathy* (reconstructing the world-view of historical actors) through ideal types (highlighting relevant cultural factors). Further, critics such as Samuelsson have failed to relate the *PESC* to Weber's other works and have thus missed the point of his exercise. Weber was not offering a history of Protestantism, nor of capitalism, but an interpretation of the origin of 'a way of life common to whole groups of people' (Moore, 1971).

Sprinzak argues that substantive criticisms of the thesis can be grouped into four types – that Weber mislocated capitalism; misinterpreted Protestantism; misunderstood Catholicism; and misplaced causality. Each of these arguments have been encountered in this chapter. They are all confidently dismissed by Sprinzak on the grounds that Weber 'never tried to prove that capitalism *had* to be the result of ascetic Protestantism', rather the latter *had* to contribute to the former. This was because he characterized a personality structure (worldly asceticism) that was bound to consume less and produce more. In defining this new personality, Weber limited his data through an ideal type of the spirit of capitalism and excluded all other direct economic and social factors that could be held responsible for the growth in capitalist mentality (Sprinzak, 1972). Again, the argument is that Weber's account is neither exclusive of others, nor is it really about Calvinism and capitalism. It is about something else – in this case the psychology of economic growth, in Moore's case a correlation between cultural factors.

The view that Weber was primarily addressing the cultural condition for the psychology of modernization is a view developed by Eisenstadt, Razzell and many others. Razzell describes Weber's achievement as having 'analysed the relationship between the disenchantment of rationalization and the evolution of the Protestant ethic'. This was accomplished, according to Weber, through the sublimation of anxiety and guilt. Both the Protestant ethic and the capitalist spirit oppose what Freud called the pleasure principle and institutionalize the ego and super-ego as psychological forces. Restraint, rational temporing of irrational impulse, denial of all institutional impulses, suspicion of all enjoyment, together generated the psychical energy for modernization (Razzell, 1977). Eisenstadt, whose interest is to examine how the thesis might be 'applied' to contemporary 'modernization' processes, suggests that in the course of the Weber controversy there has been a shift of attention from allegedly direct causal relationships to 'internal transformative capacities of Protestantism and their impact on the modern world' (Eisenstadt, 1968, pp. 6ff). This perspective is taken up by

Ernest Gellner, Clifford Geertz and David McClelland, and is implicit in many others. Moore, for example, refers to the need of underdeveloped countries to break with tradition and 'subject themselves to the insecurity of an impersonal urban market', which requires motivation 'to continuous work for a wage' and a 'measure of dedication' (Moore, 1971, p. 44). So here the real relevance of the thesis lies in its potential for generalization to the Third World (an approach to development heavily criticized by Frank (1971)).

This sort of literature, especially that emphasizing the need to read the *PESC* in the context of Weber's other work, follows what Marshall calls the 'Parsonian legacy'. Parsons saw in the *PESC* an example of Weber's view (developed more thoroughly in subsequent works), that Western Civilization has been subject to an autonomous process of 'rationalization'. Although as we have seen, Weber did not consider this to be a unilinear or straightforward process, one could trace, through the systematization of religious belief, the emergence of modern science, and even in architectural forms, a progressive 'disenchantment' of world views. Magical beliefs and charismatic religious leaders gradually gave way to instrumental (means–end related) values. Calvinism represented an extreme example of this process, since the whole cosmos was conceived of as part of a minutely predetermined Divine Plan, and no ritual or magical intervention could affect human destiny.

Marshall takes issue with a recent example of this approach to the *PESC*, in Tenbruck (1980). This version of the thesis argues that Weber outlines progressively rational solutions to the historical problem of theodicy. As magical religious and charismatic figures proved fallible in eliminating suffering and misfortune, so progressively more encompassing solutions were offered, each unifying more of reality into a systematic world view. This is how religious belief developed its inner logic, until the rationalization of belief created the ethos of worldly asceticism and this influenced world views in a secular direction. Presented like this, Weber does seem open to the charge that he attributed to 'spiritual' or subjective factors (motives, world views, etc.) causal significance.

According to Marshall there are two main objections to this widely held interpretation of the *PESC*. First, that since Weber's conception of the development of Western civilization appears in his *Religionssoziologie* which was written well after the *PESC*, it is inappropriate to read the views of the former into the latter. Secondly, this sort of discussion, which focuses on the theoretical and methodological extensions of the thesis goes no way to providing a serious evaluation. Indeed, sociologists have rarely stood up to the empirical shortcomings of the *PESC* (Marshall, 1982, p. 168), and a similar point could be made in relation to Sprinzak.

The second point seems to have more force than the first, since a 'chronological' reading of Weber is not necessarily more illuminating than one which views his work as a unity. Concentrating then on the second point – Marshall confronts the divergent approaches of historians and sociologists. We are scarcely better placed, he says, 'now than were combatants at the onset to offer informed arbitration between those who view Weber's account . . . as an immensely important and durable insight . . . and those for whom it remains an imaginative but wholly unsubstantiated flight of speculation' (*ibid.*, p. 169). The lesson, he concludes, is that history and sociology must move forward together or not at all. The disciplines share common objectives – to uncover the meaning of social actions and relationships as agents participate in them. Weber, he says, recognized that sociology was a historical discipline.

For Marshall then, the controversy, after more than seven decades, is far from over – really it will only begin to take off in a fruitful way when sociologists and historians stop evading each other and grapple with both the substantive and methodological issues involved. Unfortunately this might be a forlorn hope. As disciplinary and subdisciplinary specialization becomes more intense, historians and sociologists tend to debate with each other less rather than more. The 'Weber thesis' is regarded by many historians, especially of economics and religion, as an untenable idea, still adhered to by sociologists who lack the historical knowledge and skills to evaluate it. Most economic history courses and undergraduate texts either completely ignore the *PESC*, or refer in passing to the fact that it does not 'apply'.

Further, as quantitative methods and computer techniques become more widely used in both history and sociology, so they structure the sorts of questions that tend to be asked. Marx and

Weber were, in different ways, addressing fundamental questions about the worth and destiny of modern Western civilization – its values, economic structure and its origins. The *PESC* became a 'classical dispute' precisely because it posed these questions in a challenging and original way. Their answers, however, require historical imagination and critical insight, for which there is as yet no algorithm package. While it would be rash to join others who over the years have announced an 'end' to the debate, it is possible that rather than become the focus of new exchanges between historians and sociologists, the Weber thesis will disappear, for a time at any rate, under a welter of statistical analysis and computer printouts.

References and Further Reading

Aron, R. (1967), *Main Currents in Sociological Thought*, Vol. 2 (Harmondsworth: Penguin).

Bendix, R. (1969), *Max Weber: An Intellectual Portrait* (London: Methuen).

Bendix, R. and Roth, G. (1971), *Scholarship and Partisanship: Essays on Max Weber* (Berkeley, Calif.: University of California Press).

Benton, T. (1977), *Philosophical Foundations of the Three Sociologies* (London: Routledge & Kegan Paul).

Birnbaum, N. (1953), 'Conflicting Interpretations of the Rise of Capitalism: Marx and Weber', *British Journal of Sociology*, vol. 4, pp. 125–41.

Eisenstadt, S. N. (1968), 'The Protestant Ethic in an analytic and comparative framework', in S. N. Eisenstadt (ed.), *The Protestant Ethic and Modernization*, (New York: Basic Books).

Eldridge, J. E. T. (ed.), (1972), *Max Weber: The Interpretation of Social Reality* (London: Nelson).

Fischoff, E. (1944), 'The Protestant Ethic and the Spirit of Capitalism – The History of a Controversy', *Social Research*, vol. 11, pp. 61–77.

Frank, A. G. (1971), *Sociology of Development and Underdevelopment of Sociology* (London: Pluto Press).

Green, R. W. (ed.), (1959), *Protestantism and Capitalism – the Weber Thesis and its Critics* (Boston, Mass.: Heath).

Hill, C. (1961), 'Protestantism and the Rise of Capitalism' in F. J. Fisher (ed.), *Essays in the Economic and Social History of Tudor England, In Honor of R. H. Tawney* (Cambridge: Cambridge University Press).

Hindess, B. and Hirst, P. (1975), *Pre-capitalist Modes of Production* (London: Routledge & Kegan Paul).

Hudson, W. S. (1949), 'Puritanism and the Spirit of Capitalism', *Church History*, vol. 18, pp. 3–16.

Hyma, A. (1955), *Renaissance to Reformation* (Grand Rapids, Mich.: Eermans' Publishing Co.)

Löwith, K. (1960), 'Max Weber und Karl Marx' in *Gesammelte Abhandlungen – Zur Kritik der Gesellschaft 2* (Frankfurt: Suhrkamp).

Lukács, G. (1972), 'Max Weber and German Sociology', *Economy and Society*, vol. 1, pp. 386–98.

Lukács, G. (1980), *The Destruction of Reason*, trans. P. Palmer, (London: Merlin).

Marshall, G. (1982), *In Search of the Spirit of Capitalism: An Essay on Max Weber's Protestant Ethic Thesis* (London: Hutchinson).

Marx, K. (1974), *Capital Vol. I* (London: Lawrence & Wishart).

Mommsen, W. (1977), 'Max Weber as a critic of Marxism', *Canadian Journal of Sociology*, vol. 2, pp. 373–98.

Moore, R. (1971), 'History, Economics and Religion: A Review of "the Max Weber thesis" thesis', in A. Sahay (ed.), *Max Weber and Modern Sociology*, (London: Routledge & Kegan Paul).

Poulantzas, N. (1973), *Political Power and Social Classes*, trans. T. O'Hagan (London: New Left Books).

Rachfahl, F. (1968), 'Kalvinismus und Kapitalismus' in J. Winchelmann (ed.), *Max Weber, Die protestantische Ethik* II: *Kritichen und Antihritiken* (Munchen: Siebenstern Taschenbuch).

Razzell, P. (1977), 'The Protestant Ethic and the Spirit of Capitalism: a Natural Scientific Critique', *British Journal of Sociology*, vol. 28, pp. 17–37.

Robertson, R. (1933), *Aspects of the Rise of Economic Individualism: A Criticism of Max Weber and his School* (Cambridge: Cambridge University Press).

Sée, H. (1959), 'Contribution of the Puritans to the Evolution of Modern Capitalism', in Green, *op. cit.* pp. 62–5.

Sombart, W. (1902), *Der Moderne Kapitalismus*, 2 vols (Leipzig: Duncher und Humbolt).

Sombart, W. (1967), *The Quintessence of Capitalism*, trans. M. Epstein (New York: Howard Fertig).

Sprinzak, E. (1972), 'Weber's Thesis as an Historical Explanation', *History and Theory*, vol. 11, pp. 294–320.

Tawney, R. H. (1975), *Religion and the Rise of Capitalism* (Harmondsworth: Penguin).

Tenbruck, F. H. (1980), 'The Problem of Thematic Unity in the Works of Max Weber', *British Journal of Sociology*, vol. 31, pp. 316–51.

Troeltsch, E. (1950), *The Social Teaching of the Christian Churches*, trans. O. Wyan (New York: Macmillan).

Turner, B. (1977), 'The Structuralist Critique of Weber's Sociology', *British Journal of Sociology*, vol. 28, pp. 1–16.

Weber, M. (1974), *The Protestant Ethic and the Spirit of Capitalism*, trans. T. Parsons (London: Allen & Unwin).

Weber, M. (1978a), *General Economic History* (London: Allen & Unwin).

Weber, M. (1978b), 'Anti-critical last word on "the Spirit of Capitalism"', *American Journal of Sociology*, vol. 283, pp. 1105–31.

Chapter 5

Individual and Society

W. W. SHARROCK

When Karl Marx told us that men make history, but not in circumstances of their own choosing (Marx, 1962, p. 247), he was making a point from which hardly anyone would want to dissent. Human beings do, in important ways, make themselves what they are. They have control of their own lives and are able to shape the world around them to meet their needs. The changes they make in their environment act back upon them, altering the ways they live and behave. What happens in history happens because human beings make it happen. Of course, human beings cannot do whatever they like. They are born into a world which already exists and which has been given a shape by the course of previous history. The capacity to act is, therefore, limited by the weight of the past: people find themselves in circumstances their predecessors have made. Marx himself thought that the possibilities for the control of history were more limited at some times than others. He thought, for example, that some of the forms of social organization which human beings had made were such as to limit more than is necessary people's ability to control their own destiny.

Whilst Marx's claim might seem reasonable, even verging on the indisputable, it serves in fact to state a problem rather than to provide a solution. As often happens in sociology, a general formula seems to solve a problem but proves very difficult to interpret and apply. It is all very well to say that human beings make history, but how far and in what ways is this true? On balance would we want to say that the weight of accumulated history, social constraint and natural causality is such that people have very little freedom indeed, but only the most marginal capacity to influence anything? Or do we want to hold that human beings are capable of self-determination and can transcend the limitation of circumstance, even reshape those very circumstances?

Even if we opt for either of these alternatives the questions are not exhausted. It is all very well to claim (say) that human beings are dominated by their circumstances but how we do show this is so? How do circumstances dominate people, in what ways are history and environment constraints upon human action? If we stick to the line that people are much constrained by these factors, may we be in danger of over-emphasizing the domination of circumstance, suggesting that human beings have no 'freedom of action' whatsoever? Are we, that is, going to find ourselves advocating a 'deterministic' position? If we try to counter such a 'pessimistic' conception by a more 'optimistic' one holding that people are not just puppets on strings pulled by history and society, may we then teeter into portraying people as if they have virtually unlimited capacity to decide things?

We could devote the entire chapter to arguing these matters out in relation to Marx's own thought, working out how the numerous, complicated and various arguments which Marx and Engels put forward over numerous years and in many places actually related to each other: do some cancel others out, or can they be reconciled as complementary etc.? Marx's interpreters have trouble working out how Marx himself stands on the issues we have just raised.

Some argue that Marx thought that circumstances *determined* people's behaviour. Marx is sometimes interpreted, by friends and enemies alike, as taking the view that history is a process virtually as independent of human control as the movement of the heavenly bodies, one which is working out an inexorable progression toward the transformation of capitalism into communism. The willingness to attribute opinions to Marx on these matters is influenced by the temper of the times as much as by the nature of the texts. Once it was thought that the nature of science was 'determinist' and, accordingly, to maintain that Marxism was scientific, it must be insisted that it was no less determinist than a natural science such as astronomy. This would mean showing that historical events were as much the product of

impersonal and immutable laws as any other natural phenomenon. Thus, Marx could be thought of as an economic or
technological determinist. One factor decides the course of
human history and that factor is the growth of technology.
Economic production was the basic element of human life, and
the technology employed in production the key component in
structuring the economy. A particular kind of technology
requires certain kinds of social relations, so that change in
technology is *also* change in the social relations involved in
production, and changes in these reverberate throughout society,
resulting in the reorganization of such institutions as the family,
religion, law and government.

However, even sciences like physics which were the very
models of determinism, have ceased to be so. There has also been
reaction against the idea that the natural sciences can be taken as
compelling models of what social studies should be. The attempt
to conceive of human relations in much the same way as
physicists think of connections between physical objects seems
repugnant to many and perhaps as contributing to an all too
common tendency to 'dehumanize' human beings: a characteristic feature of capitalism noted by Marx and against which he
had inveighed. Thus, on this view, Marx was not a determinist at
all, but, instead, a *voluntarist*, who emphasized the extent to
which the world and circumstances are the product of human
action. At least in his early writings Marx had taken a view of the
tremendous creative power of humanity that is sometimes called
'Promethean', drawing a parallel with someone who challenged
the gods stressing that human beings are their own masters, not
the playthings of gods (or other super- and inhuman forces).
True, Marx does play up the importance of technology and
economic relations. But what is technology except a product of
human beings? What else are economic relations but transactions
between human beings? Had not Marx's objective been to
'demystify' economic relations, to show that these were not
relations between abstract forces but transactions between real
human beings? What else was Marx's life's work but an attempt
to make people aware of something concealed from them,
namely, their capacity to take control of their own destiny: a
control which had been lost to them?

The relations between the early and late works of Marx is a

matter of continuing controversy. Some, like Althusser (1970), say there is a discontinuity. The early work was humanistic and unscientific. The later work, however, was not about human beings but about structures of social relationship, most specifically, about the structures which make up capitalist society.

Against this, though, it can be argued that there is a high degree of consistency between the early works and the late ones (cf. Kolakowski, 1978). Marx's later, mainly economic scribblings continued the project which had been outlined in the earlier works, namely, that of exposing the extent to which people's capacity to control their own destiny had been *usurped* (cf. Kolakowski, 1978). Such a view makes the idea of (if not the word) 'alienation' the key to understanding *all* Marx's thought. People believe that they are subject to the workings or powers which they cannot change or control, such as those of the gods or of nature. They are apt to think that their social lives are ruled in the same way, to develop false beliefs about the nature of their institutions and practices. For example, people in capitalist society think they are subject to 'the laws of the market' and, as 'laws', are inclined to think that the fact of their poverty or unemployment is not something they can do anything about, any more than the rising and setting of the sun can be altered. The whole point of Marx's theory, on this view, is to show that these beliefs are illusions, manifestations of alienation, the condition in which people are unable to recognize products of their own efforts as such, to treat things they have made as though they were alien and controlling 'things'. Marx's economics was meant to show that economic relations are relations between human beings; in a word, social. 'The market' is an abstract name for social relations between people – those of buying and selling. The market is but one kind of arrangement and other ways of arranging economic activities are possible. If the market does have damaging effects on people this is not because of fixed laws of nature. People can rearrange their practices, reshape their institutions. So, one of the things responsible for people feeling they have no control of their history has been their lack of awareness of the true nature of their institutions and practices and, consequently, of their own capacity to alter them. They have obscured from themselves the fact that the market, religion, the family and so on are products (albeit largely *unintended* products) of their own activities.

Of course, even 'humanistically' interpreted, Marx was not much impressed by the capacity of *individual* human beings to control their destinies. Marx thought that history was the affair of large-scale social groupings, of great masses of people, especially those masses called classes and that in the face of such enormous complexes of activity the particular individual counts for little (cf. Wiatr, 1985). It was only through *collective* action that human beings could exercise decisive effect on the historical stage, and it was through collective revolutionary action that people could re-establish control of their destiny. For example, it is clear that if the market can be done away with, this cannot be done by a single individual since it is an integral and indispensable part of a whole society. Doing away with the market means doing away with a whole form of society and this, plainly, can only be achieved by co-ordinated action on a truly massive scale.

Marx's economics were certainly diametrically opposed to those *laissez-faire* views which have recently had something of a resurgence and which maintain that it is individuals who accomplish things, and insist upon the importance of the market as a mechanism for maximizing the effect of individual preferences (see below, pp. 135–138). Such *laissez-faire* views are not purely economic, any more than Marx's. They have a political nature. The unfettered operation of the market is thought to allow the most effective mobilization of human wisdom and knowledge, thus ensuring that the results produced are the best that can be hoped for. The operation of the market is a mechanism which ensures the perpetuation of human freedom. Consequently, operation of the market is seen as an alternative to state control, the object being to minimize the extent to which power concentrates in a central decision-making body and to maximize the capacity of individuals to decide for themselves. Marx thought that such arguments were fairy tales designed to encourage people to accommodate to a situation in which the majority were, *through the operations of the market*, at the mercy of a minority. The market, far from maximizing human freedom, served to impose misery, degradation and impoverishment.

These remarks should suffice to show the range of questions opened up by disputes over how to understand Marx and how to evaluate what he is saying, and, important for the purposes of this chapter, arguments which turn up throughout sociological litera- ture. The issues of the balance between 'determinism' and 'voluntarism', of the relative importance of 'the individual' and 'the collective' are persistent problems. To discuss them we will take up some themes from a variety of continuing sociological controversies under five headings: (1) Autonomy; (2) Compo- sition; (3) Abstraction; (4) Causation; and (5) Interaction.

Autonomy

The problem of the relationship of the individual to society is very much a political one. In introducing sociological theory it is often useful to use the arguments of Thomas Hobbes to present the 'problem of social order'. Hobbes, in his *Leviathan*, originally published in 1651, asks us to suppose that all human beings are basically selfish, concerned with getting their own way. As such, they will soon see that the best way to achieve this is by either making use of other people or doing away with them. Since it does not take a genius to see this, very soon everyone will be trying to take advantage of or eliminate everyone else. The inevitable result will be a struggle of each against everyone else. Such a state would be an absolute misery and people will, therefore, see that it is in their overall interest to accept some limitation, albeit a minimal one, on their freedom to do whatever is best for their self-interest. They will, that is, accept the need for a state to regulate their activities just enough to prevent them falling into chaos.

Hobbes's problem was a political problem about the relation- ship of the individual to the collectivity: to what extent is it better if people are left to pursue their own interests as they see fit, and, the obverse of this, to what extent is it right that others should interfere with that? Hobbes gives reason for thinking that modest restriction on the freedom to pursue self-interest is needed. Note, however, that the assumption underlying Hobbes's argument is that it is better for people to be free to pursue self-interest *unless* this threatens to become self-destructive. Hobbes, and thinkers like him, take it for granted that it is in the nature of human beings to be self-interested and that it is best if they are, by and large, able to do so. Adam Smith (1933) tried to show that, in economic matters at least, leaving individuals free to follow their self-interest would produce an outcome that is best for all. The way to produce the maximum benefit for everyone is not through the decision of any single individual, or small group of them, but by letting *everyone* have an influence on the decision. If all individuals in economic activity are left free to follow their own interests then things will work out for the best. A great mass of separate and independent individual choices will produce the best result, almost as if they had been guided by an 'invisible hand'. If such is the case, then the less the state control of economic behaviour the better.

Sociological arguments on this topic are themselves put forward as having political implications, though distinctly different ones. Both Marx and Durkheim, just for example, tried to show that views, which presented the individual and collective as being in opposition to one another, were ideological, that is, misleading doctrines which arose from and expressed a particular kind of social situation rather than being a general truth. This view of the individual as a naturally self-interested creature which flourished only when exempt from any kind of control by society was a manifestation of modern society and, indeed, of the most pathological features of that society. We now live in societies (called 'organic' by Durkheim, 'capitalist' by Marx), they argued, in which people are less and less part of social groups and are increasingly able to do what they, individually, want to do. Neither Marx nor Durkheim are opposed to the idea that people should be free from external constraint, but they do think this can, in modern societies, be taken to extremes. Far from being the best thing that can happen to individuals, it may be very bad for them.

Though the 'freedom of the individual' came to be prized above all in the Western societies of the nineteenth century, Marx and Durkheim tried to show this was an illusion. The freedom of the individual was, Marx argued, only apparent, a superficial kind of freedom. People who thought they were deciding things were, in reality, the prisoners of society, controlled and driven by it. People like Hobbes talk about 'individuals' as though they were all identical atoms, as though they were all basically the same and in basically the same position, but they are not. In the important historical forms of society, Marx said, one could distinguish two kinds of people: those who dominated and those who were dominated. In capitalist society, these two kinds are represented by employer and employee. The latter are, it is true, free in ways that slaves and serfs are not. Slaves and serfs are subject to legal constraint. The former are the property of a master, the latter are legally bound to a lord. The industrial worker is not legally bound in a comparable way. He is legally free to sell his labour-power to any employer but this freedom was nominal. Though legally free, the employee is not *in fact* free.

The industrial worker is free to sell labour to an employer, but is not assured that there will be an employer who wants to buy. Nor can the worker decide how much an employer will pay. The worker is at the mercy of the employer and is compelled to take such work as can be found. The industrial worker in capitalist society is free to be exploited by capitalist employers. Moreover, not even the employers are really free. They can follow out their self-interest all right, seeking profit wherever they can find it. But, their hunger for profit does not originate in their individual self-interest but in their role in capitalist production: the employer *must* seek ever greater profit in order to survive in the fierce competition that this very hunger creates amongst capitalists. The capitalist is *compelled* to seek profit and, in so doing, to put his own existence as a capitalist at risk.

Though the relation between the particular worker and employer may be freely contracted, it is altogether misleading to disregard the fact that these two individuals are located within a whole system of economic production and attendent social relations, which imposes upon them conditions of life and practical necessities. The relation between individual employee and employer is part of a relation between groups, between social classes, and the interests involved in their transaction are not just of individuals, but of classes. The worker, wholly dependent on wages, seeks to increase them, but the capitalist, motivated by the overriding need for greater profit must resist. The interests of workers and capitalists are diametrically opposed. Society is centred upon a conflict of interest between groups, each of which seeks to advance its own position at the expense of the other.

The idea that the best for everyone results from the pursuit of self-interest is attacked: there are built in, unavoidable conflicts between different interests, generated by relative positions within society. If we simply think of society as made up of individuals without taking into account the positions they occupy in the system of which they are a part, we can be misled into thinking that it is best for all if each individual can do as seems fit. However, if we do take such things into consideration then we can see that this is not so. Indeed, it may be that what a person thinks in their best interest is anything but. Just as in the situation Hobbes imagined, if capitalists are left free to seek only the greatest profit they can acquire, then they will collectively produce an economic chaos in which, first, many of them will be eliminated and, finally, all of them will be destroyed. It was the unfettered competitiveness of capitalism that Marx thought would be most conducive to revolution and to the self-destruction of the capitalist system.

Durkheim, too, sought to demonstrate the flaw in the idea that leaving individuals free to pursue self-interest was the best thing. Individual well being needed a balance between dependence on and autonomy from social groups. Durkheim tried to put this point most sharply in his account of *Suicide* (Durkheim, 1952). Suicide, is the greatest harm an individual can do to him or herself. And the likelihood of an individual committing suicide, Durkheim argued, is predictable from the social relations in which that individual is involved. Among the individuals most at risk are those who are 'free' of social ties and, at the other extreme, those who are most intensely bound by them. Thus, suicides are commoner amongst those who are isolated from close social ties such as those provided in a family or by some religious groups. They are also more likely amongst groups such as a military unit in which relations are very intense, so strong that the individual comes to matter less than the group and in which the individual life will be voluntarily surrendered for the sake of that group. Both too much and too little dependence upon groups is bad for the individual. The individual, therefore, needs *both* a relationship with and autonomy from groups.

As far as the highly differentiated societies that we live in are concerned, there has been, or so Durkheim argued, rather too much attenuation of social groups and too much individual liberation from the traditions and mores groups provide. There are ties between one individual and another, such as those of marriage and friendship, and there are ties, too, between the individual and the society as a whole such as those involving national sentiment and loyalty; but there are now very few groups larger than the immediate personal network of the person but smaller than the nation-state, which play a meaningful, supportive and regulative part in the life of the individual. It is to meet this kind of problem that Durkheim proposed that intermediate groups, such as professional and occupational groups, be organized to knit the individual into the community.

The objective of Marx's and Durkheim's argument is to reject the idea that there is a necessary opposition between individual and society and that the attempt to view the individual in isolation from a social context is bound to falsify and distort. A sociological dimension is indispensable to political understanding. The positions taken by Marx and Durkheim, then, are intended to play a corrective role against a previous point of view which overplayed the importance of the individual and diminished, almost ignored, that of society. The risk such a corrective view runs is, of course, of putting the emphasis the opposite way around and giving society the kind of exclusive, or at least overriding, significance that the individual was previously awarded. There are certainly those who think that this is a failing of Marx, Durkheim and the bearers of their legacy. A fallacy of individualism has given way to that of collectivism.

The danger is not just an intellectual one, but one with serious political consequences. Someone like Marx criticizes the kind of freedom that people in capitalist society have because it is only superficial freedom. He admits that it is somewhat better than the subordination of slavery or serfdom, but does not think it matches up against the real possibilities of freedom which would free individuals from all kinds of domination, economic, political and otherwise. Marx offers, through the transformation of society into socialism/communism, an unprecedented degree of human freedom.

His critics, however, think that there may be great differences between what you are offered and what you will get. Far from improving on the legal freedom of capitalist society, they are afraid that if Marx got his way the result would be even less freedom, not an unlimited amount of it. F. A. Von Hayek (1955) and Karl Popper (1945) have between them mounted a sustained critique of positions like Marx's and a defence of the freedom which is provided in a liberal society.

They regarded Marx's arguments as pointing up a dilemma between freedom and equality. Marx thought that lack of equality makes political freedom meaningless, but Hayek and Popper object that the measures necessary to eradicate inequality will also diminish freedom. The kind of political freedom which is found in the liberal democracies is, for them, to be contrasted with the situation under tyrannies and, on that comparison, there can be no doubt, they argue, that the liberal democracies are immensely preferable. A serious attempt to impose equality on society will produce a new tyranny.

Their scepticism about Marxian utopianism is based on a belief in the limitations on the power of human knowledge. For them, Marx stands squarely in a 'social engineering' tradition: that is, that by acquiring scientific knowledge of society's working and history's course we shall then be able to reorganize society to suit our purposes in the way that the engineer can shape aspects of our natural environment. Popper and Hayek, however, argue that the kind of knowledge that we can have of society and its workings is limited relative to such ambitions and that we cannot have the kind of knowledge which will enable us to predict and control the future course of society. Popper claims to have shown that this is a logical impossibility. The future depends upon new knowledge, which means that we cannot predict future states of society since we cannot predict what future discoveries will be. If we could, then they would not be discoveries since we should already know about them.

There is also a tension between the intent and the actualities of attempts at social engineering. The intent may be to achieve greater freedom but the actuality will be the extension of political control. In theory, the aim may be to give individuals greater control over their own destinies, but in practice the need will be to centralize control in order to facilitate planning, requiring, of course, the regulation of individual choices, subordinating them to the decisions of the centre.

It is at this point that the danger of emphasizing the collective over against the individual reveals itself. The virtue of individualistic views is, in the terms we are now considering, that they place the protection of the individual above the claims of the collectivity, thus discouraging the 'natural' efforts of collectivities, especially states, to seek to extend their power. For collectivist doctrines the freedom of the individual is a myth, and, instead, they place the rights of the community or society at least on a level with, if not above, those of the individual. This means that, politically, the interests of actual individuals will be readily sacrificed in the name of some collectivity. The fact that a tyranny is exercised in the name of freedom makes its methods no less tyrannical.

Hayek and Popper are not arguing for an individualism which takes no account of the social context but for one which recognizes the importance of certain kinds of institutional structure. The political freedom with which they are concerned is associated with the liberal democracies. These are societies of the kind Popper calls 'open', in contrast to 'closed' ones. The contrast is made largely in terms of the possibility of criticism, the capacity of people to distance themselves from and question the received and institutionalized structures of thought. This possibility is available in the open ones but they can regress toward a closed society, and it is in this direction which totalitarianism would take them. The open society requires the legitimate interplay of a plurality of points of view; a situation most fully realized in the institution of science, the essential nature of which is criticism (Popper, 1959).

Knowledge is a matter of trial and error, and hence Popper's corresponding conviction that it can only arise where people are free to experiment and take a critical stance toward prevalent beliefs. That there are a great many diverse prejudices, political opinions, etc. amongst scientists does not seem a drawback to Popper: this diversity is necessary for the growth of science. It is the variety of convictions which will encourage the scepticism that is the life of science. If we are to accumulate knowledge we require a society which allows a diversity of viewpoints, the very thing which totalitarian society cannot tolerate.

Hayek, too, thinks that the character of the institutional order is important, but in his case it is the market which is crucial. At its simplest, Hayek's conception of the market is as a mechanism of communication through which a highly diversified and widely dispersed range of information may be distributed. The market as a whole is uncoordinated and undirected (which is, of course, just what Marx thought was wrong with it) but it has the capacity for discriminating among and responding flexibly to people's preferences in a way that state bureaucracies and planned economies cannot. One reason why, Hayek thinks, socialist doctrines cannot succeed, is because they seek to intervene in and restrict the operation of the best mechanism for being able to know and respond to the things that people want. The result of socialist measures, however well intentioned, will be to end up imposing on people what they do not really want.

Obviously the arguments do not end here. They are clearly still alive in practical political terms, with the continuing struggle over whether we need more or less state intervention in the management of the economy and society.

Composition

If there is argument about whether the interest of the individual should be subordinate to that of the group, then the issue of whether there are indeed such things as groups and institutions is critical. If there are no such things then, presumably, to subordinate individuals to groups is to subject real things to the needs of imaginary entities. Hence, arguments about the composition of society are not irrelevant to the political arguments we have reviewed and the names of Marx and Durkheim will reappear, as will those of Hayek and Popper.

This question also bears upon the nature of sociology. If it were accepted that society was simply composed of individuals then sociology would seem to be a discipline without subject-matter. The study of society would fall within the domain of psychology as the discipline which studies individual behaviour. The theme of this section is, then, 'reduction': is society reducible to the behaviour of individuals, and can the behaviour of those individuals be derived entirely from the laws of psychology?

Marx and Durkheim, on our account, sought to reverse what they saw as a mistaken preoccupation of much nineteenth-century thought with the individual; a preoccupation which distorted the understanding of individual behaviour itself, since it treated it as a product of psychological dispositions when it should properly be understood as a result of socio-cultural circumstances. Thus, on Marx's argument, the acquisitiveness of capitalists previously regarded as a manifestation of a general human nature is, in reality, imposed by the logic of the capitalist system of production.

Marx and Durkheim both, in very different ways and for quite different purposes, wanted to maintain that society is more than just a collection of individuals. Both are, of course, ready to recognize that *in one sense* society is made up of its individual members. Neither of them imagines that if we took away all its members society would still exist, but they do insist that society is still more than just an aggregate of individuals. Society is more than the sum of individuals in the sense that we talk of something possessing 'emergent properties'; properties not possessed by constituents but which emerge from the combination of constituents. A classical example would be the production of water through the fusion (in the right proportions) of oxygen and hydrogen. Water has the property of liquidity, but neither oxygen nor hydrogen do. Thus, by analogy, the combination of human beings in association produces new properties which are distinct from those of the individuals themselves. Thus, Durkheim was notoriously involved in arguing for what he called 'social facts' (Durkheim, 1938), facts about the association and interrelation of individuals and which give sociology a subject-matter distinct from that of psychology. Durkheim's most striking effort to make this point was, again, his study of suicide, which tried to show that something which seemed to be the obvious and exclusive province of psychology – the suicidal act – was in need of sociological explanation: suicide rates are stable over time between societies and between sectors of society, the proportion of the population committing suicide showing a (surprising?) constancy. Durkheim's case is that this stability cannot be a result of the psychology of individuals, but must be understood in terms of the structure of its religious practice, etc.

However, if Marx and Durkheim pressed the idea that, in social matters, the whole is greater than the sum of its parts, their point of view was not universally accepted. There have always been those who suspect that such 'holistic' doctrines are false, not to say dangerous, given the arguments about autonomy outlined earlier.

Even amongst the three great founders of modern sociology

there was no unanimity on this point. Marx and Durkheim certainly held holistic views but Max Weber emphatically disagreed. He held what are nowadays called 'methodological individualist' views, as does Popper. Weber rejected any approach which tried to make out that society was anything more than a collection of individuals. Talk about society or about such collective entities as 'the state' and 'social classes' is all right as long as it is kept in mind that this is a shorthand way of talking and referring to complex patterns of action and relation *among individuals*. Such patterns are so complex and complicated that we obviously cannot describe the activities of each individual who makes them up, but can only talk about typical patterns of action. However, it is about the actions of typical individuals that we are talking. Thus, in talking about 'the state' we are using a shorthand expression to speak of the things that the typical functionaries of the state do, about how certain kinds of individuals act. Weber, therefore, attempted to do what Marx and Durkheim thought was impossible. Beginning with the most basic possible forms of human action he sought to show how these could be organized into progressively larger-scale complexes of organization, institutions, societies and great civilizations. This pattern can be seen in his major, unfinished work, *Economy and Society* (Weber, 1968).

Of course, a major issue here is whether 'methodological individualism' implies that the study of social life is a species of psychology. This was certainly the implication Durkheim tried hard to avoid in his own conception of sociology. However, in the main, advocates of 'methodological individualism' intend no such implication. Explanation in individualistic terms does not need to resort to psychology: how people act is to be understood in terms of the 'logic of the situation'. In short, this means that we understand how people act by seeing what situations they find themselves in and what actions could possibly make sense in response to such situations. In doing so we shall find that a great deal of human behaviour which seems quite bizarre or irrational will, in the light of the situation, seem rational. A good example of what Popper would call a 'logic of the situation' strategy is found in Weber's *The Protestant Ethic and the Spirit of Capitalism* (Weber, 1930).

For the Protestants of the Reformation, especially the

Calvinists, nothing could matter to them more than the salvation of their immortal souls. But according to their religion, they could neither influence nor know about the fate of their soul. God decided whether they were saved or not, regardless of how they acted, and they could not tell what God had decided. Such uncertainty, says Weber, about something so overwhelmingly important cannot be borne. The Calvinists' response was to convince themselves that they could at least *know* if they were saved and could take devout behaviour as a sign of salvation. If they behaved with devotion in all areas they could persuade themselves they were amongst God's elect.

Such an analysis proceeds by describing the situation and the terms in which those involved consider it. Weber describes the situation created by the convictions of the Calvinists and then asks, what – in the religious terms in which the Calvinists think – is the only way out of this dilemma? In the light of those considerations, the Calvinists' adaptation to their leader's teachings presented a rational response; dictated by the logic of the situation.

Of course, Weber's account does not exclude psychological considerations. It mentions the psychological suffering created by the tension between the need to know the fate of one's soul and the impossibility of knowing this. But it does not involve anything more than the most commonplace understandings of human psychology rather than specific or close inquiry into the personality of Calvinists. Thus, the 'logic of the situation' approach is independent of the science of psychology.

However, since methodological individualism recognizes only the actions of individuals and understands situations from their point of view, in terms of what they want and believe, then it must surely overestimate the extent to which historical situations and social organizations, institutions, etc. are the creations of individuals. Granted, individuals act in the light of their situation as they see it, to realize whatever ends they have in mind, but we surely cannot imagine that they always get what they bargain for, or that they have any conception of what they produce? A point which Marx, for example, is likely to have raised.

Methodological individualists agree that there are such things as the unintended consequences of human action. Weber's account of the Calvinist situation is precisely directed to show

how the development of a capitalist spirit of acquisitiveness was the *unintended* consequence of the attempt to escape an unbearable dilemma. Humans act in situations, but those actions are not assured to have the results they aim at. Even if people achieve what they want their actions may have effects quite other than they envisage. Of course, the patterns of action which are built up by multitudes of people over long periods of time are not necessarily intended or foreseen by those who make them, but that does not mean that we need to talk about 'emergent properties', or suggest that society has a reality over and above that of its individual members or that it operates according to its own laws. All we need to do to make adequate recognition of these possibilities is to appreciate that there can be unintended consequences *of individual actions*.

The methodological individualist position identifies itself in its name as a methodological policy. It can be seen as a view which is to be judged by results. If we attempt to understand organizations, institutions and societies as complexes of individual action rather than as wholes existing in their own right, will we get a better understanding of both the actions of individuals and the organization of these social 'wholes'? The only way to judge that argument would be to see whether 'holistic' or 'individualistic' policies are the most effective. On methodological grounds, we do not need to decide whether there really are only individuals, or whether there really are social wholes as well. It is simply a question of whether it is more fruitful to look at society *as if* it consisted only in individuals or not. The question becomes, then, can methodological individualism work out?

There are at least two lines on which it can be attacked. One is to take things further. Thus, George Homans wants to maintain that sociology *is* an outgrowth of psychology (Homans, 1967). He does not want to argue against the distinctiveness of sociology nor to say that psychological explanations can everywhere displace sociological ones. He does, though, want to argue that sociology can be 'reduced' to psychology in the sense that the laws of sociology can be logically derived from those of psychology. The laws of sociology are less general than those of psychology (or of that particular kind, called behaviourist psychology) and it is a simple fact, or so Homans maintains, that less general laws can be logically derived from more general ones.

This is the form that 'reductionism' often takes in the natural sciences where the laws of one discipline, say chemistry, can be deduced from those of a more general one, such as physics. Thus, the laws of behaviourist psychology are very general because they apply to all kinds of creatures, pigeons, rats, human beings, etc., whilst those of sociology apply to human beings. However, on Homans's assumptions, it must be the case that the possibilities of human action must be limited by the basic and general laws of psychology. Hence such laws must always be assumed by, even if not spelled out, any sociological scheme.

The other standard objection to methodological individualism is that it cannot work through its own programme. In effect, this programme aims to eliminate from our explanations terms like 'class', 'state', 'legal system' and replace them with descriptions of what individuals do. However, the question is, can such a replacement be taken any distance? It may sound plausible on first hearing to be told that we are going to replace statements like 'the state did this' with statements like 'the typical state functionary did this'. However, our second statement does not eliminate the expression·'the state' at all. If we are to simply describe what some individuals did without taking note of the fact that they were officials of 'the state' then we should not correctly understand what they did. Their actions make sense to us not because they are the actions of individuals – such as Margaret Thatcher, Leon Brittan, Ronald Reagan and so on – but because they are functionaries of the state, are people acting in the name of and on behalf of a collectivity of some sort. Hence, try as we might, we cannot become thoroughgoing methodological individualists.

This is one of those arguments which reaches a peculiar kind of impasse, in which each party is convinced that the other one agrees – in practice. Thus, holists note that methodological individualists go on using such terms as 'church', 'state', 'army' and so on, whilst the latter satisfy themselves that whatever they might say, in practice, holists keep trying to understand such things as churches, states, armies by trying to understand the typical behaviour of the individuals who make them up, and do so by trying to identify the 'logic of the situations' in which those individuals are involved (cf. the papers reprinted in parts 3 and 4 of O'Neill, 1973). It is at this point that we need to consider another theme, abstraction.

Abstraction

It perhaps seems more natural to think of there being just individuals, if only because they are tangible, directly observable: we encounter other individuals but we do not meet society, the state, etc., in person. These are abstractions, and we tend to think of abstractions as *less real* than the concrete. Thus, as discussed above, if collectivities are abstractions then it would seem wrong to put their interests before those of real individuals. However, there is room for argument as to whether that which is abstract is any less real than that which is concrete and whether, even, it might be more so? Why should we regard the legal system as any less real than the judge, the jury, the courtroom, the solicitor who charges us fees, the policeman who arrests us and so on? Indeed, further, why should we regard the judges, the jury, the solicitors, etc. as concrete individuals at all? After all, judges, juries and the rest are what they are because they are defined as such by a legal system. They are, in other words and to borrow a relevantly dramatic term, roles in a system and only exist in terms of the relationships and activities the system specifies. It may not be going too far, then, to argue that the abstract comes before and gives reality to the concrete.

We are alluding here to 'structuralist' views (cf. Pettit, 1975). The expression 'structure' plays a role in many different ways of thinking, but one of its most recent influential usages has been to identify views which derive, more or less directly, from the views about language held by de Saussure (1964). Saussure thought that the fundamental mistake in much thinking about language was to regard it as speech, a temptation arising from the concreteness of speech. We think that, as individuals who produce speech, that we make meaning and because of this also to think that we must understand meaning in terms of what an individual intends by his/her speech. However, for Saussure, our capacity to mean what we intend to mean depends on the structure of the language that we speak. Saying 'Give that to me' will only mean what it does because it is said in English and is a sentence possible within the structure of that language. Thus, for Saussure, the point of studying language is not to examine the beliefs and intentions of speakers but to describe *the whole system* within which speakers operate.

The application of this doctrine involves another important twist to the argument. We might suppose that the way to understand the meaning of a word in a language, say 'bat', is in terms of its own character. But, this too may be the wrong way to go about it, because the point about the word 'bat' is that it *contrasts* with other words like 'pat', 'cat', 'rat', etc., and that we cannot therefore understand how words mean except in the context of a whole system *of organized contrasts*. The most famous and influential application of these ideas has been in the analyses of mythology by Claude Lévi-Strauss (e.g. Lévi-Strauss, 1967).

Take an obscure-seeming myth, which tells of someone going on a journey, receiving help from various animals, having to visit the sun, etc. To make sense of it we need to look at it as being constructed as a set of 'oppositions', as a system of contrasts, such that things are related in terms of differences of animation, gender, habitation, direction, etc. Then, we should find, Lévi-Strauss suggests, that myths get their meaning from contrasts of living with dead, male with female, human with animal, land-dwelling with sky or water-dwelling, high with low and so on. Through these contrasts people are able to express and, in principle at least, resolve the contradictions and conflicts which exist in their social life. To understand the myth, though, one does not need to ask what those who tell and listen to the myth think about it. Their beliefs and intentions can be disregarded in favour of looking at the pattern of opposition which is present in the myth, and, indeed, in the whole system of myths within which this particular one occurs (e.g. Lévi-Strauss, 1967).

Rather than myths being vehicles through which human beings convey meanings, it turns out that human beings are the unconscious vehicles through which the mythical system operates. This is quite a dramatic step since it reverses a common and largely unquestioned assumption about language. On this view, language is no longer the vehicle through which we express ourselves, rather it is we who are the vehicle through which language speaks. Language speaks through us. As speakers of a language we are as unaware as the tellers of myths are of the operating principles of the system which acts through us. We are unaware of the 'laws' of myth, language and social organization.

Some of the possibilities here have been exploited by linking Marx and Sigmund Freud with these arguments. Freud is most notorious for developing the idea of 'the unconscious' to stressing that the conscious control of our behaviour is very limited and that what we do is governed by forces of which we are largely unaware. Marx, too, is one of those figures credited with showing that we are in control of forces (in his case, those of social development) of which we are unaware: thus, the kind of 'structuralist' methods we have been outlining offer possibilities of getting access to the kind of systems of control which Marx and Freud identify (cf. Coward and Ellis, 1977).

Taking these points of view as far as one can takes us to a point at which we might claim to have 'abolished the subject'. The individual is seen to be at best a product of these systems, not the source of them, and that however much our activity seems to be produced by our intention or consciousness it is in fact the resultant of the working of the system. Thus, from the point of view of a thoroughgoing structuralist analysis, we individuals may as well disappear altogether.

Causation

We have been examining arguments about the composition of society: is it made up of individuals, or of collective phenomena, or ultimately even of structures? Questions about composition have, of course, to do with explanation, as our discussion of structuralism should have shown. Thus, over the question of whether the meaning of our expressions is a product of our individual intentions or the result of a structural operation, the debate is about how we explain what individuals do. The best way to condense this area of controversy to rudimentary division is to identify two points of disagreement: (1) whether we need determinism or voluntarism; (2) whether individuals produce structures or are produced by them.

Question (1) is about the extent of constraint. Everyone recognizes that people find themselves in situations which they did not create, but disagree about how far they have room to alter such situations. Some who incline towards a 'determinist' standpoint, want to say that the press of the situation is so decisive that the consciousness and intentions of individuals are, by and large, irrelevant to determining its outcome. What happens in a given situation is due to the operation of the forces or structures which govern it and the capacity of individuals to make any difference negligible.

A good example of this kind of controversy is the 'Weber thesis' about the rise of capitalism (cf. Chapter 4). Weber treats the rise of Western capitalism as an unintended consequence of the actions of the Reformation Protestants. Had they not had the kind of religion they did, and responded to the dilemma it posed for them, we would not have the capitalism that we do. Thus, without paying attention to the beliefs of those Protestants, and the purposes that arose from them, we should not understand why capitalism developed. Some opponents of the Weber thesis reject it because this seems to give too great importance to what individuals think and aim to do. The Western world at the time of the Reformation was one in which the development of modern capitalist society was well under way, and in which the economic and political circumstances were setting up needs which had to be satisfied – needs, for example, for a free, disciplined labour force of wage workers – and which would have had to be satisfied regardless of whether the Reformation had taken place. The Protestant ethic that Weber talks about was largely an irrelevance and, in so far as it was important, then it is to be explained in terms of the need of capitalism for an appropriate attitude of systematic discipline toward work, rather than the other way about. The particular vicissitudes of people's religious beliefs and attitudes would have made no difference to the outcome.

But does this not underestimate the extent to which the outcome of situations is open and is to be decisively affected by the intentions and actions of the individuals involved? The criticism of the Weber thesis along the lines we have sketched does not necessarily invalidate what many think that Weber was trying to demonstrate by the thesis. The 'determinist' position presents things as though they were settled in advance, as though a situation dictates its own outcome and cannot be altered by individuals. How individuals act will be the result of the needs of a particular system or structure, and they will behave in ways which will unconsciously meet those needs, *whatever they may think they are doing*.

The voluntarist position argues that the situation in which people are cannot be properly identified without reference to their beliefs and consciousness. It is a most important part of sociological understanding to see situations as those caught up in them do. However, even if it was accepted that beliefs and intentions 'make a difference' this need not be taken as incompatible with the determinist argument, since it simply needs to be applied to beliefs and intentions themselves. Beliefs and intentions do not come out of thin air, but are obtained from society. Thus, we need not maintain that people's beliefs and intentions are irrelevant to what they are doing, and may even accept that beliefs and intentions are consequential to what people do. But the beliefs and intentions thay have are such as to make them 'fall in' with the forces and needs of the society. Thus, to use the Weber thesis again, it is not necessary for a determinist to say that 'the Protestant ethic' had nothing to do with the rise of capitalism but just to say that Weber's explanation of the rise of capitalism is incomplete. It shows that the Protestant ethic which gave virtue to hard work was helpful to the rise of capitalism but does not really explain why the Protestant ethic developed. Many find that Weber's account of the origins of modern capitalism makes it sound too accidental: capitalism would need something like the Protestant ethic to get it going and it just coincidentally happened that the Protestant Reformation took place in Europe at the appropriate time. The rise of the Protestant ethic itself needs to be explained, and explained in terms of the development of capitalism and its needs.

The broad position we have called 'voluntarist', for want of a better general name, thinks that the effect of the determinist argument is to deny the status of 'action' to people's activities. It is in the nature of action that it involves choice between alternatives, that there are different things that we could do and that we can elect one of them. Determinism makes it seem that we do not act because there are no real alternatives, we could not have done otherwise than we did. For voluntarists this underestimates the extent to which we are confronted by alternative possibilities and that many of the things we do are chosen rather than imposed upon us. The need is, then, for sociological strategies which preserve and give full significance to the fact that in social situations the outcome is not wholly settled in advance and in which the outcome of situations will be seen as a result of *decision-making*. Further, for them, it is also important to maintain an awareness of the extent to which, by making decisions, the members of society are making the society itself by working out their social arrangements even as they live them.

The voluntarist position is represented in its strongest form by positions often labelled 'interactionist', such as symbolic inter-actionism and ethnomethodology, though it should be said that this label is potentially very misleading about the nature of the views involved and of the likeness of the two positions. However, given such reservations, the 'interactionist' title will do if only because it is widely used.

For brevity's sake we will make three points about 'inter-actionism'.

(1) That it emphasizes the importance of the 'definition of the situation'. A determinist account of conduct suggests we are made to act as we do because circumstances force us to act. In which case, people's response to circumstances would be uniform, we would all behave in the same way in the same circumstances. Whilst this uniformity of reaction might be characteristic of earthworms or other simple forms of life, it does not appear to be true of human beings – different people respond differently to 'the same' situation. However, it is important to point out that interactionists hold that human beings respond to situations as they see them, as they define them. This means that a situation is not 'the same' for two people if they define it quite differently. Thus, for example, for patients and for medical personnel a given situation can be very different: for the patient it is a matter of urgency, a crisis, but for the medical personnel it is a routine, everyday situation requiring no particular hurry. We cannot say what the situation is independently of the points of view involved. The same, of course, goes with regard to the topic of deviance, and the famous 'labelling theory' which derives from interactionist assumptions. Is an action deviant? We cannot give a flat answer to that, because it all depends upon which point of view it is seen from. Some could look on the action as deviant, whereas others would not see it in that way (Becker, 1963). How people act depends upon how they view the situation. Hence the famous maxim 'If people define situations as real, they are real in their consequences'

(Thomas, 1966). Thus, if someone is defined as 'a witch' in a community where such things are believed in, it does not matter if *we* think there are no witches, for the person really will be cast out, burned alive or otherwise punished, if that is the fate meted out to witches in the society concerned. Thus, any inquiry must take into account the ways people define their situations.

(2) The organization of social action involves decision-making. To understand how social processes have the results they do, then we need to examine the ways decision-making is organized.

A good example, though presented more crudely than is altogether fair, is that of the sociology of education. The study of educational achievement has often taken a 'determinist' form (e.g. Sewell and Shah, Bowles and Gintis in Karabel and Halsey, 1977). It has long been noted that there is a correlation between social class and levels of educational achievement, with those from the higher social classes tending to do best in terms of achievement. Thus it was common to seek to identify factors which determined those levels of achievement, to see which factors of social class origin, family situation and so on are most strongly related to levels of educational achievement.

Interactionists objected that this made educational achievement seem an automatic result of such influence and led to a complete neglect of the role of the school in producing levels of achievement. There are, indeed, relations between social class background and educational achievement, not least because of the extent to which conceptions about intelligence, ability and motivation are related to ideas about educational achievement *in the minds of the teachers* and through the decision-making process within the school. Thus, there were investigations into the ways in which teachers and administrators allocate people within the opportunity structure of the school, the ways in which teachers would differentially respond to the behaviour and accomplishments of their pupils because of their assumptions about how typical working class or middle class, black or white kids can be expected to behave. Thus, the differential definition of the situation enters in again: behaviour which is ostensibly the same, such as, say, asking questions in class, would be responded to quite differently if it originated from different kinds of kids. If it was from lower-class kids then asking questions would be seen as a way of 'getting the lesson off track', 'wasting time', etc., and would be treated punitively, whereas if done by middle-class ones it would be encouraged as showing interest and willingness to learn. Within the school, teachers are crucial decision-makers, managing the careers and fates of their charges and we will not correctly understand how achievement is distributed unless we see how they make their decisions (cf. Cicourel and Kitsuse in Karabel and Halsey, 1977).

(3) The activities of people involve the 'working out' of social arrangements. The point of the studies of the relationship between social class and educational achievement just outlined is not to deny that there is a connection between social class and educational achievement for, plainly enough, there is. They are meant to say something about the character of the connection and about the ways in which those involved in the educational system *make* that connection. Thus, the argument is that children from different social classes have much the same levels of ability and motivation to do well in school but that their teachers overlook the abilities and dissipate the motivation of those from the lower social classes. Relations between pupil and teacher work themselves out in such a way that the teacher responds negatively to the well-motivated actions of the lower-class pupil, often failing to see the intelligence in what the child does because of cultural differences, and eventually such negative responses alienate the child, leading it to start withdrawing motivation and behaving in deliberately disruptive ways which, in turn, intensify the negative response of the teachers. There is a stable pattern of relationship between class and achievement, but that is, if these arguments are right, a product of the ways in which the parties to the classroom situation work out their relationships in the classroom. Mutual alienation builds up action by action: the child does something, the teacher responds, the child responds to that, the teacher's earlier response is reinforced, the child begins to feel that the teacher does not like it, etc. (cf. Rist in Karabel and Halsey, 1977).

Rather than thinking of people as having to behave as they do because of the circumstances in which they find themselves, the interactionist policy invites us to see people as producing those 'social facts', to use Durkheim's term, which confront them. There is a relationship between social class and educational achievement, but only because the educational decision-maker makes a connection between those things in the school and the classroom and thus the development of relations between the lower-class pupil and the school limit the former's possibility of behaving in educationally valued and successful ways. Obviously, the aim is to generalize this view and to examine the ways in which the everyday activities in social life give rise to the stable relationships which we find in society, in the way that the school itself may be seen to give rise to the relationship of educational achievement to social class. The outcomes of social situations are not inevitable results of them but are made to happen through the kinds of decisions that we take. We are, that is, building up social patterns through our relationships with each other and, in that sense, we produce them.

Interaction

The views just outlined seem to offer entirely different conceptions of society. For some sociologists this is unsatisfactory and what such an opposition represents is an over enthusiastic partiality. While each side has some truth to it, a better picture is obtainable if we put the apparently irreconcilable points of view together. Thus, in answer to the question, do individuals produce society or does society produce individuals, the answer is both!

Peter Berger and Thomas Luckmann (1966) provide the essentials of this 'integrative' strategy which they specifically design to overcome the opposition of Marx and Durkheim on the one hand, to interactionists such as George Herbert Mead (1934) on the other.

Sociologists like Marx and Durkheim tend toward the determinist end of the spectrum emphasizing a view of 'society as objective reality', which appears to all of us as something we have not made and which limits what we can do. By contrast, Mead is of a voluntarist turn of mind, emphasizing the degree to which we form society by our present actions, the way in which, through our interactions with one another, we are organizing society. Mead's view is of 'society as subjective reality', of society as something which we can shape and control.

Instead of seeing these views in opposition, they can be seen as complementary. Society is *both* a subjective and an objective reality. Society is built up out of the actions of its individual members (and, of course, the unintended consequences of their actions) and therefore the particular contributions of its members give shape to an organization of relationships. Spontaneously constructed patterns of relationship, however, become stabilized and relatively immutable, and so something which began as a 'subjective' creation, the product of the aims and actions of individuals, develops into something 'objective', into a fixed arrangement which presents itself as a given and constraining environment for subsequent action. At any point in time, then, a structure of society has already been created by preceding generations which means that its present inhabitants are presented with given ways of life and arrangements of relationships into which they will have, in one way or another, to fit. At the same time, however, that accumulated structure does not confine completely, does not inhibit all possibility of choice, decision and creation, and within that structure we can take actions which will shape the further course of the society's development, including even the drastic reshaping of the structure that we have inherited.

More recently, Anthony Giddens (1976) offered similar views, talking in terms of a 'duality of agency and structure'. These notions are designed, like those of Berger and Luckmann, to persuade us against thinking that we must view society as *either* something virtually immutable and which we cannot, therefore, modify at all, *or* as something which we can transform at our will in whatever way we want. Similarly, we must not think of ourselves as being *either* creatures who are just the play-things of structures, puppets moved by forces which are entirely beyond our control and wholly unknown to us, *or* as creatures capable of deciding everything for ourselves, completely free to act in whatever way we wish. We must recognize that we have the power of 'agency', that we can act and achieve things, but must also appreciate that we act within and upon structures, and that, in addition, those structures themselves shape us, affect the kinds of things that we want and provide us with the means (i.e. cultural rules and knowledge) which enable us to design and carry out actions.

Conclusion

It is impossible for a conclusion to draw together or reconcile the views which have been outlined above. Though some of the positions we have sketched were formulated a long time ago, no one of them can be said to be outdated, for they all have active support within contemporary sociology. In one form or another, disputes about the right view of the individual–society relationship play crucial roles in many controversies. Criticism often takes the form of a complaint that too much (or too little) importance is given to the influence of structures.

The attempts at integration which we have described in the last section may seem appealing because of the attempt to put an end to what may seem like a fruitless and wholly inconclusive argument. However, such appeal may be wholly superficial.

A journalist, Alan Watkins, once wondered why politicians thought that in saying things like 'It would be better if we all pulled together' they were producing an answer to problems rather than just restating the problem. The problem is that, though it might well be better if we all pulled together, we do not do so. Saying that society is both an objective and a subjective reality and involves both structure and agency, may sound like a conciliation of opposed views, but is it anything more than a restatement of Marx's contention that we make history, but not in circumstances of our own choosing? Does it in any way differentiate itself from many of the other positions we have sketched out? For example, it is quite misleading to see the positions outlined in the arguments above as being necessarily divided over whether society is an 'objective reality' or not. To pick one example, the dispute between 'holists' and 'methodological individualists' is not whether social life is objective, but in what sense it is so. Both accept that the life of society provides a real situation within which individuals must act. The question between them is what kind of objectivity society does have, does it consist simply of other individuals or of something more?

Thus, the issues we have raised are still open and still generate as much controversy and confusion as they have in the past. We have perhaps given enough detail on them to indicate that there is no simple way of disposing of them, no quick way through them. They are the arguments which have divided sociology over much of its past and look like doing so in the foreseeable future.

References and Further Reading

Althusser, L. (1970), *For Marx* (London: Allen Lane).

Becker, H. S. (1963), *Outsiders* (Glencoe, Ill.: Free Press).

Berger, P. and Luckmann, T. (1966), *The Social Construction of Reality* (New York: Doubleday).

Bowles, S. and Gintis, H. (1977), 'IQ in the US Class Structure' in J. Karabel and A. H. Halsey (eds), *Power and Ideology in Education* (Oxford: Oxford University Press).

Cicourel, A. V. and Kitsuse, J. I. (1977), 'The School as a Mechanism of Social Differentiation' in J. Karabel and A. H. Halsey (eds), *Power and Ideology in Education* (Oxford: Oxford University Press).

Coward, R. and Ellis, J. (1977), *Language and Materialism* (London: Routledge & Kegan Paul).

Durkheim, E. (1938), *Rules of Sociological Method* (Glencoe, Ill.: Free Press).

Durkheim, E. (1952), *Suicide* (London: Routledge & Kegan Paul).

Giddens, A. (1976), *New Rules of Sociological Method* (London: Hutchinson).

Hayek, F. A. von (1955), *The Counter-Revolution of Science* (Glencoe, Ill.: Free Press).

Hobbes, T. (1962), *Leviathan* (London: Collier-Macmillan).

Homans, G. (1967), *The Nature of Social Science* (New York: Harcourt, Brace and World).

Karabel, J. and Halsey, A. H. (1977), *Power and Ideology in Education* (Oxford: Oxford University Press).

Kolakowski, L. (1978) *Main Currents of Marxism*, Vol. 1 (Oxford: Oxford University Press).

Lévi-Strauss, C. (1967), 'The Story of Asdiwal' in E. Leach (ed.), *The Structural Study of Myth and Totemism* (London: Tavistock), pp. 1–47.

Marx, K. (1962), 'Eighteenth Brumaire of Louis Napoleon' in *Marx and Engels, Selected Works* (Moscow: Foreign Language Publishing House).

Mead, G. H. (1934), *Mind, Self and Society* (Chicago, Ill.: University of Chicago Press).

O'Neill, J. (1973), *Modes of Individualism and Collectivism* (London: Heinemann).

Pettit, P. (1975), *The Concept of Structuralism* (Berkeley, Calif.: University of California Press).

Popper, K. (1945), *The Open Society and its Enemies*, 2 vols (London: Routledge & Kegan Paul).

Popper, K. (1959), *The Logic of Scientific Discovery* (London: Heinemann).

Rist, R. C. (1977), 'On Understanding the Process of Schooling; the Contributions of Labelling Theory' in J. Karabel and A. H. Halsey (eds), *Power and Ideology in Education* (Oxford: Oxford University Press).

Saussure, F. de (1964), *Course in General Linguistics* (London: Collins).

Sewell, W. H. and Shah, V. P. (1977), 'Socio-Economic Status, Intelligence and the Attainment of Higher Education' in J. Karabel and A. H. Halsey (eds), *Power and Ideology in Education* (Oxford: Oxford University Press).

Smith, A. (1933), *The Wealth of Nations* (London: Dent).

Thomas, W. I. (1966), *On Social Organization and Social Personality* (Chicago, Ill.: University of Chicago Press).

Walicki, A. (1984), 'Marx and Freedom', *New York Review of Books*, vol. 30, no. 18, pp. 50–6.

Weber, M. (1930), *The Protestant Ethic and the Spirit of Capitalism* (London: Allen & Unwin).

Weber, M. (1968), *Economy and Society*, 2 vols (Totawa, N.J.: Bedminster Press).

Chapter 6

Laws and Explanations in Sociology

WILLIAM OUTHWAITE

There are basically two disputes around these issues. The first is a dispute in philosophy of science about what laws are. The second is a dispute about whether such laws are useful to sociology and the other social sciences, and if so, how.

I shall take it as unproblematic that sociologists want to explain things, even if only in a very broad sense of explanation which includes description, understanding (in the special sense in which this word has been used in sociology) and so on. Many social scientists have insisted on distinguishing between explanation and these other processes. (As we shall see, this is very often because their conception of explanation relies heavily on the idea of laws.) I want to begin, however, with a common-sense notion of explanation, in which there are very many different ways of explaining things. In particular, an explanation of why something is going on, that is, an answer to questions of the type 'Why are they doing that?' will often be given by a description of the activity. If you ask for an explanation of a particular crowd scene, it will often be enough to be told 'It's a football match' or 'It's an open-air Mass' or 'It's a demonstration'. There may, of course, be further questions such as 'Why is the match/Mass taking place in Stadium A rather than Stadium B?' or, more fundamentally, 'What *is* a football match/Mass, etc.?' The former question may be answered by showing that Stadium A is after all better, or at least adequate for the purpose, that Stadium B was closed for repairs, or perhaps, more interestingly, that the local council decided to keep the match/Mass as far away as possible from the city centre. This last explanation also has the interesting struct-ural feature that it explains by telling a story, or at least referring to a possible story, about a process or set of processes which brought about the situation to be explained. This is, of course, a form of explanation characteristically found in historical narratives.

The second explanation, answering the question 'What *is* a match/Mass?' etc., will involve a fuller account of the structure, purpose, etc. of these activities. This may lead as far as multi-volume studies in the sociology of sport, religion, political activity and so on.

What makes an explanation, or what makes an explanation a good one, is therefore quite a difficult question, which may require a detailed study, not just of the logical properties of the explanation but of the context in which it is offered. You can buy, for example, a joke poster which 'explains' the structure of a game of cricket in terms of a play on the words 'in' and 'out'. This has the form of an explanatory description, but it only makes sense if you already understand the rules of cricket. 'I was ill' has the socially recognized form of a good explanation for, for example, why I am late in delivering my manuscript for this volume, but a suspicious editor may want to know *how* ill, for how long, and so on.

The purpose of these introductory remarks has been to illus-trate the diverse forms which explanations take in everyday life. Once again, I assume we agree that we need, or at least want, explanations in these senses. The issue, however, is whether laws help us to explain social life, or whether they are a misleading distraction from this enterprise. But to answer this question, we need to know what we mean by laws.

In English, and in many other European languages, the term 'law' is used to refer both to scientific laws and to the 'legal' principles expressed in statutes, constitutions and so on. It is worth making this obvious point because it tells us something important about the history of the term. The laws enacted by governments aim to establish regularities in social life, by telling people what they should and should not do, and threatening to punish, by civil or criminal procedures, people who do the latter. So if there is an Ultimate Legislator who made the world behave as it does, the regularities which we observe in nature must be the result of things obeying 'His' will, just as human beings, on the whole, obey the laws of their political or religious communities.

With the advances made by modern Western science around the seventeenth century, we begin to find the idea of 'laws of nature' separating away from this original theological conception. What remain, however, are the twin ideas of regularity and necessity. (The word regularity is of course linked to that of rule, and we still speak of things 'obeying' laws, such as the law of gravity.) Regularity means that things always behave in the way described by the law; necessity means that they are somehow constrained to do so. And the people who came, in the nineteenth century, to be called scientists, discover these laws and use them to describe or explain the phenomena of nature.

But when philosophers came to analyse these laws, the ideas of regularity and necessity no longer seemed to fit together. Regularity was no problem: any exceptions to a law could be explained away by special circumstances. But necessity became an embarrassment. The most obvious way to analyse it was in terms of the natures or tendencies of things, but this came to seem either anthropomorphic, in that it made natural objects sound like people deciding to do things, or trivial, in the sense that it added nothing to the original statement of the regularity of things. The classic expression of the latter criticism is Molière's mockery of the claim that opium makes people sleep because of its 'dormative power' (*virtus dormativa*). For the dominant philosophical movement known as empiricism, we can only be sure about our experiences. On this basis, David Hume (1711–76) developed an analysis of causal laws which, in modified forms, has remained the dominant orthodoxy. All we observe, and therefore, for empiricism, all we can know, are conjunctions of events. When one billiard ball hits another, with adequate force and in a clear space on the table, the second ball moves. But the idea that there is a necessary connection here, for Hume, is just a habit of mind. I shall return later to this philosophical opposition between 'realists' who stress the *necessity* of causal relationships, and 'empiricists' who rely only on their *regularity*.

At the time of the emergence of the sciences as we know them, in the seventeenth and eighteenth centuries in Europe and North America, these differences in the analysis of causal laws were glossed over; what mattered was that people were now discovering laws of nature, and even laws governing social life. The social sciences in their modern form have developed in the shadow of, and with constant reference to, the sciences of nature. Not that the progress of the natural sciences was entirely smooth and unproblematic. Philosophers of science, and especially philosophers of social science, have tended to adopt an idealized picture of the natural sciences which has been very heavily qualified by recent work in the history and sociology of science, largely inspired by Thomas Kuhn's classic book *The Structure of Scientific Revolutions* (1962). The progress of science is discontinuous, conjectural and fraught with controversy. The status of scientific laws, in particular, is itself controversial. Albert Einstein wrote in 1923: 'As far as the laws of mathematics refer to reality, they are not certain; and as far as they are certain, they do not refer to reality.' And this theme has recently been developed further in a challenging book by Nancy Cartwright, *How the Laws of Physics Lie* (1983), where she argues that 'Really powerful explanatory laws of the sort found in theoretical physics do not state the truth' (p. 3). It remains the case, however, that the natural sciences, when they are successful, bring about dramatic changes in our understanding of reality, disclosing entities and mechanisms which are quite inaccessible to common-sense. Machiavelli, and, more importantly, even his less perceptive contemporaries had a quite good understanding of power relations in society, but they did not and could not have a corresponding understanding of, say, sub-atomic structures. Even the most sceptical historian of science cannot deny the 'revelatory power', as Giddens has described it, of modern natural science. Judged by these standards, the only issue is whether we should see the social sciences as disabled or 'differently abled'.

The dispute over the status of laws in sociological explanations is inseparable, then, from the broader issue of how far the social sciences should model themselves on the natural sciences. The idea that they should, a position best described as naturalism, was already well entrenched by the eighteenth century, while the work of Vico (1668–1744) is an important anticipation of later anti-naturalist arguments. It was in the nineteenth century, however, that the dispute really got going, with the opposition between the positivists and their critics. This dispute between positivists, mainly French and English, and anti-positivists, working mainly in Germany, fed directly into the debates which have raged in English-language sociology and elsewhere, over the past twenty years (see Outhwaite, 1975). Though the detailed arguments have changed on both sides, the basic issue remains the same.

The Original Dispute

The term 'positivism' is notoriously ambiguous, but was first used by Auguste Comte (1798–1857) to describe his view that the only valid knowledge arises from scientific observation and that the individual sciences, including the science for which he coined the term sociology, form a single hierarchical system of knowledge. Comte's ideas were tremendously influential in, for example, the philosophical system of John Stuart Mill. In sociology, the influence was even stronger. Until the turn of the century, 'sociology' virtually meant the work of Comte and of Herbert Spencer. Theories of society which treated it as a kind of organism were a particularly drastic expression of this positivist naturalism. Anti-naturalist views, however, came to form a strong oppositional current in the philosophy of history, and subsequently in the social sciences, especially in the German-speaking countries. J. G. Droysen launched a powerful attack on positivist history, especially as represented by the English historian H. T. Buckle. Droysen's anti-naturalism was based on the difference between nature and mind or spirit, and the way in which the expressions of the latter can be understood. This notion of 'understanding' (*verstehen* in German) as something distinct from the observation of natural phenomena was taken up by Wilhelm Dilthey in his theory of the human sciences. In a parallel anti-naturalist move, expressed in more methodological terms, Windelband and Rickert distinguished between the generalizing method of the natural sciences and the individualizing method of the 'cultural sciences' (history, philology and so on). The latter are not interested in regularities, said Rickert, but in individual cultural phenomena which bear some relation to human values. From this position, clearly, the search for an exact science of lawlike regularities in social life, if not a mistake, was likely to provide a worthwhile basis for the study of human history.

The term 'exact science' became the focus of the 'methodological dispute' carried on in Germany between the 'historical
school' of economists and those who wanted to develop a more
abstract form of economic theory. The historical school of
economics, like the historical school of law, stressed that
economic and legal relations must be seen as part of complex
historical totalities; they cannot be abstracted out and reduced to
a simple set of elements, such as the simplifying assumptions
about motivation which one tends to find in economic theory.
But if the historical school rejected the pursuit of exact laws of
economics, it was distinctly sanguine, as its critic Carl Menger
pointed out, in accepting large-scale laws of social development.
In other words, whereas classical positivism had paid lip-service
to the idea of exact science but was really more interested in laws
of human development, it now became clear that one had to
choose between the two. Modern positivist empiricism turns its
back on historical complexity (and possible laws of development
to be sought therein) and seeks to simplify, to analyse, to
abstract.

Menger took the conciliatory line that there were simply two
approaches to science, a 'realistic-empirical' one and an 'exact'
one. The former, inductive, approach can only yield approxi-
mate regularities; phenomena cannot be ordered into 'strict types
and laws', but only into 'real types and empirical laws'. But there
is another, 'exact' mode of investigation which

> seeks to ascertain the simplest elements of everything real. It strives
> for the establishment of these elements by way of an only partially
> empirical-realistic analysis, i.e. without considering whether these
> in reality are present as *independent* phenomena ... In this manner
> theoretical research arrives at ... results ... which, to be sure,
> must not be tested by full empirical reality (for the empirical forms
> here under discussion, e.g. absolutely pure oxygen, pure alcohol,
> pure gold, a person pursuing only economic aims etc. exist in part
> only in our ideas).
>
> (Menger, 1963, pp. 60f)

One of the central themes of the controversy between Menger
and G. Schmoller was the analysis of economic motivation.
Schmoller criticized the 'psychological' assumptions of the
classical economists, while Menger replied that to take self-
interest as a basic motivational postulate was merely a convenient simplification: economics did not deny the existence of

other motives, any more than pure mechanics denied the existence of air-filled spaces.

I have discussed this economic debate in some detail because it is one of the sources at least of Max Weber's attempt to resolve this dispute with the concept of 'ideal types'. This concept, introduced into sociology by Simmel and Weber, has become the central element of several of the most prominent approaches to the subject. Weber broadly accepts Menger's distinction between history and theory, or between an 'empirical–realistic' and an 'exact' approach, but he differs from Menger in the account he gives of the difference. First, the difference between the two approaches is grounded not so much in differences in the reality with which they deal (the sociohistorical totality vs a distinct aspect or side of reality) as in differences in the knowledge-interests with which we approach the phenomena. The 'economic' character of a phenomenon is not an objective property of it, but merely a function of our cognitive interest. However, it should be noted that Weber goes on to distinguish between strictly 'economic' phenomena, those which are 'economically relevant' (e.g. certain aspects of religion) and those which are 'economically conditioned', such as the social stratification of the artistic public. Secondly, underlying this difference between a 'systematic' and a 'historical' approach is a more important difference between the kind of knowledge which is desirable and possible in the natural sciences and that which is appropriate to a science like economics. To expect to deduce concrete, quantitative predictions from economic 'laws' is a 'naturalistic prejudice'; economic 'laws' can only have an ideal-typical form. Their failure to apply in individual cases does not impugn their heuristic value.

For Max Weber, then, sociology is a generalizing science in the sense that, unlike history, it looks for 'general regularities in what takes place'; its theories do not so much consist of lawlike statements as make provisional and conditional use of them. Sociology is a consumer, rather than a producer of laws. In addition, of course, these regularities must be 'understandable' if they are to provide an adequate explanation. They must be 'meaningfully adequate' as well as 'causally adequate' in the sense of empirically well supported. A good example of this is the connection he believed to exist between Protestantism and the spirit of capitalism. Starting from the alleged fact that Protestants were more innovative in their economic behaviour than Catholics in early modern Europe, he goes on to offer a meaningfully adequate explanation of this fact in terms of their anxieties about their salvation. Another example which Weber himself uses is Gresham's Law that bad money drives out good. This is causally adequate, in the sense that we can observe its operation in cases where a debased currency is in circulation, and meaningfully adequate in that we can see that it makes sense for an individual to pass on the bad money and hold on to the good.

Weber, then, saw empirical regularities as things to be explained rather than as explanations in their own right. An adequate sociological explanation will always be historically specific and involve a reference to the purposes and orientation of the action of real or 'typical' individuals. Although the consequences of these actions will often be unintended, as in the case of Protestant theology and the 'spirit' of capitalism, these consequences could not have come about if individual actors had not acted in certain ways and for certain reasons.

Weber's *verstehende* sociology can be contrasted with the more naturalistic conception of the subject to be found in Marx and Durkheim. Durkheim was wedded to a set of rather dubious analogies between biology and sociology, in which forms of society are analysed as 'social species', with laws which govern their operation and set the parameters of their 'normal' or equilibrium states. He was, however, unable to provide any convincing foundation for the distinction between normal and pathological phenomena within human societies let alone one for distinguishing between normal and pathological societies.

In the case of Marx, Engels and later Marxist writers, the position is a good deal more complicated, but there are two basic themes to note. First, Marx's critique of political economy very often takes the form of an attack on the way in which economists have misrepresented the phenomena of the capitalist mode of production as corresponding to universal natural laws, and therefore historically unchangeable. But when economists claim that pre-capitalist, for example, feudal, relations of production are somehow less natural than those of capitalism, they should really be showing how the class antagonisms of feudal society caused it to fall apart and mutate into capitalism.

Is not this as good as saying that the mode of production, the relations in which the productive forces develop, are anything but eternal laws, but that they correspond to a definite development of men and their productive forces, and that a change in men's productive forces necessarily brings about a change in their relations of production?

(Marx, 1975a, p. 114)

It is clear that Marx, in criticizing the economists' conception of eternal natural laws, himself invokes the idea of lawlike tendencies governing the operation and transformation of forms of production. As he put it a couple of years later, in the famous 'Preface' to the *Critique of Political Economy*

In the social production of their existence, human beings inevitably enter into definite relations, which are independent of their will, namely relations of production appropriate to a given stage in the development of their material forces of production.

(1975b, p. 425)

Marx's later work is full of references to the 'laws of motion' of capitalist production and bourgeois society. Engels took this kind of language much more seriously than Marx did. He devoted a good part of his work, with Marx's acquiescence if not his active encouragement, to developing a general Marxist theory of nature and history. In natural philosophy, he formalized the dialectic into three somewhat vacuous 'laws':

(1) the law of the transformation of quantity with quality, according to which gradual quantitative changes give rise to revolutionary qualitative changes;
(2) the law of the unity of opposites, which holds that the unity of concrete reality is a unity of opposites or contradictions;
(3) the law of the negation of the negation, which claims that in the clash of opposites one opposite negates another and is in turn negated by a higher level of historical development that preserves something of both negated terms.

(Roy Edgley, 'Dialectic' in Tom Bottomore, 1983, p. 212)

Engels's construction of a dialectical materialist theory of nature is in my view a mistake; it turned an extremely powerful theory of history into an overblown natural philosophy. Even more serious, however, were the practical effects of Engels's tendency to overplay the status of Marx's notion of laws of social development. His speech at Marx's funeral is the clearest expression of this: 'As Darwin discovered the law of the development of organic nature, so Marx discovered the developmental law of human history.'

There is no doubt that Engels's emphasis on these general philosophical and evolutionary themes added to the appeal of Marxism among workers and intellectuals who had imbibed the evolutionism, and often the positivism, so prevalent in nine-teenth-century thought. In the long run, however, it made Marxism more vulnerable intellectually, and it encouraged Marxists to adopt a somewhat passive political position of waiting for the inevitable, evolutionarily guaranteed, collapse of capitalism. Marx basically conceived laws as tendencies, in a way which is close to the realist position described below (Sayer, 1979), and this should have suggested a more cautious formula-tion of his theories.

The Modern Law-Explanation Orthodoxy

In comparing the views of these 'founding fathers' with the mid-twentieth-century disputes about laws and explanations in sociology, one can of course observe a much more detailed and explicit philosophical conception in the latter period. At the same time, however, it can be argued that this development was not only a false trail in philosophical terms, but had a particularly disabling effect on the social sciences. In this section, I shall try to disentangle what I take to be the underlying dispute from the positivist assumptions within which it has been formulated. As I shall argue later, the replacement of positivism by a realist philosophy of science leads to a reformulation of the dispute, though not to its dissolution.

For the moment, however, we are in the 1950s and 1960s where, at least in the English-speaking countries, there was little visible challenge to a positivist philosophy of science whose roots were in the logical empiricism of the Vienna Circle of the 1920s. As the term implies, this movement was born of an intellectual marriage between the empiricism of Hume and Mach (1838–1916) and the modern mathematical logic of Frege, Whitehead and Russell. Scientific theory was analysed in mathematical terms as the interpretation, or filling-out, of a set of formal relations between variables. As in Comtean positivism, science was understood to form, or be on the way to forming, a harmonious, unified system, but with the crucial difference that the logical positivists, as they generally came to be known, were reductionists. They believed that the language, and ultimately the laws of all other sciences, could ultimately be reduced to the language of physics. And whatever this reductionist programme was supposed to involve, it was clear that physics was the science which best fitted the Viennese model of mathematized theory.

This produced the rather curious situation that textbooks of this period in the philosophy of social science tended to consist mainly of examples from the physical sciences, using them to illustrate *the* nature of theories, laws, explanations and so on. In the concluding chapters of such books there would be a set of apologetic remarks about the underdeveloped state of the social sciences, and some recommendations for increasing the level of precision and rigour therein. The problem was that the social sciences seemed to be caught in a vicious circle. Their theories, laws and explanations were unsatisfactory because their concepts were not precisely specified; but the concepts were imprecise because of the absence of well-established theories. The orthodox position on law and explanation, then, was one of those orthodoxies whose efficacy is inversely related to the amount of scrutiny they receive. Social science, like any other science, *had* to be devoted to the pursuit of explanations, and explanations *had* to involve covering-laws. This was the ideology of a practice which in reality was mainly concerned with the collection of empirical findings. It was agreed that these findings ought to be generalizable, but this requirement tended to be conceived in terms of the technicalities of obtaining a representative sample and measuring the statistical significance of the results obtained. If one looks at one of the classic texts in this tradition, Berelson and Steiner (1964), one is struck, first by the extreme banality of most of the 1,045 'findings' and, secondly, by the authors' avoidance of any serious discussion of their status. 'In the terminology of the behavioral sciences, what we here call findings might elsewhere be called propositions, generalisations, laws, or principles' (p. 5). The authors were of course primarily concerned to record these findings in an encyclopaedic form, rather than to mould them into a systematic social science, but their data are fairly clearly the product of what C. Wright Mills called 'abstracted empiricism'. All this meant that the status of *theories* in the social sciences was left radically unclear. Theories, as we have seen, had to consist in general laws; they also had to be testable, in terms either of the original positivist theory of verification or Karl Popper's influential reformulation, in which a proper scientific theory was one which could in principle be falsified by empirical evidence. These two requirements were difficult to reconcile. It was easy enough to reduce theoretical propositions to a simplified form in which they could be tested, but this did not yield general laws of an interesting kind. Conversely, very general theories such as those developed by Talcott Parsons or, for that matter, the classical theories of Marx, Weber, or Durkheim, could not be tested in a direct way. What was needed here was a more sophisticated understanding of the status of theory which did not, in my view, emerge until the 1970s. In the earlier period, the fact that theories existed could be invoked as a sort of talisman which ostensibly guaranteed the generalizability, and hence, given the law–explanation orthodoxy, the significance, of the empirical findings.

If we turn to the more reflective writers in this tradition, we can see various modifications of the orthodoxy which reduced its distance from what was actually going on in the social sciences. Robert Brown (1963, 1973), for example, while remaining wedded to a covering-law conception of scientific explanation noted that much of the work of social scientists was actually concerned with discovery rather than explanation, and that many of their explanations did not, for good reasons, adopt the strict form laid down by the covering-law philosophers. Genetic explanations make no explicit reference to laws, but are concerned, rather, to show how something came about, in the form of a historical narrative which accounts for the events to be explained. Explanations in terms of the intentions and dispositions of actors, and their reasons for acting in particular ways, also need not refer to lawlike generalizations. If there is a generalization in cases such as this, it is the trivial one that if someone has a reason for doing something and an intention or disposition to do so, there is a prima-facie likelihood that he or she will try to do it. This could not be analysed as a causal relation, given the orthodox view that such relations could only be sought between logically distinct events, but it nevertheless sustained an explanation.

One particular modification of the orthodoxy deserves separate attention. In its classical form, it was upheld by the American sociologist George Homans, and its most prominent modern supporter is W. G. Runciman. This involves passing the buck from sociology to psychology, with the claim that the latter science is the source of the lawlike generalizations which are 'consumed', in Runciman's formulation, by sociology and the other social sciences. Common-sense understanding of human behaviour, formalized in behavioural psychology, provides explanatory propositions for all the other social sciences. This position seems to me highly unsatisfactory, in that it exaggerates the scientific status of psychological generalizations, and also exaggerates their scope. Max Weber was surely right to insist that rational action explanations have nothing specifically psychological about them, though his methodological individualism, an insistence that sociological explanations must ultimately be formulated in terms of typical patterns of individual action, is at least contentious and in my view mistaken. Be that as it may, the buck-passing strategy was a possible way of reducing the pressure on the law–explanation orthodoxy.

Against the Orthodoxy

Attacks on the orthodox position can be roughly divided into four types. The first three critiques, which I shall call idiographic, hermeneutic, and rationalist, deny its validity for sociology and the other social sciences, while the fourth, realism, claims that it is wrong about science as a whole. In so doing, realism provides a way of reformulating the original dispute between the orthodoxy and its critics.

The idiographic critique has already been discussed in relation to Rickert. It is that 'cultural sciences', as he called them, are not concerned with general laws, but with the explanation of individual phenomena. Rickert stressed that this notion of cultural science, and its opposite, the generalizing approach of the natural sciences, were ideal types and that actual research would involve varying mixtures of the two approaches. It is easy enough to show, for example, that an account of an individual event, say the Russian Revolution, will inevitably involve relating it to other revolutions and discussing general tendencies of social life which are at work both inside and outside periods of revolutionary change. The reference to other revolutions is implied by the decision to apply to it the general term revolution.

Despite these considerations, and the fact that few if any sociologists have explicitly adopted a Rickertian approach, I think it can be shown that an important part of sociology *is* concerned with individual cases. The description and explanation of these cases is seen as having a value which is quite distinct from that of one scientific experiment among others. Comparison and generalization may be valuable, but they arise out of a detailed understanding of particular social phenomena. This position does not involve a direct critique of the law–explanation orthodoxy, but it does push it somewhat into the background.

In anthropology, of course, the individual ethnographic study has always had a crucial role. Within sociology, the position is a good deal more complicated. American sociologists in the first half of this century talked a good deal about 'the case study method' as one method among others. But there has I think been an important change in the last twenty years or so, expressed variously in the revival of historical and comparative sociology and in the emergence of 'phenomenological' sociology. This is best illustrated in a changed view of classical sociology. Whereas Parsons (1968), in *The Structure of Social Action*, was concerned to stress the convergence of the 'classics' towards a general theory of action, destined to be formalized (and even perhaps tested), modern sociologists would, I think, be more likely to see the theories of Weber and others, not so much as foothills beyond which a modern, scientific sociology would attain great peaks of knowledge, but as efforts, however flawed, in the same genre as any theories we might ourselves develop. Weber's ideal types, for example, which were earlier seen as preliminaries to the real scientific work of constructing scales on which to measure variables, are now seen much more, as he himself saw them, as aids to the categorization of concrete phenomena, with the implication that this is often as far as we will usefully be able to go in our sociological theorizing.

The idiographic critique has strong affinities with the second alternative, which I am calling hermeneutic or interpretative. Here again, there is a long anti-positivist tradition stressing the need to understand social phenomena from the standpoint of the human beings involved in them. A detailed exploration of the 'life-world' of the actor is at least as important as, and for more radical critics a substitute for, the pursuit of lawlike regularities. In the former case, we find writers like Alfred Schutz, who was worried by Weber's too-rapid jump from the subjectivity of actors to his own ideal types, and stressed that the general propositions of, say, neo-classical economics or Parsonian sociology must be related to the concrete perceptions of the people involved in the social relations thus described. In the second, more radical camp, Peter Winch has claimed that causal generalizations are essentially irrelevant to the real purpose of social scientific inquiry, this being to understand, from an insider's perspective, the *point* of what is going on. Once we have understood a 'form of life' in this way, we have explained it in the only sense in which this term has a meaning. And if Winch's programme suggests that these forms of life are somehow closed off from one another, it can be augmented with Gadamer's conception of a 'fusion of the horizons' of different perspectives, such that they are brought into relation with one another, but in a way which remains nothing like an external perspective from which they are brought under a set of general explanatory laws.

There is no need here to go into the details of this hermeneutic tradition. We should note, however, that Winch gives particular importance to the idea of members of a society following rules. These rules, prescribed by a society and made intelligible by its system of beliefs, are part of the actors' life-world; they prescribe the right and wrong ways of doing things. At the same time, of course, they provide social scientists with the regularities which they wrongly sought at the level of empirical generalizations based on external observation. To give a simple example, the way to understand the flow of traffic at a roundabout is to grasp the rules followed by the drivers, made up of formal systems of priorities and tacit understandings about how to drive safely. Rules can of course be broken but, as long as they exercise some significant influence on behaviour, they form the essential reference point for understanding it.

It has often been objected that Winch puts more weight on the notion of rule-following than it can reasonably bear. What, asked Alasdair MacIntyre, is the right way of going for a walk or smoking a cigarette? But as ethnomethodology has shown, *ad nauseam*, one *can* identify rules governing the most mundane activities. The more serious objection, I think, is that a Winchian programme does not enable us to say much about *why* a society has the belief-system, and hence the rules, which it does. The rules followed by a priest celebrating Mass are explained by Roman Catholic belief, but this does not explain why some societies, or individuals within a given society, are more attracted by this belief-system than others. We may of course be able to identify a higher-order belief-system which makes Catholicism more credible than Protestantism or atheism, but whatever the merits of such an explanation it is clear that the notion of rule-following is unlikely to have much purchase at this level.

Perhaps, however, there are universal rules, those of rational action. Here we come to the third strand of opposition to the law–explanation orthodoxy. In Martin Hollis's ringing phrase, 'rational action is its own explanation' (Hollis, 1977, p. 77). In other words, we can in principle give an adequate description of an actor and his or her circumstances such that a certain course of action appears as the right thing to do. This gives us a model of autonomous action, in which people, given their natures and their situations, rationally choose a course of action. The clearest examples of this occur in highly structured situations such as chess games, but it can be extended, as in game theory and decision theory, to much more complex situations. It is of course an open question how far people do act rationally or autono-mously in this sense, but if and when they do, we have a notion of explanation which retains the idea of necessity (since the best move is necessarily the best move), but where the general laws are normative rather than empirical.

But does this model really provide explanations? Even if we make, for the sake of argument, a set of highly implausible assumptions, viz. that people *do* act rationally much of the time, that for an actor in a given situation there is usually a single best way (or a small number of equally good ways) to act, and that actors and/or observers can decide whether they acted in this way, it is not so much the rationality of the course of action which explains it, as the fact that the reasons for the action were causally efficacious in producing it. This suggests that a better way of thinking about the whole business is to say that rational-choice theories provide us with a *rationale* for an action, whose efficacy remains to be demonstrated. At this point, however the rationality of the rationale, as it were, no longer seems to make much difference. When Max Weber's Protestants turned their anxieties about their salvation into an economic ethic, their behaviour makes a kind of sense, though it is very doubtful if we should want to call it rational. This is because, apart from anything else, human rationality is usually thought to involve some idea of reflection, the idea that we can reconstruct, even if we did not go through them at the time, the steps of reasoning which led us to act rationally. And the Weberian Protestants could not do this without getting into a terrible conflict with their formal theological principles. In other words, their rational response to their situation, if that was what it was, required that they did not examine its rationale too closely.

The upshot of all this, I think, is that although the notion of the rationale of an action, in the sense of the reasons for it, will always deserve close attention in history and the other social sciences it is unhelpfully restrictive to expect that a rationale will be rational in the sense of consistent or non-contradictory, or conversely to expect that the real action will, in Hegel's phrase, be rational. For most practical sociological explanations, I suspect, the notion of a self-explanatory rationality collapses into the general notion of rule-following discussed in the previous section.

Before leaving this topic, I should stress that I do not mean to imply that the rationality of beliefs or actions is irrelevant to sociological explanation. This latter position has been strongly urged in the history and sociology of science, in opposition to the rationalistic assumptions often made within this field. But although the social causes of true belief and rational actions need to be identified just as much as those of false beliefs and irrational actions, it is still the case that false or inconsistent beliefs are potentially unstable, that people may in favourable circumstances become aware of their falsity, and may thus be led to explain why these beliefs were or continue to be held. Most of the time, of course, belief-systems are so complex, involving a selective structure of factual statements, evaluations, stipulative definitions, etc., that it will not be easy to judge their truth or falsity. And this is of course merely a special case of the general problems of rationalist explanations: they work best in artificially simple situations, and do not generally offer much more than hypothetical models, whose greatest use is in the clarification of our understanding of the nature of a situation and alternative possibilities for action.

What follows from these three critiques? This depends, of course, how fully one embraces them, and I shall leave my own views on this matter until after my discussion of the realist critique. Before doing this, however, it may be useful to draw up a provisional balance-sheet. All three critiques shift the emphasis of social theory away from its somewhat obsessional concern with generalizations and towards the, in some ways more 'traditional', study of concrete phenomena, whether these are beliefs, actions, or events of some other kind. In their strongest form, the idiographic and hermeneutic critiques may reject all general explanatory propositions, while the rationalist allows them only at the periphery, in the 'social context' of action. But this leaves the orthodox methodologists in control of the 'general' domain, albeit with the scope of their claims somewhat limited. All three critiques accept by implication the orthodox view that causal relations must be universal. It is this principle which, in the present context, is the central focus of the realist critique, to which I now turn.

A Realist Alternative?

Realist philosophies of science have a long history, but they enjoyed a considerable revival in the 1970s as the positivist orthodoxy came to seem increasingly untenable. A number of writers, notably Rom Harré and Roy Bhaskar, contributed to this development in the philosophy of natural science and its extension to the social sciences (see Keat and Urry, 1975; Benton, 1977). According to realism, science involves the attempt to describe the real structures, entities and processes which make up the universe and which exist independently of our descriptions of them. For many realists, causal statements, and hence laws, need to be analysed in terms of tendencies arising out of the causal powers of entities, structures and mechanisms. To illustrate this conception, let us go back to Molière and the dormative power of opium. From a realist point of view, there is nothing fundamentally wrong with this explanation, once it is filled out in a non-trivial way. What we need in order to do this is precisely what is provided by the modern sciences of chemistry, physiology and pharmacology, namely, an analysis of the chemical properties of opium and its effects upon the nervous system. These effects will of course vary at the individual level, but they are sufficiently general for it to make some sense to talk about a lawlike tendency. Realists play down the regularity in laws in favour of their grounding in real, operative mechanisms which may or may not produce observable results. This is because the world consists of 'open systems', in which a multiplicity of causal mechanisms are at work at any time. My ceiling lamp, for example, shares the general tendency of heavy objects to fall to the ground, but this is held in check by the fitment which holds it to the ceiling. But the continued absence (I hope) of any observable movement does not mean that these forces and resistances are not constantly in play.

The empiricist objection to this analysis is of course that it involves reference to unobservable entities, and thus goes beyond our direct experience. Once we do this, the way is open to all kinds of arbitrary claims, as when I assert that God sent me to university this morning and is about to make me cook my supper. But realists point out that the work of science is precisely designed to demonstrate the existence of non-obvious determinants of observable events. It does this either by rendering them observable, or, more importantly, by isolating their causal effects in experimentation. Viruses, for example, originally had the status of hypotheses, constructed to explain processes of infection which were not the result of bacteria. Now, their existence is no longer in doubt, and they can even be observed with an electron microscope.

One clear advantage of the realist position, then, in the case of the social sciences, is that it does not insist that social laws should be universal; all we need is that they should represent recognizable tendencies. A further advantage is that realism brings natural causation and human action into a closer relation with one another. For among the things with powers and liabilities are of course human beings who choose to exercise their powers in certain ways. On the other hand, it is clearly much harder to specify the entities, such as power structures, which enter into social explanations, and the fear of descending into metaphysics is to that extent better grounded. The Freudian unconscious, for example, if it exists, is an excellent example of a real structure producing a wide range of observable effects, from slips of the tongue, through dreams, to neuroses. But we have no satisfactory way of deciding whether or not it exists, and this is reflected in the interminable and inconsequential battles between Freudians and anti-Freudians.

Let me now address these issues in more detail. As we saw a moment ago, the realist account of law is grounded in productive mechanisms rather than regularities. 'The citation of a law presupposes a claim about the activity of some mechanism but not about the conditions under which the mechanism operates and hence not about the results of its activity, i.e. the actual outcome on any particular occasion' (Bhaskar, 1978, p. 95). In other words, the alternative view which sees constant conjunctions as necessary, or necessary and sufficient to sustain law-statements, has confused laws with their consequences – consequences which in fact only occur in rather special circumstances when the operation of the law is not impeded by any other countervailing or complicating tendencies, that is, when it operates in a 'closed system'. Experiments in the natural sciences characteristically take the form of establishing a closed system, for example, creating a vacuum to remove the effects of the atmosphere on a particular process under investigation.

Closed systems, then, allow the precise identification of specific causal mechanisms and their interactions. As a result, they make possible precise predictions. Not much more needs to be said about this here, since it is clear that there are no closed systems in the domain of the social sciences. One cannot therefore expect the social sciences to generate more than the most conditional and imprecise predictions about their subject-matter. This explains why, when the law–explanation orthodoxy asserted the symmetry of explanation and prediction, deriving both from a general covering-law, it had very little to offer the social scientist. Let us, then, forget about prediction for the time being, and look more closely at explanation. Here, it may be useful to consider the relationship between social science and meteorology. Weather forecasts, like social forecasts, are (to say the least) not entirely reliable. The reason will be clear from the foregoing distinction between closed and open systems: weather systems, especially in areas like the British Isles, are exceptionally complex and unpredictable. But meteorology is based on a quite sophisticated and precise set of physical laws, and for all its difficulties with prediction, it can provide quite full and satisfactory explanations of weather patterns, after the event. The tragedy of the meteorologist is of course that we are not particularly interested in these.

In the case of the social sciences, however, it is difficult to attain a similar degree of certainty in explanation, or even in the identification of the elements which would enter into an explanation. In other words, the basic problem is not one of methodology, but of ontology: social scientists disagree about the entities which make up the social world and about the relations between them. The natural sciences, of course, do not have entirely stable inventories of entities either, but in their case the disputes are more frequently over the existence of some particular disputed entity, such as a 'new' sub-atomic particle. But even the most dramatic discoveries in particle physics are unlikely to change our accounts of what happens at the macroscopic level of, say, a chemical reaction in a test tube, though it may cause us to reformulate our account of the physical processes underlying the chemical change.

In the social sciences, the basic entities are in principle all open to dispute at any one time. The concept of class, discussed in an earlier chapter, is a good example. One of the most basic concepts of both Marxist and much non-Marxist social theory is rejected altogether by some theorists and defined in radically different ways by those who accept it. In the case of the unconscious, discussed earlier, there is again an internal dispute on its nature and mode of operation, and an external dispute on whether or not it exists at all.

The lesson of all this, I think, is that social theorists must avoid what A. N. Whitehead called 'misplaced concreteness'. We learn fairly quickly that a social class, say the French petty bourgeoisie, is not directly observable like a class in a school or college. This is not just because it is too big to observe directly. The extension of the term is not precise, however much we may try to specify it, in the sense in which the number of people possessing French identity cards at 11 a.m. on a particular date is a determinate, if unknown number. 'The French petty bourgeoisie' is a theoretical term, introduced because it picks out a set of people with certain similar conditions of life which differentiate them, in causally significant ways, from members of other classes.

The reference to causality, and hence to explanation, is important here. We demonstrate the existence of entities either by (direct or indirect) observation or by the inferential process sometimes called retrodiction. Here the argument takes the basic form:

(1) B has occurred, exists, etc.
(2) A, if it existed, would explain B, in virtue of some known or plausibly inferred mechanism M.
(3) There are no plausible alternatives to A, so far as we know.
(4) Therefore B was probably caused by A.

The discovery of viruses took basically this form: they were initially postulated on a causal criterion, and subsequently rendered observable.

It will, I think, be clear that this degree of precision is not to be expected in the social sciences. First, as we have seen, entities picked out by the basic concepts of the social sciences are not observable; these concepts are necessarily theoretical. But these concepts are theoretical in a second and more important sense: the entities which they pick out are in a sense second-order entities; they are structures which govern and in turn are reproduced by human action. This is the residual truth of social scientific individualism: the thesis that the ultimate objects of these sciences are human individuals and their actions. This thesis needs, in my view, to be very heavily qualified, as I shall show in a moment. First, however, I need to specify what I take to be involved in a realist account of the social sciences.

It is helpful to distinguish realism about theories from realism about entities (Hacking, 1983, p. 27). The most adequate formulation of the first thesis is that theories are attempts to describe and explain a reality which exists independently of them; they are to be judged by their success in doing this. To put it a bit crudely, true theories state what is the case. A realism about entities simply asserts that some thing or things exist. Most often, of course, the two will go together: theories assert or imply the existence of entities, so the theory can only be true if the entities exist. Conversely, many entities are only 'known' via one or more theories; their existence as described depends upon the truth of the theory or theories. Often, however, one or the other will be in command. We may be strongly committed to a theory and yet doubtful about asserting the existence of an entity implied by the theory: this is often the case in physics. Conversely, we may strongly believe in the existence of an entity, such as the atom, but be unsure how to theorize its nature.

Now I want to argue that the entities denoted by the explanatory concepts of the social sciences (class, ideology, exploitation, social structure, etc.) are squarely in the former category. In other words, a term has no direct reference independently of the theory or theories which use it. The complicating feature in social theory is that it is tied to lay, folk or common-sense theories in a much more direct and intimate way than most advanced theorizing in the natural sciences. As sociologists like Simmel and Schutz rightly insisted, the theoretical constructs of the social sciences are second-order constructs, built on the constructs in play in social life itself. Human beings are thinking animals; their social relations presuppose that they have some conception of these relations. Even behaviourist theories do not so much deny this as brush it aside as irrelevant (at the cost of being able to give any coherent account of, for example, the use of language). Social scientific concepts are therefore theoretical at two levels: first, like the concepts of the natural sciences, at the level of scientific practice, and secondly, at the level of the actors' own theories of what they are doing.

The distinction between theoretical and observational terms, concepts, entities, etc. was fetishized in empiricist philosophies of science, and it is not my intention to perpetuate this fetishism. From a realist point of view, empiricists were mistaken in their search for a pure observational language and their suspicion of unobservable, 'theoretical' entities. But the adoption of a realist philosophy of science does not license a realism about any particular entity postulated within science. And in the social world, a realist conception of theory has to take account of the particular mode of being of social facts, their ontological dependence on human actions and on human conception of their actions. This means that the understanding of a form of life has to take the place of the operations of experiment and measurement which give us our grasp on the entities described by natural science. The upshot is that a realism about social scientific theories cannot rely on a simple-minded realism about determinate entities. It must take its stand on the explanatory power of the theories themselves.

Some writers have pushed this thesis further than I would wish to do. Pierre Bourdieu, for example has argued that any 'scientific investigation' needs to be prefaced by the conventionalist qualification 'Everything happens as if . . . ' (1977, p. 209, n. 49). From a rather different standpoint, that of Critical Theory, Norman Stockman has attacked

> the realist assumption that the theoretical concepts of the social sciences refer to 'theoretical entities' in the same way as those of the natural sciences. But the reflexivity of ordinary language, to which the concepts of the social sciences are indissolubly bound, precludes the formulation of unambiguous demonstrative and recognitive criteria for the referents of theoretical concepts.
>
> (1983, p. 217)

In my view, which I cannot defend in detail here, this is to put the difference rather too strongly. Once we recognize the distinctiveness of theorizing in the social sciences, grounded in the nature of their subject-matter, we can see that they have after all developed a number of theoretical and explanatory frameworks of considerable value, based on a provisional but quite wide-ranging understanding of social structures and mechanisms. The ontological dependence of these structures on the action of individual human beings does not mean that our explanations can only be formulated at the level of individual action. This can be illustrated in terms of the realist notion of causal powers: many of the powers of human individuals cannot be understood except in terms of the social structures in which they participate. I can pick my nose all by myself, but I cannot make a telephone call, draw a cheque, confer a degree or declare war alone. Similarly, my reasons for writing a cheque are not the same as the reasons for the existence of a banking system.

Let me briefly fill out this conception by means of a critical discussion of the reductionist programme known as 'methodological individualism', the claim that basic or 'rock-bottom' social explanations must be in terms of individual action. This principle, as we have seen, plays an important part in micro-economic theory, in Weberian sociology and in more recent phenomenological and ethnomethodological research programmes in sociology and social psychology. What these programmes do, in essence, is to confuse an aspect of a complex process, and in particular the means by which it is accomplished, with the process as a whole. A currency exchange rate, for example, in a floating market system, is the product of a mass of individual transactions, performed by actors ranging from central banks to individual persons. Now it is trivially true that the action of, say, the Bank of England in purchasing sterling to support the exchange rate is accomplished by some authorized individual sending a telex or making a phone call, but this is of no practical relevance to an explanation of the Bank's action. Only a fetishism of the immediately observable would lead us to say that this is 'where the action is'.

The more interesting cases are where we do find it useful to unpack a complex social process and to look at individual decisions. Take the example of class, ethnic or gender discrimination in employment. Once we have identified a global imbalance in the recruitment of women or ethnic minorities to certain jobs, we will want to know how this process works. Again, it is trivially true that it takes the form of decisions by employers to hire or not hire (or fire or not fire) particular individuals or categories of individuals. But how far these decisions *explain* the process will depend crucially on a more general feature of the situation, namely whether the employers discriminate, either *ad hoc* or as a matter of principle, between equally qualified candidates (and if so, whether on the basis of their own prejudices or those which they impute to their other workers, their customers, etc.), or whether the social distribution of qualifications is such that they are rarely confronted with a direct choice between equally qualified middle-class and working-class, black and white, male and female candidates. In the latter situation the explanation of the class, ethnic or gender imbalance will have to be sought further back, in the structure of educational systems and so forth. In other words, the extent to which a focus on individual action and decision contributes to an explanation will depend on structural features of the situation. It will also depend of course on the nature of our intellectual interest; some sociologists choose to specialize in the study of small-scale processes, either in general or in a particular case, while others are more interested in 'macro' studies. It should be clear, however, that there is no basis here for opting in all cases for a micro or a macro approach. The nature of the object should determine the most appropriate methods of investigation.

This argument about levels of explanation can also be applied to the 'classic dispute' between partisans of 'explanation' and 'understanding'. The pursuit of natural laws of society, formalized in the law–explanation orthodoxy, held up to sociology and the other social sciences an unrealistic ideal of the nature of scientific theory and explanation. Social scientists who accepted it were led to misunderstand their own practice and that of classical social theory. At the same time, the orthodox position generated an oppositional movement, equally one-sided in its preferred alternatives of idiographic explanation, understanding and description. By abandoning the law–explanation orthodoxy, we can come to a more adequate awareness of the place of description, hermeneutic understanding and also explanation in sociology and the other social sciences.

References and Further Reading

Benton, T. (1977), *Philosophical Foundations of the Three Sociologies* (London: Routledge & Kegan Paul).
Berelson, B. and Steiner, G. A. (1964), *Human Behaviour: An Inventory of Findings* (New York: Harcourt, Brace and World).
Bhaskar, R. (1978), *A Realist Theory of Science 2nd edn* (Brighton: Harvester).
Bhaskar R. (1979), *The Possibility of Naturalism* (Brighton: Harvester).
Bourdieu, P. (1977), *Outline of a Theory of Practice* (Cambridge: Cambridge University Press).
Brown, R. (1963), *Explanation in Social Science* (London: Routledge & Kegan Paul).
Brown, R. (1973), *Rules and Laws in Sociology* (London: Routledge & Kegan Paul).
Brown, R. (1984), *The Nature of Social Laws: Machiavelli to Mill* (Cambridge: Cambridge University Press).
Cartwright, N. (1983), *How the Laws of Physics Lie* (Oxford: Clarendon Press).
Edgley, R. (1983), 'Dialectic' in T. Bottomore (ed.), *A Dictionary of Marxist Thought* (Oxford: Blackwell).
Gardiner, P. (ed.) (1959), *Theories of History* (New York: Free Press).

Hacking, I. (1983), *Representing and Intervening* (Cambridge: Cambridge University Press).

Hempel, C. G. (1965), *Aspects of Scientific Explanation* (New York: Free Press).

Hollis, M. (1977), *Models of Man* (Cambridge: Cambridge University Press).

Keat, R. and Urry, J. (1975), *Social Theory as Science* (London: Routledge & Kegan Paul).

Kuhn, T. (1962), *The Structure of Scientific Revolutions* (Chicago, Ill.: University of Chicago Press).

Marx, K. (1975a), *The Poverty of Philosophy* (Moscow: Progress).

Marx, K. (1975b), *Early Writings* (Harmondsworth: Penguin).

Menger, C. (1963), *Problems of Economics and Sociology* (Champagne, Ill.: University Press).

Outhwaite, R. W. (1975), *Understanding Social Life* (Lewes: Jean Stroud).

Outhwaite, R. W. (1983), 'Toward a Realist Perspective' in G. Morgan (ed.), *Beyond Method* (Beverly Hills, Calif.: Sage).

Parsons, T. (1968), *The Structure of Social Action* (New York: Free Press).

Ryan, A. (ed.), (1973), *The Philosophy of Social Explanation* (Oxford: Oxford University Press).

Sayer, D. (1979), *Marx's Method* (Brighton: Harvester).

Stockman, N. (1983), *Antipositivist Theories of the Sciences* (Dordrecht: Reidel).

Winch, P. (1958), *The Idea of a Social Science* (London: Routledge & Kegan Paul).

Chapter 7

The Meaning and Use of Official Statistics in the Explanation of Deviance

PETER EGLIN

Introduction: a Short History of the Dispute

In 1963, Kitsuse and Cicourel published 'A Note on the Uses of Official Statistics', an article which in retrospect can be seen as the beginning of what has become a classic dispute in sociology. They argued that contemporary theoretical and methodological problems in the sociology of deviance arose 'as a consequence of the failure to distinguish between the social conduct which produces a *unit* of behavior (the behavior-producing processes) and organizational activity which produces a unit in the rate of *deviant* behavior (the rate-producing processes)' (p. 132).

It is perfectly proper to seek a sociological theory explaining why some social groups commit more deviant acts than others. But it would be wrong to suppose that such a theory would explain the social distribution of rates of officially recorded deviance, for such official records are 'produced by *the actions taken by persons in the social system* which define, classify and record certain behaviors as deviant' (p. 135). The problem is, say the authors, that the bulk of extant studies take their data from official statistics on the assumption that statistics are records of units of behaviour reflective of the 'behavior-producing processes', more or less ignoring the extent to which the figures are units of deviant behaviour reflective of the organizational activity of unofficial and official personnel (the public, police, coroners, etc.). They conclude by recommending that future studies address the questions: 'what forms of behavior are organizationally defined as deviant, and how are they classified, recorded and treated by persons in society?' (p. 139).

The call was taken up initially, and most prominently, in an article on 'normal crimes' by Sudnow (1965) and in books by Douglas (1967) on suicide and Cicourel (1968) himself on juvenile delinquency. In place of the traditional questions of what causes variation in the social distribution of crime, suicide and delinquency, these studies addressed the topics of how court systems define and classify offences (Sudnow), how deaths are certified and registered as suicide (Douglas) and how juveniles become processed as one or other type of delinquent. That is, they either recommended or carried out studies of the *organizational activities of officials*, namely 'plea-bargaining' by lawyers (Sudnow), death inquiries by coroners (Douglas) and decision-making by the police, probation officers and judges of the juvenile justice system (Cicourel). While Douglas set out the argument in detail and illustrated it with historical and contemporary examples, Sudnow and Cicourel provided detailed case studies in support of the claim that official statistics of deviance are hopelessly flawed as measures of some purported 'true' or 'real' volume of crime or suicide since their meaning is inseparable from the defining, sorting, recording and classifying activities of the officials who 'create' them.

The initial reaction to these works was meagre. Few of the major journals reviewed the two books. But in 1973 Hindess addressed them directly in his *The Use of Official Statistics in Sociology*, to which Cicourel replied in the new introduction to the otherwise unchanged 1976 edition of his 1968 book. Meanwhile the dispute had surfaced in a debate between Atkinson (1973) and Bagley (1972, 1974) in the journal *Sociology* over the meaning of suicide statistics, while in 1975 the whole dispute was given its own textbook treatment in an Open University Social Science Statistical Sources Unit on *Suicide and Crime* by Cresswell. It was reviewed again in a chapter by Miles and Irvine (1979) in *Demystifying Social Statistics*, in the course of book-length studies of suicide by Atkinson (1978) and Taylor (1982), and in the report of an empirical study devoted to *Understanding Crime Rates* by Bottomley and Coleman (1981). Apart from these signal contributions, from about 1971 the dispute came to occupy a chapter or chapter section in textbooks on deviance (e.g., Box, 1971), especially those in criminology (e.g., Bottomley, 1973). In writings setting out the virtues of one or another theoretical position it became a favourite vehicle for argument. As for empirical studies it had become clear by at least 1980 that over the period since 1963 two quite divergent research strategies had been adopted towards the dispute. An 'externalist' strategy seeking a traditional structural theory of deviance causation transformed the organizational processes revealed by the likes of Douglas and Cicourel into additional 'variables' needing to be controlled for in studies based on official statistics. In contrast an 'internalist' strategy produced a welter of ethnographic studies of official decision-making, particularly that of the police (e.g., Black, 1970), but extending to official records of non-deviant phenomena such as those of medicine. At least three different emphases can be discerned in these works. One preserves the symbolic interactionist focus on the relationship of organizational process, deviant definition and official statistics, and extends it to, for example, the use of official statistics in the construction of social problems. A second develops the ethnomethodological interest in how any particular instance of a deviant phenomenon is identified as such, and in the methods of reasoning informing that identification. A third returns to a typically Marxist concern with the structural sources of the definitions employed by organizational personnel in making the decisions reflected in the official figures.

Rather than going on to provide a more detailed historical account of the twists and turns of the dispute over the last twenty-odd years, in what follows I will attempt to sketch out the arguments more clearly, if more abstractly, and to relate them to the sociological perspectives (Cuff and Payne, 1984) or sociological 'games' (Anderson *et al.*, 1985) in which they have their life and being. To put some flesh on the abstract bones of the discussion I begin, however, with some facts and figures about suicide.

An Initial Example: Suicide

In 1963 in the Canadian province of Ontario twenty young people from 15 to 19 years of age committed suicide. Of these, 15 were boys, 5 were girls. More recently, in 1980, 83 persons of this age group committed suicide. This time 65 of them were boys, 18 were girls. The 1980 combined figure for boys and girls is over four times higher than that of 1963. For one fifteen-year period between the early 1960s and the early 1980s, in Canada as a whole, the number of suicides of older teenagers rose fivefold, leading the country's major newspaper *The Globe and Mail* to print a front-page story on 16 June 1982 with the headline 'Suicides by Teens up by 400%'. (A fivefold increase is the same as one of 400 per cent.)

In comparison, in England and Wales in 1963, 93 persons aged from 15 to 19 years committed suicide, 61 of them boys, 32 girls. In 1980, 123 persons of this age group committed suicide, 84 of them boys, 39 of them were girls. The increase is about 32 per cent. There were no headlines.

Now the reader with or without a pass in the 'O' level General Paper will point out that the figures for Canada and for England and Wales are not really comparable because the populations of the two countries are different, Canada having twenty-odd million people, England and Wales more than twice as many. And without knowing the precise figures it is a good bet that the proportional difference is about the same for the two countries' 15–19 year age groups. Moreover, from 1963 to 1980 the population of young people has surely increased in Ontario, in Canada and in England and Wales. Therefore the figures from one year to the other are not strictly comparable. How are we to know, then, whether there is really more (older) teenage suicide in 1980 than in 1963, or more in one country than in another?

The suicide *rate* is a simple statistic which represents the actual number of suicides in any year as a proportion of the population in that year. The resulting fraction is then multiplied by some constant (one million in the UK, 100,000 in Canada) to give a manageable number. In what follows, rates for each country will be expressed as 'per 100,000'. If we are interested in the rate for a particular age group, then it is best to calculate the rate as a proportion of the population in that age group. Thus,

$$\text{SR (15–19)} = \frac{\text{SN (15–19)}}{\text{P (15–19)}} \times 100{,}000$$

where 'SR (15–19)' means the suicide rate for the 15–19 year age group, 'SN (15–19)' means the number of suicides in that age group, and 'P (15–19)' means the population of persons aged 15–19 years. Thus, the suicide *rate* among the older teenagers in Ontario in 1963 was 4 per 100,000 or 4/100,000 or simply 4. In 1980 the rate was 9.8. The increase in rate is almost 2½ times (not half so dramatic as the fourfold increase in the raw numbers). In England and Wales the suicide rate for the 15–19 age group was 2.6 in 1963 and 3.0 in 1980 (and 2.7 in 1984, the latest year for which figures are available). The 'suicide rate' allows us, then, to make statistically meaningful comparisons from one time to another and from one place to another.

The reader can be forgiven for wondering why an essay bearing this one's title should now become something that looks suspiciously like the bluffer's guide to epidemiology. The reason is this. While there are many sociologists for whom the above represents a perfectly legitimate way of starting to determine what patterns of variation there might be in the social distribution of some phenomenon such as suicide or crime – say across different time periods, countries, age groups, genders and so on – with a view to explaining what causes the patterns to vary as they do, there are many other sociologists who would dispute every claim contained in the above, starting with that asserted in the first sentence, and embracing the procedure of inquiry itself, its theoretical goals and the methodological assumptions upon which it rests. While the dispute is grounded in fundamental differences of sociological perspective between 'externalists' and 'internalists' (Anderson *et al.*, 1985), differences that run through the whole of sociology, in the field of deviance it is expressed most characteristically in the question of the meaning and use of official statistics. *Who says* 20 older teenagers in Ontario committed suicide in 1963 (or 110 in England and Wales in 1984)? *How do they know?* These are the critic's initial questions. Every claim in the opening discussion should be prefaced with 'according to official statistics'. The whole should be accompanied by a description of how and for what purpose the statistics were collected. Only with that in hand can it be said what any particular numerical claim *means* and what *use* the sociologist may put it to.

Defenders of the sociological use of official statistics are not likely to disagree with these correctives. Indeed virtually every sociological article based on the analysis of official statistics incorporates a (brief) discussion of their method of collection leading to a statement of their 'relative reliability'. Typically authors find and claim that with the appropriate methodological strategy and care in interpretation the figures can be used as a measure of the 'real' amount (prevalence or incidence) of the phenomenon in question. Critics, however, are likely to reply that it is not possible to separate the statistics from their method of collection, that the two are hopelessly confounded, so that the figures tell us as much about the decision-making of the officials who determine whether a given death is a suicide or a particular action is a crime as they do about the occurrence of those events 'in themselves'. Clearly, the two positions have sharply different implications for further inquiry. With confidence in the statistics the researcher can discover that, say, males commit suicide about three times more frequently than females, or that young, working-class, urban, black males commit more crimes than any other comparable social group. The task then becomes one of constructing a theory, typically a social-structural one, to explain what causes these patterned variations in the distribution of deviance. But the critic is likely to turn to investigating not the characteristics of the social position of the group with high (or low) suicide or crime rates but the activities of the officials whose task it is to detect, report, record, classify and count each instance as, say, a suicide or accident, or as a type of crime. The one sociologist is looking for anomie or alienation in the structure of society, the other is seeking for organized practices in the decision-making of coroners and police officers.

The Dispute in Detail

THE RELIABILITY QUESTION

The dispute over the meaning and use of official statistics in studies of deviance has turned principally on the issues of the reliability and validity of the statistics as measures: how well do the official suicide and crime rates correspond to the real prevalence and incidence of these phenomena in society? A measure's reliability is the degree to which it gives the same reading when being used to measure the same phenomenon or object at different times or by different observers. For example, the reliability of litmus paper as a measure of the presence or absence of acid depends on it changing to the right colour every time it is exposed to acid, no matter who is doing the experiment nor under what conditions (subject to known limits). Similarly the reliability of an official suicide rate is given by the degree to which the procedures for calculating it produce the same results when applied to the same deaths by different observers or under different conditions (subject to known limits). More concretely, when faced with the same death would two coroners 'measure' (classify) it as the same type of death, whether suicide, accident, homicide or 'open'? And if they would not, can we specify the conditions under which the variation would take place? How strong a 'yes' can be given to either of these questions will then indicate how reliable the rate is.

A standard starting point for criticizing the reliability of official statistics is provided by the 'funnel-and-sieve' metaphor for the operation of the criminal justice system. At the open top of the funnel are poured in all putative criminal acts. As they fall through the funnel they encounter a series of sieves which filter out certain of them until a much reduced number emerge at the narrow end. The sieves represent stages in the process. The first is the screening judgements of the public itself, not all perceived offences being reported to the police. For example, the so-called victimless crimes such as soliciting for prostitution or illegal gambling are not typically subject to being reported to the police since the 'victims' are the consumers of the service. In stark contrast, victims of rape or sexual assault may not report the offence to the police for fear of reprisals, humiliation or of simply being disbelieved. Other victims, say of theft, may feel the loss too insignificant to be worth reporting, may think it unlikely the police will catch the offender, or, in the case of department stores and other companies, simply accept a certain percentage loss to employee theft as a business cost which will be passed on to the consumer in the price of the product. An unknown proportion of 'offences' will, then, never reach the police. Of those that do a further proportion will be filtered out by the sieve representing the complex array of decisions made by the police as to whether to make an arrest, lay a charge, record the offence or 'unfound' it. For example, a recent Canadian study found up to one-third of reported rapes were 'unfounded' by police, that is, were treated and regarded by them on the basis of preliminary investigation as not having happened.

And again, as I write, the annual crime statistics published by the British Home Office are being reported on the news with emphasis on the 30 per cent increase since last year in the number of rapes. But in news interviews the commissioner of the Metropolitan London police, Kenneth Newman, is saying the rise is almost entirely the result of a change in the police *recording* procedure: the police now record as *real* offences incidents reported by women which in previous years the police would have 'unfounded', that is, more or less not believed had happened. (The apparent similarity between British and Canadian police recording practice in rape cases is itself an interesting phenomenon!)

Further sieves represent the judicial decisions to prosecute (or dismiss), plea-bargain, go to trial, convict and sentence. Of the large numbers entering the mouth of the funnel only a very few drop out of the bottom into prison. That the 'lost' cases are so numerous, and that they represent an unknown proportion of the initial collection of putative criminal acts, are the points raised in criticism of the reliability of official crime statistics by their detractors.

In defending their use, supporters argue that the mere size of the 'dark number' of unreported or unrecorded crimes is not a problem. After all, the absolute number of offences is usually not of interest. The standard research questions are comparative ones: are there more offences than there were twenty years ago, or in the USA than in Canada, or among working-class youth than among middle-class youth? The issue is one of 'relative reliability'. As long as the amount of 'error' can be reliably estimated the figures retain their utility. The second charge, that the size of that error is unknown, is then more serious. But that too can be answered. The characteristic response is that the proportion may be unknown but is not unknowable. Other sources of data can be pulled in. Rather than relying solely on 'crimes known to the police' one can ask offenders and victims directly. Since the late 1960s, the self-report and victimization surveys have become a standard part of 'externalist' research strategy in criminology. They have tended to show much higher rates of crime and delinquency than are evident in official statistics and a more even spread across the population. Thus, for example, on the basis of such studies it has been argued that middle-class delinquency is as prevalent as working- or lower-class delinquency, but subject to lower rates of arrest and criminal prosecution. This is consistent with Cicourel's ethnographic findings that police tend to prefer the 'criminal' route when dealing with lower-class delinquents and the 'therapeutic' route with those of middle-class origin. The latter are perceived as having stronger family resources for keeping the youth out of trouble whereas for the former the court and juvenile penal institutions are chosen to act as substitute parents. By thus controlling for what some would conceptualize as 'police bias' these more direct forms of measurement permit an estimate of error to be made for the reliability of official delinquency statistics and thus allow their continued use. Similarly, community mental health surveys increase the reliability of official mental health statistics, and from similar means suicide researchers are able to say with some confidence that official suicide statistics underestimate the 'true' rate by about half.

The question remains, however, whether an error estimate calculated for some set of, say, national statistics in some given year will be generalizable to other times or other places. Criticism of the reliability of official suicide statistics has here been particularly strong. Douglas, in particular, has documented many nineteenth-century cases in which, for example, a change from sacred to secular authorities responsible for death certification has led to a sudden increase in official suicide rates. Lower official rates of suicide in Catholic than in Protestant countries and in rural than in urban areas have been argued to follow from higher rates of concealment in more 'integrated' communities. Scotland's official rate is lower than England's, it is said, because of the former's procurator-fiscal system of death certification. Difference in method of death registration is also said to account for the variation in suicide rate among the otherwise similar Scandinavian countries. San Francisco's high official suicide rate has been associated with its very high autopsy rate for coroners' cases. Alberta's suicide rate jumped in the late 1970s in response to the change from a coroners' to a medical examiners' system of death certification. In his autobiography a former Metropolitan Toronto Chief Coroner writes:

> Prior to 1963 it had been the practice in Ontario to conceal suicides 'for the family's sake' and so the rule had been laid down that unless an actual suicide note was found, accident or natural causes was put on the death certificate. I reversed this ruling and from 1963 on, accurate statistics were kept. This resulted in an immediate apparent dramatic jump in the number of suicides...
>
> (Shulman, 1976, p. 141)

Indeed, the Ontario official suicide rate, which from 1950 to 1964 was stable at between 8 and 9 per 100,000, started to rise steadily in 1965, not levelling off until the early 1970s at 13 to 14. But it is difficult to attribute this to Coroner Shulman's ruling since the same pattern occurred in the aggregate rate for the country as a whole (unless, of course, coroners in the other Canadian provinces followed Ontario's example). In England and Wales between 1957 and 1975 the official suicide rate declined from 11.8 to 7.5 with the exception of a marked rise from 1961 to 1962 (and three smaller ones in other years); domestic gas was detoxified during this period, while in 1961 suicide was decriminalized in the United Kingdom.

But again the 'externalist' research strategy is evident in researchers' responses to this sort of criticism. Particularly in the work of British researchers since 1968, numerous attempts have been made to control for the effects of the sort of confounding 'variables' discussed by critics. Since most of these researchers are not sociologists but psychologists, psychiatrists and epidemiologists the bulk of this work has appeared in a variety of medical and epidemiological sources such as the *British Journal of Psychiatry*. A useful review is Sainsbury (1983). Sainsbury himself controlled for the effect of different national methods of death certification by comparing the rank order of suicide rates for immigrant groups in the United States with the order of rates for the groups' countries of origin. Since the United States was assumed to have a uniform system of death registration any difference in the rates attributable to variations in such procedures in the countries of origin should, other things being equal, disappear in the groups' rates in the United States. The rank order was, however, not significantly different. Sainsbury therefore concluded that the official statistics in question were reliable and that the national differences reflected 'real' differences in suicide rate. Similarly the purported effect of different coroners on suicide rates was tested by comparing changes in suicide rate over a given period in districts where the coroner had changed with those in which s/he remained the same. Again a finding of no significant difference prompted the conclusion that the official figures were a reliable measure of the 'true' rate. Related studies have reached similar conclusions in the cases of the difference between Scotland and England and Wales, and among Denmark, England and Wales, and Ireland. Since one of the critical arguments turns on claimed variation in countries' rates of concealment, suicide researchers have adopted the practice of adding to a country's official suicide figures those deaths classified as 'open' or 'undetermined' and in some cases those attributed to certain of the categories of 'accident' most easily associated with suicide, such as 'self-poisoning'. The assumption is that some suicides are 'concealed' by being classified in these other ways. The standard finding is that taking these modes of death into account does not tend to alter countries' relative ranking in terms of suicide rate. For example, the authors of a recent study comparing suicide in Ireland, England and Wales, and Denmark conclude as follows:

> Because combined death rates for suicide, undetermined and accidental deaths do not remove the differences between countries it is suggested that the Danish suicide death rate reflects a genuinely higher rate of suicide in that country.
>
> (Walsh *et al.*, 1984, p. 472)

As for the claim that changes over time are an artefact of legal and administrative changes bearing on death certification, Jennings and Barraclough (1980) find from a review of such changes in England and Wales this century that none, including the 1961 decriminalization, can explain the 'large observed fluctuation in the suicide rate'. Finally, much stock has been placed in the finding by Brugha and Walsh (1978) that the rate of under-recording (they say 'under-reporting') of suicide by coroners in Dublin in 1900–4 was the same as in 1964–8. That is, if the rate of under-recording is temporally constant then a reliable estimate of error can be calculated and the reliability of the official statistics be preserved.

It is possible to continue the dispute by pointing to additional 'factors' that bring into question the assumption of temporal constancy of under-recording, but as long as the battle is fought over reliability it remains on ground that is favourable to the 'externalist' position. It is always possible to handle inaccuracy or inconsistency in the application of the rules for measuring (classifying) cases by assuming that most error is random, by controlling for sources of systematic variation, and by taking refuge in the very stability of the rates themselves. The dispute becomes more pointed, however, over the question of validity; it is to this I now turn.

THE VALIDITY QUESTION

It could be said that the argument over the reliability of official statistics of deviance makes sense only so long as it is presupposed that they are in principle a 'true' measure of the phenomenon in question. It would not seem to be of much use to have great confidence in the reliability of the procedure for categorizing and counting cases if one was not sure what they were cases of. Thus all the coroners in the world could agree on the rules for classifying deaths and could apply the rules consistently so that the same (type of) case was always classified in the same category, and yet if the rules did not properly distinguish the true cases of suicide from the accidents, homicides and natural deaths, then the resulting tallies and rates would be uninterpretable. One would not know whether they were true counts of suicide or of some combination of suicides and other types of death. Moreover, some of the true cases might not be covered by the rules and so be left out of the count. The question of whether a measuring procedure isolates all and only those cases of the phenomenon is called the problem of (measurement) validity. It can be taken to have two aspects: one concerns the definition of the category in question, what I have been calling the 'rules', while the second concerns the operational procedure for fitting the definition (or rules) to the cases. Thus 'suicide' may be defined as 'self-inflicted death in which the victim intended to die'. The definition comprises two rules, namely (1) that the victim be the agent of his/her death, and (2) that intent be present. The 'operational procedure' would then comprise the methods by which, in any particular case, the 'facts' of self-inflicted mortal injury and intent to die are established.

It is over the question of validity that the debate about the meaning and use of official statistics begins to touch fundamental issues which divide sociologists and to reveal quite sharp differences in resulting research strategies. But before these matters can be dealt with it is necessary to consider briefly a related topic that arises at this point. This concerns the relationship between the sociologist's definition of the category of deviance in question and the definition employed by the officials categorizing and classifying cases as part of their work.

It is likely to be the case, and according to a quite orthodox model of sociological method *ought* to be the case, that the categories of behaviour being studied by the sociologist are *theoretically* derived. Thus, from his theory of suicide Durkheim (1952) deduced four types, namely egoistic, altruistic, anomic and fatalistic suicide. Each is defined in terms of the degree of integration or regulation characterizing it, these characteristics being theoretically derived. Moreover, Durkheim's definition of suicide is his own: it comprises deaths which are (1) self-inflicted, in which (2) the victim *knows* the normal result of his or her action with certainty. The problem is, however, that neither Durkheim's definition of suicide nor the types he isolated were employed by the officials categorizing the deaths which he took for his data. 'Intent' rather than 'knowledge' was the officials' criterion (Douglas, 1967, p. 379) and categories such as 'egoistic' and the rest were not to be found on any form of death certificate. Similarly, Merton's (1938) four categories of *deviant* adaptation to the disjuncture between culturally prescribed goals and socially institutionalized means, namely 'innovation', 'ritualism', 'retreatism' and 'rebellion', are not to be found as categories in the criminal law nor (in any simple way) in official classifications of mental disorder. Thus there is no simple match of official crime or mental illness statistics and Merton's categories of deviant behaviour (Kitsuse and Cicourel, 1963). The same case can be argued for such sociological categories as 'white-collar crime', 'systematic check forgery' and 'official deviance'. The categories of both the criminal law, for example, fraud and forgery, and civil law, for example, 'restrictive trading practices' are defined on a different basis. (Though it must be said that this is not always the case: the sociological categories of 'consensus crime' and 'conflict crime' are defined on the same basis as the legal categories of 'crimes that are *mala en se*' and 'crimes that are *mala prohibita*'.)

The question of the relationship of observers' (here sociologists') categories and actors' (here officials') categories is a fundamental one in social science and is discussed as such in Chapter 6. Since the issues raised by the problem of the validity of official statistics do not turn on it in this form, I will not discuss it further here. Suffice it to say that sociologists in this predicament employ a variety of strategies – from ignoring it at one extreme, through employing some translation procedure (such as adding on the 'open' and 'accident' verdicts to get a 'true' count of 'suicide'), to simply asserting the identity of observer and actor categories by 'methodological fiat' at the other extreme – in order to effect a *de facto* correspondence of the two. However this issue is resolved, the problem of validity still remains. It is now appropriate to specify what that entails.

The question is whether a given official statistic, such as a crime rate or a suicide rate, is a *true* measure or representation of the prevalence of the deviant phenomenon, that is of the actual crimes or suicides, being studied. I have said the question has two dimensions, that of the definition of the category, and that of the operational procedure fitting the definition to the cases. The matter of definition itself has two sides. (This distinction crosscuts the two 'rules' that make up the definition.) The first concerns the external boundary the definition draws between the defined category and those categories bordering it. The second relates to the internal configuration of the category: do the rules comprising the definition specify a set of properties that are in fact shared by the cases to which the category is intended to apply?

One part of Douglas's critique of sociologists' use of official suicide statistics turns on the argument of cultural variation in the definition of suicide, where what is being referred to is the question of where the boundary is drawn between suicide and other forms of death such as homicide or accident. The clearest cases pertain to the (first) rule about suicide being self-inflicted death, and come from contrasts between cultures that are relatively far apart. In that form of Japanese ritual death known as *seppuku* the central figure disembowels himself (*hara-kiri*), but death is 'hastened' by the action of the second who decapitates him with a sword. The point here is *not* that for the European concept of suicide-as-self-killing there is a problem of whether this is suicide or homicide (indeed execution), but that the Japanese classification of modes of death does not match the European one; the boundaries are not being drawn in the same places. Similarly the practice among the Inuit of Canada of what is most readily translated as 'assisted death', in which an old person is helped to kill himself or herself, say, by shooting, overlaps the boundary between the Western concepts of suicide and homicide. The question of who pulled the trigger, which is crucial for categorizing the event in Western terms, may be immaterial to the Inuit concept of this as a type of death. Where, then, there is cultural variation in classifying modes of death, comparing 'suicide' rates becomes problematic.

Douglas had in mind, however, more subtle differences in the definition of suicide within Western (European) culture itself. Over the last two thousand years suicide has been regarded as an ecclesiastical sin, a moral offence, a criminal act, a rational act, an irrational act, a sign of mental illness. Moreover, in terms of the second rule, definitions have varied according to the relative importance attached to 'intent to die', 'knowledge of the likely consequences of one's acts', 'motivation to be dead' and so on (see Douglas, 1967, Appendix II). According to the selected definition such actions/events as martyrdom, or self-killing by the insane, may or may not be counted as suicide. If such definitions tend to vary by historical period then problems arise for the comparison of official suicide rates across time.

The issue becomes more critical when it is allowed that historical differences may, in a sense, be present in the variety of meanings suicide has at any particular point in time. Thus, though all cases in a given year may meet the prevailing criteria (say, self-inflicted death with intent to die), they may fall into different types such that we might begin to wonder whether they are all instances of the 'same thing'. For example, in what way is the act of Captain Oates, who walked out into the snow to die to save his colleagues on the beleaguered Scott expedition to the South Pole, the same as that of Marilyn Monroe who (let us assume here) killed herself with an overdose of drugs? In the case of Monroe it has been found relevant to investigate her entire biography for signs of that kind of trouble and unhappiness sufficient to cause the depression assumed to cause her death. Yet none of this, as far as I know, has been undertaken for Captain Oates, nor, even if it were done and were productive of similar findings, would we be inclined to see it as relevant to an understanding and indeed identification of what he did. The one action has become virtually a mythic exemplar of bravery, selflessness and courage, the other a sad case standardly described in terms of misery, confusion, self-destructiveness, unhappiness, drug and alcohol dependence, and so on. The suicides of religious ecstasy, of guilt and shame, of fear and trembling, of boredom, of defeat, of revenge, of intolerable loss, of political protest, of military action – while all may bear the title 'suicide', reflection leads one to doubt that all share the same set of defining properties, other than 'self-killing' and 'intent to die'. And 'intent' here clearly means different things in the different types of case. While there may be a set of 'family resemblances' (Wittgenstein) across the range of types this does not preclude the inclusion of actions of qualitatively different sorts. For the purposes of national mortality book-keeping the internal config- uration of the collection of suicides may be irrelevant, but it is hard to see how that could be true for sociological theorizing. One using as data the official suicide statistics – or, indeed, the official crime statistics, for the same argument can be made there – runs the risk of 'distinguishing what should be combined, or combining what should be distinguished, thus mistaking the real affinities of things, and accordingly misapprehending their nature' (Durkheim, 1952, p. 41).

The problems created by the external variability and internal 'open texture' of the definitions of suicide or crime for estab- lishing the validity of official statistics are exacerbated by variabil- ity in the procedures for 'operationalizing' the definition. For even where countries or historical periods share the same formal definition of the deviant act, the working procedures by which officials apply the formal definition to cases may *embody* different operational definitions of the act. If I am here returning to a consideration of such things as variation in death registration procedure already encountered in the discussion of reliability, it is nevertheless with a different point in mind. The reliability question entails that one interpret procedural differences as introducing 'error' into the measurement of what is presumed to be a (potentially) determinate population of real acts or events, a population that exists independently of the instrument used to measure it. In terms of validity, however, the argument is that differences in procedure embody differences in the very concept of the deviant act itself. Thus, for example, when Ontario's coroners started counting as suicides certain deaths where no suicide note was found they were not changing from a 'mistaken' to a 'correct' procedure for categorizing suicide but changing the definition of suicide itself. Thus, to a certain extent comparing official Ontario suicide rates before and after 1963 is to compare (slightly) different things. Similarly, to compare Canadian suicide rates with those of England and Wales is to compare slightly different things, for in England and Wales evidence sufficient for a suicide verdict must be 'beyond a reasonable doubt' (the criterion used in criminal law), whereas in Canada it need only tip 'the balance of probabilities' (the criterion standardly used in civil law).

Responding to the Validity Problem:
'Externalist' and 'Internalist' research strategies

While I have been discussing the difference between formal and operational definitions of deviant acts in relatively abstract terms, but with accompanying examples, for such things as crime and suicide, the difference is of course represented concretely in the co-existence of sets of formal rules or definitions such as the criminal code and sets of operational definitions such as those represented by the workings of the criminal justice system. In recognition of the validity problem researchers have set about investigating how the operational definitions embodied in judicial procedure or death registration procedure affect the interpretability of the official statistics. But the manner of these investigations and the interpretation of findings has varied significantly according to the fundamental research strategy adopted. To show this I will report briefly some of the 'factors' revealed by these studies of officials' operational definitions, then describe the contrasting lessons drawn from them.

Broadly speaking, officials such as police officers, lawyers and coroners 'operationalize' the definitions of the formal categories of the criminal law and the 'Coroners Act' against a background of

(1) culturally derived common-sense knowledge of criminal and suicidal types, of methods of operation, antecedent circumstances, motivation, location, time and occasion, and

(2) organizationally relevant 'demand characteristics' of their work, such as the time and resources at their disposal given the flow of cases, the occupational division of labour, the local political environment, the type of department, and so on.

(1) It has been argued, for example, that coroners and other officials perceive 'students' to be a particularly suicide-prone category of persons. The discipline required to study, the forgoing of earnings, being away from home, the anxiety engendered by both the anticipation and experience of examinations – these are the conventional sources of stress expressed in such headlines as 'Pressures Drive Students to Despair'. Clearly to the extent that coroners hold these views they derive less from professional expertise than from the 'general knowledge' coroners share with other members of society. Such views dispose decision-makers to locate the conditions considered antecedent to the intent to die more readily in students, than in non-students of the same age, sex, class and so on. Thus the 'operational definition' of the second 'rule' comprising the formal definition of suicide, namely 'intent to die', incorporates a 'bias' towards a certain category of persons, namely 'students'; and the same can be argued for the 'elderly', the 'mentally ill', 'the recently bereaved', 'the terminally ill' and so on. The possible source of invalidity is here compounded by the further possibility of a process of 'deviance amplification' whereby the official expectation of greater suicide risk among students becomes incorporated into students' own self-perception and leads them to commit suicide more often.

Again the 'externalist' response is to treat this 'suicide meaning' attached to 'students' as an additional variable, the possible biasing effects of which are to be controlled for. In this way a validity issue is treated as a reliability issue for which computing an appropriate error factor is taken to be the appropriate remedy; the integrity of the official statistics is thereby preserved.

(2) In the United States, for example, it appears to make a difference to the interpretation and disposition of 'incidents' involving 'juveniles' whether the local police department has a juvenile bureau or not. Where not, police officers are likely, other things being equal, to handle many such incidents informally on the street with no record being made. But in departments with juvenile officers regular police officers are likely to report incidents to them whereupon the incidents are investigated. This might entail a visit to the juvenile's home to interview the parents, or to the school to talk to the headmaster or principal; since this counts as work for the juvenile officer it will almost certainly entail the making of a record. Whether or not prosecution ensues or, from the point of view of the juvenile officer, the matter is disposed of informally, an 'offence' is recorded, a file is opened. Later, perhaps, more incidents occur such that after the fourth or fifth the juvenile receives a severer disposition than had been handed out to that point.

For a criminologist pursuing an externalist research strategy such findings constitute a recommendation to control for additional variables in future studies. To understand the varying delinquency statistics from one jurisdiction to another one must control for 'type of department' (i.e. ± juvenile bureau), and to understand the distribution of sentencing statistics for the 'same' juvenile offence one needs take account of 'prior record'. In this way in recent years criminologists have come to control a growing range of what are conceptualized as 'intervening variables' representing the operation of what are seen as 'sources of bias' in the operation of the criminal justice system and which thus affect the interpretation of the crime statistics. Reflecting standard conceptions of what is sociologically significant most effort has been devoted to isolating the effects of class (or socio-economic status), gender and race. Thus when studies reveal, for example, that when seriousness of offence and prior record are controlled females receive lighter sentences than males for the 'same offence', it is taken as indicating discrimination in the 'operational' application of the formal categories of the law.

In contrast, those pursuing an internalist research strategy read the significance of the (1) cultural and (2) organizational 'factors' revealed in studies of official decision-making quite differently.

Far from introducing sources of bias these are seen to constitute the very *means* by which officials (1) *identify* acts as deviant, as falling under the formal rules, and (2) provide *accountable* verdicts. They are the very stuff comprising the reality of suicides-and - crimes - for - all - practical-social–cultural–medical–legal–organizational purposes. While for the purposes of discussion I have separated cultural and organizational matters the hyphenated expression in the previous sentence is meant to indicate that they are in every particular case inseparable.

What is being meant here? There are three points:

(1) To say, for example, that 'coroners treat students as suicide-prone' is not to say that 'student' appears on a check-list of categories which provides the coroner with a score by which suicide is determined. Rather, to note in a particular case that the dead person is a student is to have one or more possible means of seeing that this *could be a real suicide*. It is not that the belief that students are suicide-prone introduces a 'bias' into coroners' decision-making and thus into the statistics, but rather that the conditions of student life provide one or more scenarios consistent with culturally informed notions of when, where, why and by whom suicides are performed; such conditions provide a means to 'see' that a suicide has in fact occurred.

Thus to the category 'student' are closely tied such activities as 'studying' and 'taking examinations' with both of which Western culture readily associates such social-psychological states as 'pressure' and 'stress' (through, say, fear of failure): and these are standardly seen as possible precursors of suicide. Whether or not it is true that in general 'students are suicide-prone', the employment of such an assumption in its scripted form permits the decision-maker to see that the remains before him or her could constitute a suicide. Moreover, such a reading of the remains as a particular case of 'pressures drive students to despair' is one that is recognizable to any other culturally competent member of society; it does not need to be specially justified; anybody can see that this is such a case as fits the bill; it thus provides the coroner with a defensible verdict.

A second illustration can be given more briefly. 'It's about five in the morning, you know, that suicides are most common', says Inspector Banner to Sherlock Holmes in a celebrated case. Via this assumption (together with that by which significance is attached to the method of death, here namely hanging) the inspector interprets the dead body before him as a good candidate for suicide – its estimated time of death was five in the morning. Again, the point is not that such beliefs introduce bias into the decision-making, but that they provide part of the means by which the death is seen to be a suicide in the first place. (For Conan Doyle, of course, this reasoning merely provides a foil for the display of the superior powers of Holmes who proceeds to show that the apparent suicide is 'in fact' a brilliant and diabolical murder. The 'extraordinary' nature of Holmes's deductions rests, nevertheless, on the mundane credibility of Banner's and our reasoning.)

(2) The meaning of any category or attribute such as 'student' or 'Black' or of any action such as 'shoplifting' or other form of stealing, or of any physical-cum-mental state such as 'under the influence of drugs', will not necessarily be the same from one case to another. For one gross example, some studies of sentencing decisions in American courts appear to show that in aggregate Blacks are not treated differently from Whites. But the aggregate picture conceals dual, if balancing, forms of discrimination, one in which Blacks are treated more punitively than Whites and one in which they are treated more leniently. In the one class of cases, so the argument goes, the offence is adjudged to be more serious because a Black committed it, whereas in the other class of cases the offence is perceived as less serious because a Black committed it. Again, my point is not to display official bias, arising here from racial discrimination, but to point out how the meaning of a person-category can change from one case to another and thus *constitute* those cases as of different gravity and therefore, in effect, as different offences. To return to the juvenile in trouble with the law, the keeping of a file on a person comprising a list of offences and other 'contacts' with the police, what the Americans call a 'rap sheet', provides a context for interpreting the 'meaning' or 'significance' of any subsequent 'incident'. Thus, stealing a small sum of money from a locker at school might on the first occasion be regarded as a prank, on a third or fourth occasion as a real theft indicating perhaps developing criminal intent or as 'attention-getting behaviour arising from trouble at home', and on the thirtieth occasion as, say, theft warranting 'habitual offender' status and portending a life of adult crime or as 'klepto-

mania' arising from a mental illness rather than criminal intent. The 'same' action thus may count as 'nothing', as '(not serious) theft', as '(very serious) theft' or as 'not-theft-but-a-symptom-of-insanity', these possibilities depending upon the position of the action in a sequence of such actions. Each will give rise to a different official record and will contribute to the counts of different categories of statistics. In carefully documenting such instances in the case of 'Audrey' and his other subjects, Cicourel (1968) was trying to show that rather than representing inaccuracy and inconsistency in the recording practices of official personnel such records and statistics are precisely the normal, natural product of the routine operation of the juvenile justice system.

(3) The interpretive possibilities provided by the categories describing persons, actions and social-psychological states are further articulated in terms of the organizational requirements for rendering a verdict. Thus, for example, what 'student' amounts to in terms of judicial procedures or those of a coroner's inquiry or inquest is what can be attested to in the form of available and admissible evidence, for example, a record of marks, a letter from the headteacher, the testimony of teachers and fellow students. And while such matters are constrained by formal legal rules the latter are subject to interpretation in the light of the local organizational culture. Studies of plea-bargaining are particularly illuminating here.

Sudnow's 1965 study, the first explicitly to follow the programme set out in Kitsuse and Cicourel (1963), provides classical examples of how public defenders assess the features of each case, such as where, how and by whom the offence was committed, so as to determine whether it matches the characteristics of offences that are 'normal' for that jurisdiction. In this way, as in points (1) and (2) above, they assess what 'sort' of an offence it is, where that assessment is critical both to whether or not defendants are encouraged to plead guilty to a reduced charge and to what that reduced charge will be. Thus, for example, child-molesting is routinely reduced to 'loitering around a schoolyard'. But whether in fact the defendant had loitered around a schoolyard is immaterial to the use of that charge. Rather the lesser charge draws a prison sentence sufficiently shorter than that for molesting to make it appealing to the defendant but nevertheless long enough to satisfy the court officials that the offender would 'receive his due'. What is relevant to the dispute over official statistics is both that the conviction statistics will register cases of loitering where none in fact took place, and that in terms of the operation of the criminal justice system no error is thereby involved.

More recent work by Maynard (1984) based on the close examination of tape-recordings of plea-bargaining sessions between attorneys in an American court system shows how (1) both public defender and district attorney use defendant attributes such as sex, age, marital status, number of children, religiosity, occupational status and ethnicity along with other features of the circumstances of the case to determine *what* offence, if any, took place, where, (2) the meaning of any attribute depends on its relationship to the collection of others and where (3) both these matters are assessed in terms of how the case would look in court, before a jury; where, too, that assessment trades on their knowledge of possible legal defences, local precedent, judges' preferences and the like. A case against a Spanish-speaking defendant may be dismissed not because of some bias for or against Mexican-Americans but because of the difficulties of pursuing a prosecution in court against someone who does not speak English.

Conclusion

I began by saying that the dispute over the meaning and use of official statistics in the sociological explanation of deviance started with the 1963 article by Kitsuse and Cicourel. They took issue with the way official statistics were being used in the sociology of deviance and in criminology, particularly in the school of anomie theory founded by Robert Merton (1938), despite the latter's awareness of the limited reliability of this form of data. Their article was part of the developing interactionist approach to deviance, an approach which focused attention both on the social processes of rule creation by which categories of deviance are defined, and especially on those of rule enforcement or application comprising the operational procedures by which organizational personnel routinely identify and process particular cases.

But it could be said that their article originated the dispute in a different sense, that is, by setting out the terms which made it possible or in which it was to be conducted. Thus by separating out the so-called 'behavior-producing processes' from the 'rate-producing processes' they provided a means of defining and assessing rival sociological positions. For those seeking a causal explanation of the behaviour-producing processes, that is, of those processes producing variation in the social distribution of (deviant) behaviour, it was mistaken to use official deviance statistics as their data without taking account of the rate-producing processes embodied in the way those statistical data were assembled by the organizations producing them. But their article did not make it illegitimate to seek a causal explanation of the behaviour-producing processes. Indeed it incorporated that as the third area comprising their (interactionist) programme for the study of deviance. What was illegitimate was the use of the official statistics of deviance for that purpose because the degree of unreliability and invalidity of the statistics was too great. The proper approach to an understanding of the rate-producing processes was through studying the defining and classifying activities and practices of organizational personnel.

The subsequent course of the dispute can be seen to have been conditioned by this original formulation of it. For this formulation contains an ambivalence, one visible in other parts of Cicourel's work (1964, 1968, 1976) and in Douglas's book (1967). Thus we have seen how externalists have responded to the critique by seeking ways to improve the reliability and validity of the official statistics through, for example, introducing additional sources of data as reliability checks and controlling for biasing variables. Kitsuse and Cicourel could not object to this, for if, as they state, it is proper to seek an explanation of (deviant) *behaviour* then it must be possible to identify that behaviour; and if ways can be found to improve the reliability and validity of the statistics as measures of that behaviour then their argument does not appear in principle to rule out doing that. In this way externalists can continue to treat official deviance statistics as they have done since the early nineteenth century, that is, as both 'errorful and essential' (Hagan, 1984, p. 36). However imperfect those data may be, they exist as measuring instruments independent of the behaviour they measure.

On the other hand we have seen how a characteristically internalist response to the validity problem leads to the position that the sociologist's identification of deviant behaviour cannot be separated from the rate-producing processes; that, indeed, the very decision-making practices that lie behind the production of the suicide and crime rates actually *constitute* the cases that make up the figures as instances of *deviant behaviour* in the first place. To put it more technically, the 'objects' being isolated, identified, classified and counted cannot be separated from the 'instruments' being used so to measure them. The idea of seeking a causal explanation of the behaviour-producing processes is then brought into question: the 'units of behaviour' theorized by externalists as resulting from the behaviour-producing processes are inseparable from, are conceptually tied to, are indeed constituted by the 'units of deviant behaviour' theorized by internalists as resulting from the rate-producing processes. This, too, is a lesson that can be drawn from Kitsuse and Cicourel.

At this point I must declare an interest. As an ethnomethodologist I come down in favour of the internalist position. I cannot see how the 'constitutive argument' can be overcome, unless it is that externalists and internalists are engaged in different forms of sociology so that the constitutive argument fails to *be* a critical one for the externalist position. For the externalist stance in this dispute entails the view that the sociologist may know better what is suicide and crime than the very members of society working as officials in the large organizational and bureaucratic apparatuses specifically charged with determining these matters. When suicidologists such as Brugha and Walsh (1978), for example, consult coroners' records and decide for themselves which deaths are 'really' suicides – which may involve re-classifying deaths officially coded as accidents or undetermined – they are supposing that the death certification process is in error, that if only one of their profession was at hand at each death inquiry the 'true' facts would be discovered. But to the extent this line is taken it involves the identification of a class of cases which are *not* those 'society' has otherwise judged to be its suicides. It produces a sociology not of the society under study but of one constructed by the sociologist (or, more likely, by the physician, psychiatrist, psychologist or epidemiologist).

It seems to me equally bizarre that the sociologist or criminologist should claim to know better what is a case of rape, theft, assault or malicious damage than the citizens, police, lawyers, judges and other officials specifically empowered to decide these matters. From this (my) point of view an instance of the *crime* of rape (now redefined in Canada into three forms of sexual assault) has not occurred until a conviction as such has been registered. And, as we have seen, the criminal offence for which a person is convicted may not be that for which s/he was originally charged. The resulting 'crime' is then very much a creation or production of the criminal justice system (including citizens acting as reporters, victims, witnesses and jury members), that is, of the rate-producing processes. But it would be supremely presumptuous for the sociologist to suppose that sh/he could do the job better than the system or, more fundamentally, that s/he could do it without recourse to the same *sort* of reasoning about evidence, intent, motive and so on that goes into official decision-making. In this sense externalist data derived from the sociologist's own judgements as to what is deviant are as much a social construction as those statistics produced by official agencies. In so far as both sociological and official data creation are ways in which 'deviance' is reproduced as a social fact they become of interest as topics of investigation to the internalist student of deviance.

Part of internalist methodology is the principle of charity of interpretation (Anderson *et al.*, 1985) whereby practitioners look for the 'good organizational reasons' behind the production of social facts, rather than 'competing with the natives' (here, the officials). I have tried to adopt this principle in presenting externalist research strategy towards the official statistics dispute. Furthermore, since, like the suicides of Captain Oates and Marilyn Monroe, externalist and internalist sociologies are not quite the same sort of thing despite sharing the same name, I have not attempted to push the dispute to a resolution in any of its areas of contention. For though there *are* areas where comparison and mutual criticism are possible, in the end the protagonists are playing different sociological games, living different forms of sociological life.

On one issue this essay may stand accused of lack of charity. The contribution of the Marxist or 'structural-conflict' perspective has not been discussed. There are three principal reasons for this. With one major exception Marxist treatments of the 'official data problem' have not dealt with deviance but with economic and political matters. The exception, an essay by Hindess (1973), is both confused and intemperate; when the confusions are sorted out and the bluster circumnavigated it may be seen to add little or nothing to the dispute (Roche, 1974; but see Miles and Irvine (1979) and Bottomley and Coleman (1981, pp. 12–14) for more favourable assessments). Finally, while assertions such as the following – 'data are therefore conceived of as social products: statistics are not *collected*, but *produced*; research results are not *findings*, but *creations*' (Irvine *et al.*, 1979, p. 3) – imply an appreciation of the internalist position, the writing rapidly moves to what amounts to an externalist attempt to explain historically the development of the definitions and operations comprising the procedures for producing official data. And the explanation is always the same: official data (and sociologists' unreconstructed use of them) are part of the ideological apparatus whereby the hegemony of the dominant bourgeois class in capitalist society is instituted and exercised. Programmatic assertion of a familiar political line tends to substitute for analysis.

The Marxists' programmatic concern for the practical mechanics of political control has, however, exposed a lacuna in the work produced by the main protagonists in the dispute. For all that it has been *about* the meaning and (sociological) use of official statistics in the explanation of deviance, the dispute has not engendered any *significant empirical* study – allowing for the American studies, reviewed by Bottomley and Coleman (1981, pp. 82–5), of the alleged Nixon manipulations – *of* the actual uses that official statistics of crime and suicide are put to by those who produce them or, apart from sociologists, consume them. Despite strenuous efforts at constructing, reconstructing and deconstructing them, the sociology of official statistics is yet to be written.

Endnote: I would like to thank the Medical Statistics Unit of the Office of Population Censuses and Surveys for providing the official suicide data for England and Wales.

References and Further Reading

Anderson, R. J., Hughes, J. A. and Sharrock, W. W. (1985), *The Sociology Game* (London: Longman).

Atkinson, J. M. (1973), 'Suicide, Status Integration and Pseudo-science', *Sociology*, vol. 7, pp. 437–45.

Atkinson, J. M. (1978), *Discovering Suicide: Studies in the Social Organization of Sudden Death* (London: Macmillan).

Bagley, C. (1972), 'Authoritarianism, Status Integration and Suicide', *Sociology*, vol. 6, pp. 395–404.

Bagley, C. (1974), 'On the Validity and Meaning of Suicide Statistics', *Sociology*, vol. 8, pp. 313–16.

Black, D. J. (1970), 'Production of Crime Rates', *American Sociological Review*, vol. 35, pp. 733–48.

Bottomley, A. K. (1973), *Decisions in the Penal Process* (London: Martin Robertson).

Bottomley, A. K, and Coleman, C. (1981), *Understanding Crime Rates: Police and Public Roles in the Production of Official Statistics* (London: Gower).

Box, S. (1971), *Deviance, Reality and Society* (London: Holt, Rinehart & Winston).

Brugha, T. and Walsh, D. (1978), 'Suicide Past and Present – the Temporal Constancy of Under-reporting', *British Journal of Psychiatry*, vol. 32, pp. 177–9.

Cicourel, A. V. (1964), *Method and Measurement in Sociology* (New York: Free Press).

Cicourel, A. V. (1968), *The Social Organization of Juvenile Justice* (New York: Wiley).

Cicourel, A. V. (1976), 'Introduction', in *The Social Organization of Juvenile Justice* (London: Heinemann), pp. xi–xxi.

Cresswell, P. (1975), *Suicide and Crime* (Milton Keynes: Open University Press).

Cuff, E. C. and Payne, G. (eds), (1984), *Perspectives in Sociology* (London: Allen & Unwin).

Douglas, J. D. (1967), *The Social Meanings of Suicide* (Princeton, NJ: Princeton University Press).

Duncan, B. and Eglin, P. (1979), 'Making Sense of the Reliability and Validity of Official Crime Statistics; Review and Prospect', *Canadian Criminology Forum*, vol. 2, pp. 7–19.

Durkheim, E. (1952), *Suicide* (London: Routledge & Kegan Paul).

Eglin, P. A., Abwunza, J. and Hallman, W. (1984), 'Producing the "Teenage Suicide Epidemic": the Ontario Coroners' System and Suicidologists', *Wilfred Laurier University Research Paper Series, No. 8459* (Waterloo, Ontario).

Garfinkel, H. (1967), ' "Good" Organizational Reasons for "Bad" Clinical Records', in H. Garfinkel, *Studies in Ethnomethodology* (Englewood Cliffs: Prentice-Hall).

Gusfield, J. R. (1981), *The Culture of Public Problems: Drinking–Driving and the Symbolic Order* (Chicago, Ill.: University of Chicago Press).

Hagan, J. (1984), *The Disreputable Pleasures: Crime and Deviance in Canada* (Toronto: McGraw-Hill).

Hindess, B. (1973), *The Use of Official Statistics in Sociology* (London: Macmillan).

Irvine, J., Miles, I. and Evans, J. (eds) (1979), *Demystifying Social Statistics* (London: Pluto Press).

Jennings, C. and Barraclough, B. (1980), 'Legal and Administrative Influences on the English Suicide Rate Since 1900', *Psychological Medicine*, vol. 10, pp. 407–18.

Kitsuse, J. and Cicourel, A. V. (1963), 'A Note on the Uses of Official Statistics', *Social Problems*, vol. 11, pp. 131–9.

Maynard, D. W. (1984), *Inside Plea Bargaining: The Language of Negotiation* (New York: Plenum).

Merton, R. K. (1938), 'Social Structure and Anomie', *American Sociological Review*, vol. 3, pp. 672–82.

Miles, I. and Irvine, J. (1979), 'The Critique of Official Statistics', in J. Irvine *et al.* (eds), *op. cit.*, pp. 113–29.

Roche, M. (1974), 'Review of *The Use of Official Statistics in Sociology* by B. Hindess', *Philosophy of the Social Sciences*, vol. 4, pp. 99–102.

Sainsbury, P. (1983), 'Validity and Reliability of Trends in Suicide Statistics', *World Health Statistics Quarterly*, vol. 36, pp. 339–48.

Shulman, M. (1976), *Coroner* (Markham, Ont.: Pocket Books).

Smith, D. (1975), 'The Statistics on Mental Illness: (What They Do Not Tell Us About Women and Why)', in D. Smith and S. J. David (eds), *Women Look at Psychiatry* (Vancouver: Press Gang).

Sudnow, D. (1965), 'Normal Crimes: Sociological Features of the Penal Code in a Public Defender's Office', *Social Problems*, vol. 12, pp. 255–76.

Taylor, S. (1982), *Durkheim and the Study of Suicide* (London: Macmillan).

Walsh, D., Mosbech, J., Adelstein, A., Spooner, J. and Dean, G. (1984), 'Suicide and Self-poisoning in Three Countries – a Study from Ireland, England and Wales, and Denmark, *International Journal of Epidemiology*, vol. 13, pp. 472–4.

Chapter 8

Nature and Society: The Organization of Space

JOHN URRY

Introduction

One of the most widespread, and perhaps dangerous, beliefs held by those born and bred in industrial societies is the idea that industrialism, through its technology, its science, its energy, has conquered nature. At last it seems human society is no longer dependent upon the whims or dictates of nature but can control, manipulate and exploit it to its own service. Nature is ours to tame, protect, or destroy, but at least it is ours. This view invites a contrast with human society before industrialization in which life was very much at the mercy of nature, indeed, as it still is in many parts of the world today. Nor is this merely a point about the dramas of nature, hurricanes, drought, volcanic eruptions, typhoons and so on, cataclysms which could destroy town and village, devastate nations even. It is rather a point about the prosaic but fundamental facts of life which shape human society, determining the location of towns and villages, the character and organization of work, diet, the size and distribution of populations, the ease and direction of travel, trade and migration and the social differentiation to be found within and between human societies. Thus, so it is often argued, for the whole of human history up until the culmination of industrialism, human society had been dependent on nature for its work, food, shelter and communication.

However, even during the onset of industrialization the demise of 'nature' did not go unlamented. Even in the late eighteenth and early nineteenth centuries a number of writers were bemoaning the ways in which 'nature' was being destroyed by the new, and growing, industrial society, especially with the consequent rise of new and massive urban areas. 'Nature' resided in the countryside not in the monstrous wens of industrial society. 'Nature', according to Wordsworth, was something to be communed with or yearned for:

> In nature and the language of the sense
> The anchor of my purest thought, the nurse,
> The guide, the guardian of heart and soul
> Of all my moral being.

Rural communities, it was felt, were organically related to the physical environment and so closer to nature than urban and industrial life. Towns and industry were 'outside' of nature, literally unnatural.

As a general claim, the idea that industrialism had conquered nature on close inspection becomes little more than a slogan shouted by the more extreme celebrants of science and industrialism or, alternatively, a dread voiced by the more incurable romantics. Part of the problem, and an important part at that, is that it is not clear quite what we are to mean by 'nature' in this context. Of the varied meanings the term has taken, the following are worth mentioning. To begin, there is 'nature' as referring to the essential quality or character of something, as it could be said that it is the nature of human beings to use language or for dogs to bark. We also have the idea of 'nature' as the underlying force which directs and controls all events in the world. In addition, there is 'nature' as the physical as opposed to the human environment. Against this is 'nature' as the entirety of animate and inanimate objects in the world, including human beings. And, for a final example, 'nature' is seen as belonging to the countryside, the rural as opposed to the urban.

In order though to see the significance of different conceptions of nature we may consider the peace-camp established by women at Greenham Common (see Gold, 1984). On the one hand, the women there speak about their aim to protect the planet, protect nature, from nuclear warfare. They especially emphasize how they as women have a special responsibility for ensuring that their children, or the children of other women, have a world to inherit and not one destroyed by nuclear warfare.

Implicit here is the view that it is women who are in some ways closer to nature, more sensitive to it, because biologically only they have the capacity to reproduce human beings. Science and technology, as represented by the Cruise missiles, which are located at the American air base, are seen as unnatural and masculine.

Yet, on the other hand, the development of Cruise missiles in many ways represents something as much part of nature as the modern technologically regulated process of childbirth. After all, sophisticated weapons like Cruise, based on the knowledge of how to split the atom, represent some of the most striking and effective examples of the understanding of nature that can be found. Science and technology are fundamentally based on laws of nature. Moreover, Greenham Common itself is no more unaffected by human intervention than is a Cruise missile. It is no more nor less 'natural' than a Cruise. Greenham used to be a stretch of common ground used for the grazing of cattle and sheep. For centuries this area was supported by the wool trade and then by textile machinery driven by local streams. The land was worked by substantial farmers. Riots of agricultural workers occurred there in 1830 and the Grenadier Guards searched and found many of the rioters there. The American air force arrived during the Second World War and the area was used in preparing for the invasion of Europe in 1944. It became a permanent air base in 1951. It therefore has a history of human intervention. Greenham Common in the 1980s is not 'natural'. It is the result of certain kinds of human intervention just as Cruise missiles represent a different form of such intervention.

The picture is, then, a confused one and, as should be evident, bound up with metaphysical, philosophical, moral as well as empirical matters. So much so that it is difficult for us to see quite in what ways the interplay between 'nature' and society can be sociologically investigated. In this chapter I want to reduce the 'big' question of the relationship between 'nature' and society to more manageable proportions by concentrating on two 'natural constraints', that is, space and time which, I shall argue, are still vital parameters to the organization of social life. To put it generally at this stage, these act as limits on what we can produce, whom we can meet, whom we can form relationships with and so on. Social life involves spending *time* with other people, and it involves crossing *space* to be in their company. Time and space are thus two central aspects by which 'nature' constrains social activity.

In the following I shall consider how various sociologists have analysed the spatial constraints upon social activity. I shall consider three classical contributions to this debate, Marx, Durkheim and Simmel, and suggest that development of their ideas especially in the alleged contrasts between the 'rural' and the 'urban' have not been terribly convincing. However, there are more recent analyses of how 'space' affects our social activities and these will be considered in some detail. It will be suggested that it is only recently that the analyses of 'nature', of 'space' and 'society', could be in part brought together as various boundaries between academic subjects were broken down.

How, then, did the classical sociologists understand the way in which nature, particularly in the form of 'spatial constraints', structured social life?

Karl Marx (1818–83)

The writings of Marx, and to a lesser extent, of Friedrich Engels (1820–95) represent the first really serious attempt to understand the transformations of nature that were entailed by the twin nineteenth-century processes of capitalist industrialization and urbanization. Their writings are particularly remarkable since they were produced in an intellectual vacuum; no contemporaries of theirs really understood much of their work, let alone contributed to it. Their 'materialist' analysis was quite simply unique.

Marx's starting point was that there is a material world, of natural resources, land, machinery, factories, skills and so on, and that this world is directly fashioned by human labour. Labour is therefore uncontroversially part of nature. We should not therefore talk of human beings, on the one hand, and nature, on the other, but rather of the interactions within nature which include human actions and especially that of human labour. Marx considers such labour of critical importance. Labour transforms the world of material objects, and in that transformation makes people truly human and, therefore, authentically part of the natural world. The production of such objects is the basis for developing truly human powers, powers that distinguish humans from animals.

There are a number of aspects of such human labour which need to be noted. First, unlike animals, human beings are able to think out, to plan, to conceptualize what they are going to produce and how to produce it. Not only do they execute tasks, they also conceptualize them. Secondly, unlike the merely instinctive and habitual labour of animals, human beings can monitor and reflect upon what they are doing. As the task is being undertaken they may consider whether the best methods are being employed and reflect upon how the process could be improved. Human labour is reflexive; the labour of animals is merely instinctive. Thirdly, human labour is necessarily social. It must involve interaction with others either directly or indirectly. Human labour always involves some social division of labour, so that people produce in part *for* others and in part *with* others. People never produce on their own and without any regard for what others are producing. Transforming nature through human labour, then, is always a socially patterned activity. Fourthly, this human labour necessarily involves understanding the physical laws of nature. Animals by contrast do not know such natural processes. Humans gradually acquire knowledge of these processes; a knowledge that is produced and generated in various social contexts. Knowledge of those physical processes is never acquired through a single individual's reflection but through a complex social process of producing and transmitting knowledge. Fifthly, there are systematic connections between particular means of transforming the physical environment and the specific social relations within which this occurs. These sets of connections are known in Marxism as different modes of production, which are comprised of forces of production such as technologies, factories, land, skills and so on, and relations of production, such as lords and serfs in feudalism, or capitalists and workers as in capitalist production.

As is well known, Marx and Engels devote particular detailed attention to one mode of production, namely, the capitalist. This mode is to be found when the relations of production are those of capitalist and worker, and where surplus-value, the value of unpaid surplus-labour, is appropriated by the capitalist from the worker. Capitalist forces of production consist of the growth of machinery, workshops, factories and new industry-based technologies and skills. Such a mode of production is no longer based on the land and involves massive changes in the organization of production, with large factories owned and controlled by capitalist employers, and in the organization of people, with the growth of large, newly created towns and cities. Central to this mode is the production of commodities, that is, objects like chairs or services like a haircut, which have both a use to the consumer and can be bought and sold in the market. Under capitalism people are connected to each other largely through the exchange of such commodities. Indeed, labour is itself a commodity, bought and sold, exchanged and moved around. The relations between the prices of such commodities constrain our behaviour. We are limited to what we can buy and sell by the prices which different commodities are able to command in the market. However, it is essential, Marx notes, to realize that the laws governing capitalist production are not natural laws, they are not eternal but are historically based. They stem from a given set of social relations, namely capitalism. None the less, they are experienced as a set of 'natural', inevitable, laws constraining economic and social life.

But, Marx says they are *not* natural at all but social, and to view them as natural is to 'fetishize' commodities. Commodities, even ones like the steam machine or the computer, do not possess 'natural' powers as such. Rather the powers they do possess are derived, on the one hand, from the socially produced forms of knowledge they happen to embody, and on the other hand, from the specific social relations within which they are located, that is, whether, for example, they function as 'capital' as opposed to 'labour'. Overall, Marx maintains that capitalism represents a massive increase in overcoming the constraints of both animate and inanimate nature. Capitalism allows for the extraordinary growth of the forces of production, of the increase in the human mastery of the physical environment. However, this mastery is achieved in a manner which is dehumanizing, 'alienating' and conflict-producing. Workers, although using machinery and tools previously undreamt of, are alienated from those means of production, from the products that they produce, from the work itself, from other people in this necessarily 'social' activity and from one's very human nature which is to work creatively and in an authentically free relationship with others.

This growth of a capitalist mode of production transforms the patterns of economic and social life previously established. One central feature of this consists of the exceedingly rapid growth of industrial towns and cities. Marx considered that the division between town and countryside had been a feature of all societies where there was some development of the division of labour. However, up to the Middle Ages the countryside was the more important aspect of society. Of the ancient city-states of Greece and Rome, Marx noted that they were fundamentally based upon landownership and agriculture. There was 'ruralization of the city' (Grundrisse, 1973, p. 479). In the Middle Ages though this slowly began to change, especially as, first, agriculture itself came to be much more based on producing commodities for sale in the market and much less tied to producing for relatively self-sufficient communities; and, secondly, small-scale industrial production was gradually established in the countryside. The 'modern (age) is the urbanization of countryside' (Grundrisse, 1973, p. 479). The contradiction then between town and country, although necessary for the growth of capitalism, is itself mini- mized as new industrial towns emerged in the countryside. However, these towns then developed exceedingly rapidly. In 1801 one-fifth of the British population lived in towns, by 1911 this had increased to four-fifths. As a result new conflicts arose between town and countryside.

Marx and Engels also wrote more generally of how in capitalist society there is the:

> Constant revolutionising of production, uninterrupted disturbance of all social conditions, everlasting uncertainty and agitation distin- guish the bourgeois epoch from all earlier ones. All fixed, fast- frozen relations . . . all swept away, all new-formed ones become antiquated before they can ossify. All that is solid melts into air, all that is holy is profaned . . .
>
> (1888, pp. 53–4)

Bourgeois or capitalist society, then, is one of intense change, particularly of where people live and how their lives are organized over time. As production is revolutionized in order to bring about massive savings of labour-time, people's relation- ships to each other across space are transformed. There are a number of changes, namely: (1) capitalism has 'pitilessly torn asunder the motley feudal ties that bound man to his "natural superiors"'; (2) the need for a constantly expanding market 'chases the bourgeoisie over the whole surface of the globe and destroys local and regional markets'; (3) the 'immensely facilitated means of communication draws all . . . nations into civilisation' – hence reducing the distance between societies; (4) enormous cities are created and this has 'rescued a considerable part of the population from the idiocy of rural life'; (5) political centralization is generated as independent, loosely connected provinces 'become lumped together into one nation'; (6) masses of labourers 'organised like soldiers' are 'crowded into the factory', the proletariat 'becomes concentrated in greater masses'; and (7) the development of trade unions is 'Helped on by the improved means of communication that are created by modern industry and that place the workers of different localities in contact with one another' (1888, p. 65). Overall they argue that the aim of capitalist production is to annihilate space with time, and hence to overcome all spatial barriers to capitalist industrialization.

Emile Durkheim (1858–1917)

In *The Division of Labour in Society* Durkheim is concerned to understand what causes changes in the division of labour which brings about transition from one type of social solidarity to another. He considers that there are two kinds of solidarity, mechanical and organic. The former is to be found in simple societies were there is a strong similarity between people. There is a minimal division of labour and solidarity is sustained through a highly effective collective conscience, a set of moral values, which treats the collectivity as sacred. Individuals are subject to this all-encompassing collective conscience which permeates all aspects of individual life, which is highly intense and which rigidly sustains conceptions of what is right and wrong. There is very little development of individual variation and personal identity or uniqueness. Such a mechanical solidarity can be identified by the existence of a 'repressive' legal system. Crimes in such a society are felt to be offences against the whole society, not just against the individual concerned.

The decline of 'repressive' and the growth of what Durkheim

calls 'restitutive' law marks the shift towards organic solidarity. Under this legal system the emphasis is placed upon attempting to rectify the wrong that has been committed. The law does not provoke a generalized moral outrage, and it reflects a society that derives its solidarity from the complementary difference between individuals, especially resulting from a much more developed division of labour. In such an advanced society mechanical bonds of similarity have been replaced by 'organic' relations of interdependence. The force of the overwhelming collective conscience is replaced by a more positive pattern of co-operation stemming from mutual dependence, by the fact that because everyone is more specialized so everyone needs other people more clearly. For Durkheim these bonds of interdependence, resulting from specialization produced by an advanced division of labour, are more effective than those produced under mechanical solidarity. In societies based on organic solidarity, there is a much more weakly developed collective conscience. It is less intense, less rigid and more scope is given to individual conscience, aptitude and motivation. Sentiments relating to the collectivity become the focus of vague feelings and ideals as opposed to rigid notions of duty and obligation.

Although Durkheim thinks that modern society contains various undesirable characteristics, particularly the likelihood of 'anomie', which is one of the social causes of suicide, in general the growth of organic solidarity is a progressive phenomenon. It is not that, for Durkheim, people in modern societies are more self-interested, but, rather, that individuals feel moral obligations to each other and, indeed, are unable to live together without recognizing this reciprocal character of the obligations between each other.

So far then we have seen that for Durkheim there are two kinds of society. He then argues that it is the growth in the division of labour, of dramatically increased specialization, that brings about the transition from one to the other. It is in this transition from mechanical to organic solidarity that his analysis of the city and of space becomes important. Two factors give rise to this increased division of labour: increases in 'material density' and in 'moral density'. By the former he means that the density of population in a given area increases, both because of the development of new forms and speed of communication so that by 'abolishing or lessening the vacuums separating social segments, these means increase the density of society' (1984, p. 203), and because of the growth of towns and cities. 'Moral density' refers to the increased density of interaction and social relationships within a given population.

The increase in the division of labour is due to the fact that different parts of society lose their individuality. The partitions between them become more permeable. And this occurs for Durkheim because of heightened material and moral density. There is a drawing together of individuals who once were separated from one another. Social relationships become more numerous and complex. Durkheim says that as the 'division of labour progresses the more individuals there are who are sufficiently in contact with one another to be able mutually to act and react upon one another' (1984, p. 201). This drawing together and the active exchanges resulting from it are what generates a heightened division of labour and hence organic rather than mechanical solidarity. The increased moral density resulting, from either expanded social interactions, or from new communications which bring together individuals from different places, will generally have the effect of raising the levels of specialization. People seek to satisfy new needs, or to separate off some particular segment of an existing market. Spatial proximity generates heightened competition and normally an increase in the division of labour. However, Durkheim also notes that because cities normally grow through immigration rather than through natural increase, this means that new residents will have a weakened attachment to traditional beliefs and values. Hence the collective conscience will be less strong and this will generally facilitate the new organic solidarity of interdependence. Two further points should be noted. First, cities are also on occasions centres of social pathology. Secondly, local or geographical loyalties will be gradually undermined with the growth of the new occupationally based division of labour, he suggests that 'geographical divisions' will generally become less and less significant in awakening feelings of attachment and loyalty.

Georg Simmel (1858–1918)

The final classical writer considered here is that of Simmel, a brilliant German essayist who examined the spatial form and consequences of city life especially in his essay 'Metropolis and Mental Life' (1971, pp. 324–39).

Simmel's conception of sociology is rather different from either Marx or Durkheim. He is normally known as an advocate of 'formal sociology'. He is concerned to analyse certain of the forms of everyday social life and is not particularly interested in larger-scale patterns of social and historical change. One particular element in this formal analysis was to consider the effects of the number of people on social life. For example, are social interactions between just two people in a dyad different from interactions between three? In the latter, one out of three is typically an outsider, 'two's company, three's none'. He further argues that certain of the unpleasant features of modern life, of 'alienation', for example, result from sheer numbers which necessitate considerable distances between individuals. As a result, formal means of control, like the law, become necessary and partly replace personal interactions.

In 'Metropolis and the City' (1971, pp. 324–39) these comments are developed in detail. Simmel makes a number of points about life in the modern city. First, because there is such a richness and diversity of experience, because of the multitude of stimuli, it is necessary to develop an attitude of reserve and an insensitivity to feeling. Without the development of such an attitude people would not be able to cope with such experiences. Reserve in the face of superficial contacts with the crowd is necessary for survival. Otherwise people would become literally neurotic. The urban personality is necessarily unemotional, reserved, detached – blasé, in other words.

Secondly, at the same time the city assures individuals of a distinctive type of personal freedom. Simmel, like Durkheim, contrasts the modern city with the small-scale community. It is in the latter that 'the individual member has only a very slight area for the development of his [sic] own qualities and for the free activity for which he himself is responsible' (1971, p. 332). Such groups cannot, he says, give room to freedom and to the peculiarities of the inner and outer development of the individual.

And this is even so in the life of the 'small town dweller'. It is only in the large metropolis that great opportunities are available for the unique development of the individual, particularly because of the cosmopolitanism of the modern city. This is partly because of the wider contacts available to each person in the city – there is an enlargement of the circle forming each person's social milieu – and, partly because cities are themselves interconnected with other cities, and so each individual is placed in exceptionally wide social contacts with people in the rest of the country and in other countries. Simmel maintains that 'economic, personal and intellectual relations in the city . . . grow in a geometrical progression as soon as . . . a certain limit has been passed' (1971, p. 334).

A third central feature of the city is that it is based on the money economy. Money is indeed both the source and the expression of the rationality and the intellectualism of the city. Both money and the intellect share, he says, a matter-of-fact attitude towards people and things. They are indifferent to genuine individuality. The typical city dweller is guided by his (sic) head and not by his heart, by calculation and intellect, not by affection and emotion. Money contributes to a levelling of feeling and attitude, to express everything in terms of a single measure. Simmel says that money with 'its colorlessness and its indifferent quality' hollows out the core of things, their peculiarities, their specific values and their uniqueness and incomparability in a way which is beyond repair' (1971, p. 330). Even the impressive features of human development, great works of art, new technologies, the wonders of science, and so on, all become devalued, colourless, and distant from the 'sophisticated' individuals that have given rise to them.

Fourthly, and connected to this, Simmel notes how the money economy generates a concern for precision and punctuality. This is both in the general sense that the money economy makes people more calculative about their activities and their relationships. 'What am I getting out of this' becomes a common consideration. And a concern for precision stems from the fact that the city contains so many people doing so many different things. In order for these to take place in an even moderately efficient manner there has to be some scheduling of different activities. This necessitates accurate time-keeping, precise arrangements, and a prohibition on spontaneity. Meetings with other people have to be timetabled, they are typically brief and infrequent.

Finally, the city exacts a considerable price for the freedoms that it allows the individual. This is partly because the city permits a much greater division of labour and this may lead to a distorted development of the individual. People often have to develop one side or aspect of their personality in order to find an appropriate occupation or skill. Other people develop a kind of contrived, exaggerated personality in order to stand up to the demands of city life. Generally, Simmel considers that the city dweller 'becomes a single cog as over against the vast overwhelming organization of things and forces which gradually take out of his [sic] hands everything connected with progress, spirituality and value' (1971, p. 337).

These, then, are the classical contributions concerning the way in which the 'natural constraints' of space and time are reflected in forms of social organization, particularly to do with modern industry and the modern city. The question they address is: in what ways do nature and/or the spatial organization of the modern industry and the modern city determine the patterns of social life? We will now consider what sociology in the twentieth century contributed to our understanding of this question. In general we shall suggest that until recently much of the literature had not really improved upon these classical contributions. It is only in the last twenty or so years that writers are now beginning to resolve some of these issues. We shall consider twentieth-century contributions by considering, first, the nature of town and country, or the 'urban' and the 'rural', and secondly, more general debates on nature, space and society.

Town and Country

The nature of city life was explored by many sociologists, especially those working in the University of Chicago in the period between the wars. Much of this research was collected together by Louis Wirth in his article 'Urbanism as a Way of Life' (1938). He argued that there are three causes of the differences in social patterns between rural and urban areas, and these are size, density and heterogeneity. On the first, size, he argued, like Simmel, that the larger a settlement, the greater the variation between different areas and the more there will be segregation of different groups in different parts of the settlement. Furthermore, such increases in size reduce the chances of any two people knowing each other and this leads to a greater indifference of people toward one another. It is not that one necessarily knows fewer people in cities, or that community-type relationships completely disappear. It is rather that relationships are impersonal, superficial, transitory and confined to some particular aspects of social life. Living in large settlements, then, involves greater social distance, a lack of spontaneous interactions, and the development of more formal agencies of control and regulation.

The effect of increased *density* reinforces the effects of size. In particular it leads people to relate to each other on the basis of their specific roles rather than their personal qualities. People view each other in an instrumental fashion. We see people not in a direct and spontaneous way but in terms of the specific things which they can do for us. Different areas develop in cities made up of those playing these different social roles. There is a mosaic of social worlds. Increased density also leads to more formal regulation and control, especially by laws, rather than by the appropriate customs which occur in less dense societies.

Increased *heterogeneity* means that people in cities participate in many different social circles, none of which commands their complete involvement. Individuals enjoy a different level of status within these separate circles, so much so that the urban person is unstable, disorganized and insecure. At the same time the only way that individuals can change anything is through representation within large-scale organizations from which most people feel separated and powerless.

Writers associated with the Chicago School developed more specific analyses particularly associated with the competition for land within cities. They argued that as the population of towns grows, there is an increased specialization of people into different economic positions, and that these different groups of people came to live in different sections of the town. In particular, the pressure for space at the centre creates an area of high land values, and this determines the cost of land and housing in the rest of the town. These differences in land values (which means higher rents or higher prices for buying land or houses) provide the mechanism by which different groups are distributed throughout the urban area. Burgess, for example, suggested that cities are divided into concentrically organized zones (see Park and Burgess, 1967). As the city expands each circle is invaded by the people and activities from the zone next to it. Thus the central business district expands into the neighbouring area, called the zone of transition (generally where immigrants live), which then expands into the neighbouring zone of working-class housing and so on. A particularly important role is played here by the zone of transition which is located in the inner-city. It is suggested that as the central business district expands, the area next to it deteriorates particularly because people cannot gain access to cheap and reasonable housing. The original inhabitants move out and the new immigrants take their place. There is therefore a pattern of expansion of the central business district leading to higher turnover in the zone of transition, leading to new immigration, leading to social decline, crime and housing decay, leading to further expansion of the central business district, and so on.

In recent research in Britain some evidence is found for the concentric zone model. In Sunderland, for example, it was found that the northern part of the town demonstrated this pattern of concentric circles, while in the south there was a wedge-shaped pattern of development (see Robson, 1969). Some supporting evidence for the concentric pattern was found in research on London. However, patterns of segregation within towns also depend on the ways in which roads and railways have expanded, and on political decisions regarding the location of council housing and on more general planning policies.

These views of what urban life is like have been influential particularly in generating conceptions of rural life. Redfield developed both the notion of a 'folk society' and of the idea of a folk-urban continuum. The overall trend of societies is from the increasing collectivism and stability of the folk or village, to the individualism of the city. Somewhat similarly in *Communities in Britain* Frankenberg (1966) summarized many studies of rural communities. He suggests that the following are the main features of rural areas:

(1) organized as a *community* with people frequently meeting together and being related to each other in many different ways. People play different social roles in relationship to the same other person. Each person has a close-knit network of social contacts;

(2) most inhabitants work on the *land* or in related industries. There is a high proportion of jobs which overlap and there is relatively little division of labour. Most workers are relatively unspecialized farm labourers;

(3) most people possess a status fixed by their family of origin. It is different to change one's status through achievement. People are strongly regulated to behave in ways appropriate to one's status. This status spreads from one situation to another, irrespective of the different activities in which one engages;

(4) economic class divisions are only one basis of social *conflict*. Strategies develop to handle such conflicts. Social inequalities are presumed to be justified, often in terms of tradition.

These ideas of town and country, or the urban and the rural are very powerful. Much literature and culture stems from or relates to attempts to represent conceptions of town or country, conceptions that invariably imply a contrast between them. But such contrasts are often deceptive and do scant justice to the details of human history. What is supposedly 'rural' has varied enormously, and has generally been thought about in ways which have been blind to the very people who did most of the work in such areas, namely, agricultural workers. Moreover, the (olde) village is a relatively recent creation, deriving in England from eighteenth-century movements of enclosures and agrarian improvement. It had only just come onto the historical scene before the 'unnatural' town of the industrial revolution conjured up some of the most dramatic and 'romanticized' of contrasts. William Cobbett, the nineteenth-century essayist, perhaps has done more than anyone to indoctrinate us with our feelings about the rural, that it consists of a beneficent landowner, a sturdy peasantry and a village community, self-supporting and static. As the poet Gray said of Grasmere in the Lake Distict: 'This little unsuspected paradise, where all is peace, rusticity and happy poverty.'

Continuity is a particularly powerful image here. Because the countryside involves working the land, and that land has in a sense been here forever, so there appears to be something eternal about rural life, its rhythms and patterns that city life can never reproduce. Indeed because of its aesthetic claims, the lie of the land, the thatched cottages, the grazing livestock, there is the presumption that life here must be meaningful, worthwhile, and able to support a socially beneficial pattern of life for all members, rich and poor. This is incidentally one of the clearest messages from the radio programme, 'The Archers'.

Likewise the town or the city is not itself a simple phenomenon, or wholly evil. Cities are 'man-made', and just as there is no 'real' countryside so there is no 'real' city. Moreover, much of the hostility to city life is in effect a hostility to something else, to capitalism or communism, to industry or to bureaucracy. Cities have been variously seen as being centres of light, wisdom, and learning; and centres of sin, evil and darkness.

Sociological formulations have in part followed these simple contrasts. However, recent research shows them to be largely false. In Britain, extensive investigation has been carried out on a number of rural communities. Newby argues that there is one aspect of the 'rural' which does distinguish such communities and that it is the ownership of property and the organization of relationships of property that shapes the nature of the rural social structure (1979, 1980). The crucial issue determining one's place in the social structure of rural areas is whether one owns land, rents land, or works for someone who owns or rents land. In urban areas it is generally held that differences of occupation structure one's place in the social structure. In rural areas what is crucial is the ownership of, and access to, land. In the nineteenth century most land in Britain was owned by very few landowners and was worked by tenant farmers who in turn employed a large number of agricultural workers. Over the course of this century there has been an extensive increase in owner-occupation so that about 60 per cent of farm land is now farmed by its owners, there has been a substantial increase in the ownership of agricultural land by large institutions especially those within the City of London, and the average farm size has considerably increased. As a result there has been an irreversible 'rationalization' of agriculture. Instead of it being a 'way of life' centred in a *Green and Pleasant Land* (see Newby, 1980), it has become a business where farms are organized to produce profits. This has been particularly heightened by the growth of so-called agri-business where large food-processing companies, like Bird's Eye, Ross, Walls and so on, control and direct individual farmers. Agriculture has become 'industrialized' particularly with the growth of factory-farming. What is rural then about areas dominated by factory-farming?

One aspect of these developments has been the increased mechanization of farm work. This has had quite dramatic effects in reducing the workforce employed on farms, at the same time that the size of most farms has increased considerably in terms of the acreage farmed. About one-half of all farms in Britain now employ only one farm worker, and quite a few employ none at all, the work being done by the family members. Because of this reduction in the size of the labour force the one or two workers have to be skilled at most of the jobs to be done around the farm. In other words, mechanization has *increased* the variety of skills that must be mastered – it has reduced rather than increased the division of labour. This reduction in the average numbers of farm workers has also weakened the bases of agricultural trade unionism, reduced the bureaucratization of farms, and lessened the social distance between farmers and their workers. Indeed the connections between farmers and their worker(s) have also been strengthened by the arrival of people from urban areas. The result has been to produce an 'encapsulated' rural community particularly organized around the farm and farming and defined in opposition to the newcomers. Farmers and farm labourers form a community within a community and this has reinforced a kind of 'nostalgia' for the past when rural societies were thought to be organized as relatively undivided 'communities'.

At the same time some other research has explored the nature of urban areas. Here it has been clearly shown that what have been called 'urban villages' can exist within large cities. The best-known study here is that of Bethnal Green which was researched in the 1950s (Young and Willmott, 1957). At the time it was a relatively compact borough of about 50,000 people concentrated within a very small area (about 2 square miles) with no major roads running through it. Also almost three-quarters of the male labour force were manual workers and most of the non-manual workers were shopkeepers and publicans. The way in which living in Bethnal Green has similarities with rural life is summarized in the following:

Life in an Urban village
One consequence of this immobility is that everyone is surrounded by people very like himself, most of whom he has always known. Bethnal Green has many points of similarity with a village, or rather with a whole series of overlapping and interlocking villages. The opportunities for close, long-term relationships are greater than is usually the case in a large metropolitan residential area. The likelihood of an inhabitant having neighbours who are strangers, or whose way of life is very different from his own has until recently been very slight. This immobility also makes it essential for him to be on good terms with his neighbours, as they are likely to be there, for better or worse, for most of his life.

(quoted Frankenberg, 1966, pp. 185–6)

Communities of this sort have also been found in working class towns dominated by a single industry. In a famous study, *Coal is Our Life*, Dennis, Henriques and Slaughter argued that the 'community' that they discovered stemmed from the over-whelming significance of the coalmining industry and from the shared experiences which this produced for the male miners (1965). In particular, these community relations were reinforced by the local nature of mining knowledge and experience. The colliers' skill, seniority, and even knowledge of technical terms were often not transferable from pit to pit, let alone village to village, district to district, or coalfield to coalfield. This was a factor which bound miners to their home towns and to their home collieries. Such community relations were also reinforced through the shared misfortunes of mining disasters, which particularly bound the men in the community together.

Finally, studies of suburban living have demonstrated the variability of the suburban pattern. Gans, in a famous study *The Levittowners* (1967), showed that suburban residents in America have a way of life which is 'quasi-primary'. That is to say, it does involve close ties but these are neighbours rather than kin. This he attributed to those residents in the suburb being both middle-class and at a similar stage in their life-cycle, that is, having young children. In a British study, Willmott and Young (1960) depicted a suburban style of life, which they believed was characterized by mobility away from kin, a life centred on the home, close relationships with neighbours and friends, more egalitarian marriages, and participation in formal organizations. However, they also found that it was generally the middle class that had this particular way of life.

Overall, two conclusions stand out. First, communities in rural areas are not necessarily organized in terms of the rural model primarily because major changes have occurred in the dominant form of employment, namely, agriculture. Second, in urban areas it is possible to find communities which look rather like those supposedly found in rural areas. The differing densities of population in rural and urban areas do not generate greatly different forms of social life. Does this mean that the classical writers I discussed were all wrong? Certainly the simpler claims of especially Durkheim and Simmel do not stand up very well, particularly in the way in which they were developed by Wirth and Redfield. Analyses merely of the density, or spatial concentration, of population do not seem to explain much of importance. However, there are other aspects of nature and space that are of significance and these I shall now consider.

Nature and Space

In this section I shall begin by noting that nature has become less and less important a determinant of social life. Industrial societies are increasingly based on what has been called 'created space'. Towns, cities, industries are all far less dependent on the physical environment than they once were. Consider building materials which once affected what could be built and where. Now many new buildings are constructed out of large shapes of concrete, moulded in factories, and then transported to a site for construction. Or consider economic activity. Most people work in services (about two-thirds of the employed population of most 'developed' countries: in banks, hospitals, schools, cleaning firms, restaurants, etc.) and these do not require any physical resources apart from those which can be obtained anywhere. Also, much of manufacturing could be carried out almost anywhere. There are some exceptions. A tourist industry normally has to be constructed around some kind of attraction which is often physical. However, the recent tourist development of Wigan and Bradford suggests that even this is a fairly flexible condition!

Does this mean therefore that everywhere has become the same as everywhere else? In some ways they have. The shopping centres found in many British towns and cities bear a marked similarity to one another. Most towns these days have industrial estates on the outskirts. All towns have become more dependent on employment provided by large public institutions. Places dependent on some aspect of the physical environment, like the coalmining village discussed above, have become much rarer. Both industry and services are more dependent, not on the physical environment, but on the location of consumers for their products. And consumers are of course widely spread through the country rather than being concentrated in a few very specific places (unlike coal, for example). In some ways then this would bear out Durkheim's claims that local and regional identities would decline in importance as large-scale industry and the national state have increased in significance. Does this therefore mean that as physical nature has declined in importance so also has space become less significant? Can we dispense with issues of space and simply analyse social life in terms of general processes which affect all places in roughly the same way?

In the rest of this section I shall argue that we cannot. There are a number of significant ways in which space remains of central importance in the structuring of modern societies. First of all, when we noted above that according to Marx the aim of capitalist production is to annihilate space with time, what Marx ignores is that this can only be achieved through new spatial patterns, of railways and large industrial cities, for example. Hence, new spatial patterns are necessary in order to overcome existing spatial patterns. These new spatial patterns result from four interconnected processes which characterize economic activity in modern industrial society:

(1) The tendency for firms and industries (what Marx calls 'industrial capital') to see-saw from place to place seeking advantage in terms of cheaper labour, larger markets, better transport and communications and so on.

(2) The tendency for such capital to become less and less attached
     to particular places because specific raw materials, markets or
     energy sources, happen to be located in given places; that is,
     capital becomes more 'spatially indifferent' as the physical
     environment becomes less important in determining
     location.
(3) The tendency for certain characteristics of the labour force to
     become of increased importance to capital. These character-
     istics include its skills, costs, supply, organization, reliability.
     These are of relatively heightened importance both because
     labour cannot be produced capitalistically compared with,
     say, machinery, and because labour is relatively fixed since it
     lives in and tends to be attached to particular places.
(4) The increased ability of firms to be able to split up different
     parts of their activities, so that they can be located in different
     parts of the country, and in cases in completely different
     countries. Neither Marx or Durkheim foresaw a world
     division of labour in which a single company could produce
     in fifty or a hundred different counties.

   As a result of these processes the characteristics of the labour
force in different places are of great importance in attracting firms
to invest in one place rather than another. The character of the
place in turn is important in affecting the nature of the labour
force to be found. Particular places attract labour forces which are
more or less highly skilled, more or less organized into trade
unions, more or less industrially militant, more or less used to
industrial work and so on. Just to take one example, high
technology firms tend, in Britain, to establish new research
laboratories in places like Cambridge or Berkshire because there
are already there considerable numbers of highly qualified
scientists, engineers and computing experts. And as more firms
establish plants so further higher-skilled workers are attracted,
and this in turn tends to ensure better quality shops, improved
schools and health facilities, superior cultural activities and so on.
There is a kind of spiral by which relatively favoured and
prosperous places get even more favoured and prosperous. Places
therefore are most definitely different and this affects how the
economy and society works.
   Thus far I have talked about differences between places. There

are also important spatial processes that are to be found within a place. The first of these involves the explanation as to why there are towns and cities in the first place. They stem from a fundamentally spatial problem, namely that of distance (see Ball, 1984). If two people are working in different places and they need to talk face-to-face, one or both of them have to travel to a place to meet. If they need to be in frequent contact it clearly makes sense for them to be near each other fairly permanently. Likewise if a particular firm regularly supplies components to a large factory there will clearly be advantages if they are located nearby so as to save on transport costs. And again, if customers are travelling into the centre of a city it clearly saves them a lot of time, and hence makes future visits more likely, if all the main shops are located fairly close together. This especially applies to specialist shops, such as those selling hifi equipment where customers like to compare brands and prices across a range of shops before making a purchase. These are all examples of economies of agglomeration resulting from the costs of moving either people or objects across space. However, there are some diseconomies of agglomeration, particularly of high rents and congestion. Modern offices are often now subdivided. The headquarters remains in the city centre, so that the company executives are physically close to other executives. While more routine type of office work is moved to cheaper sites elsewhere since those carrying out such work do not have to meet face-to-face with those doing similar routine work in other organizations. It is also important to note that changes regularly occur in the cost in time and money involved in crossing distances. Until the late eighteenth century, for example, there were no regular coach services connecting London with any other part of the country. London and Bristol, London and York, Bristol and York, and so on, were exceptionally distant and for most people were far further apart than London and Hong Kong, for example, are today. Likewise, of course, the development of the telephone has enabled a kind of face-to-face communication now to occur simply by dialling a few numbers. Distances have been extraordinarily reduced and hence some of the pull of the economies of agglomeration have been correspondingly reduced.

This is so far another reason. Not only must some activities be connected together within a town or city, but also they have to compete with each other for space. No two plants or offices can be located in exactly the same place and hence there is necessarily a process of spatial differentiation. This means that different activities are distributed across the city using different spaces. This is a dynamic process resulting from the economies of agglomeration and the competition for land and buildings. This competition has the effect of generating considerable inequalities of both housing and of other urban resources such as health care, education, community centres and so on for different social groups, within the city.

One of the best-known studies of these inequalities was that conducted in the 1960s in Sparkbrook, Birmingham (Rex and Moore, 1967). It was argued that there were four different social groups in the city and that each occupied a very different relationship to the market for houses. They were distributed spatially through the city and were tremendously affected by processes of spatial change. These groups were (1) the upper middle class owning their own homes; (2) the working class generally renting smaller terraced houses; (3) the lower middle class, renting but wishing to become owner-occupiers; and (4) recent immigrants to Britain especially from the West Indies. As the city grew the population generally migrated from the central to the outlying areas, particularly because of the desirability of acquiring a house in a suburban area. Group (1) moved to large houses in the 'inner suburbs', (2) moved to a 'new public suburbia' of extensive council estates, and (3) moved to fairly distant semi-detached suburbs. As a result much of the nineteenth-century housing close to the city centre of Birmingham was abandoned and quickly became occupied by (4) new immigrants.

Rex and Moore argue that there was a shared value held by people living in cities which is to want to move to the suburbs. Different groups have different access to resources which may enable them to make such a move. Three different groups are termed by Rex and Moore, housing classes. Such classes consisted of people in similar positions in the housing market. There is, of necessity, competition and conflict between different housing classes for access to the generally preferred form of housing. Rex and Moore point to two determinants of this competition: (1) the size and security of a household's income, and (2) the need for housing and length of residence. Black immigrants to Britain were in the lowest housing class. This was because under (a) they generally had low and insecure incomes so they could not obtain a mortgage for buying their own suburban house; and under (b) they generally had not been living in Birmingham long enough (5 years) to obtain council housing, and, if they had, then were generally offered substandard short-life housing in the inner city.

Immigrants were thus forced to seek accommodation in the inner-city, either renting privately or buying the large deteriorating houses usually via short-term loans at high rates of interest. This in turn encouraged multi-occupation as immigrant landlords sought to get some return from their purchase of these decaying properties. This however led to a further decline in the quality of housing and a tendency for white families to move out.

There was therefore a struggle between social groups for access to the central scarce resource, namely owner-occupied suburban housing. Moreover, this struggle was not simply determined by the housing market itself. The state played a crucial role in segregating immigrants into depressed inner-city areas as a result of it only making available council housing to the white working class. It also played an important role in preventing the expansion of immigrant landlordism into neighbouring districts – a policy which reinforced these areas as immigrant ghettoes

Conclusion

In order then to investigate social relations within different areas we need to take account of changes in the spatial distribution of productive and state economic activities, in the spatial distribution of population, and in the spatial distribution of land and buildings. Although the physical environment has declined in importance in directly producing particular patterns of social activity, the distribution of social relations across space does nevertheless remain of central significance in modern societies. Marx was wrong to think that space is simply annihilated by time in industrial capitalism. Durkheim and Simmel were wrong in thinking that simple contrasts can be drawn between the rural community and the urban, organic metropolis, depending on different densities of population. All three writers raised but did not resolve crucial issues involved in analysing the transformations of time, nature and space which occur with changes in modern industrial society.

References and Further Reading

Ball, M. (1984), 'The Spaced Out Urban Economy', in D. Massey and J. Allen (eds), *Geography Matters: A Reader* (Cambridge: Cambridge University Press).

Dennis, N., Henriques, F. and Slaughter, C. (1965), *Coal is Our Life* (London: Eyre).

Durkheim, E. (1984), *The Division of Labour in Society* (London: Macmillan).

Frankenberg, R. (1966), *Communities in Britain* (Harmondsworth: Penguin).

Gans, H. (1967), *The Levittowners* (Harmondsworth: Penguin).

Gold, M. (1984), 'A History of Nature' in D. Massey and J. Allen (eds), *op. cit.*

Marx, K. (1973), *Grundrisse* (Harmondsworth: Penguin), trans. M. Nicolaus.

Marx, K. and Engels, F. (1888), *The Manifesto of the Communist Party* (London: Foreign Languages Press).

Newby, H. (1979), *The Deferential Worker: A Study of Farmworkers in East Anglia* (Harmondsworth: Penguin).

Newby, H. (1980), *Green and Pleasant Land* (Harmondsworth: Penguin).

Park, R. and Burgess, E. (1967), *The City*, (London: University of Chicago Press).

Rex, J. and Moore, R. (1967), *Race, Community and Conflict* (London: Oxford University Press).

Robson, B. (1969), *Urban Analysis* (Cambridge: Cambridge University Press).

Simmel, G. (1971), *On Individuality and Social Forms* (Chicago: University of Chicago Press).

Willmott, R. and Young, M. (1960), *Family and Class in a London Suburb* (London: Routledge & Kegan Paul).

Wirth, L. (1938), 'Urbanism as a Way of Life', *American Journal of Sociology*, vol. 44, pp. 1–14.

Young, M. and Willmott, P. (1957), *Family and Kinship in East London* (London: Routledge & Kegan Paul).

Index